THE DIVINE LANGUAGE

OF

COINCIDENCE

**How Miracles Transformed My Life
After I Began Paying Attention**

SOPHIA DEMAS

www.mascotbooks.com

The Divine Language of Coincidence: How Miracles Transformed My Life After I Began Paying Attention

I have tried to recreate events, locales, and conversations from my memories of them. In order to maintain their anonymity in some instances I have changed the names of individuals and places. I may have changed some identifying characteristics and details such as physical properties, occupations, and places of residence.

The views and opinions expressed in this book are solely those of the author. These views and opinions do not necessarily represent those of the publisher or staff.

For more information, please contact:
Mascot Books
620 Herndon Parkway #320
Herndon, VA 20170
info@mascotbooks.com

Library of Congress Control Number: 2020907905

CPSIA Code: PRV1020A
ISBN-13: 978-1-64543-211-1

Printed in the United States

I dedicate this book to:

My parents, John and Anna,
for planting my garden;

My husband, Frank,
for lovingly cultivating it;

and

Our daughter, Eleni,
for enriching it with beauty and heart.

Contents

THE DIVINE LANGUAGE
OF COINCIDENCE

Why I Wrote This Book

This is a story of my spiritual evolution that began at the age of nineteen. At the time, I had been obsessing over two existential issues common to young people on the threshold of adulthood. I couldn't see the forest for the trees, and my anxiety grew. Within the space of a few months, a dream followed by a set of fortuitous events helped resolve my dilemmas and, as a result, I had a transformational change of perception. This life-altering experience had to be more than random kismet. It made me start paying attention, and I began to recognize these "coincidences" as messages.

Sensations began to surface, sometimes suddenly, in the form of compunctions, gentle tugs, and strong urges directing me to act or keeping me from taking action. An inner voice offered guidance. The more I acted on it, the more beneficial the outcome, and the more I relied on it. My gut was slowly becoming a trusty advisor.

There were times when I wanted something so urgently that I blindly ignored the string of red flags flapping in my face. Regardless, I would continue the pursuit while obstacle after obstacle impeded my path and kept the object of my desire from reach. Yet, soon thereafter, or two years down the line, I discovered that the very snag that had kept me from attaining my goal had saved me from peril. I began thanking God for those obstacles, and instead of asking for something specific, I asked for what was best.

More good things began to happen, and I found myself thanking God a lot. The more I said "thank you," the more I was given. People would tell me how lucky I was, adding, "These things only happen to you." I sloughed off these comments, but I had to admit that sometimes I felt as if I had been born under a lucky star.

The graces I received through apparent synchronicities and serendipities began to seem more intentional. I began calling them "miracles." Along with love, faith was a word I had heard my mother use forever, and I wondered what it meant. When I finally entered that realm, I knew. I had become a believer and attributed these mysteries to God. Not the one with the flowing white hair and beard on a throne in heaven or the God who bellows from a burning bush, but an entity that pervades all realms and all living things, with whom I was having a personal relationship.

Grateful for my cosmic connection, I felt a need to help those whom happiness had eluded, those who were not raised by loving parents and did not have merry little childhoods. My sense of connectedness made me reach out to the disenfranchised. The happiness that permeated my being had led me to help those who were depressed, grieving, anxious, incarcerated, or stuck in prisons of their own making. I never felt alone in these endeavors. Mentors and grants showed up to help me. I felt as if I were a sailboat and an invisible force was propelling me in exactly the direction I needed to go.

When a medium told me that I was going to write a book, I shot her down by telling her that sequestering myself off somewhere to write was not going to happen. I was intent on exercising my God-given free will. The Universe, however, had other plans. The door of my mind must have been left ajar, allowing God's will to intervene, upend my staunch resolutions, and change my perception. It was letting go of my stubbornness and underwent a change of mind that has brought me such unimaginable fulfillment and joy. The greater will knew better what was best for me, and it joined forces with my inner voice. Thankfully, I listened.

Still, I was wary. Can these gifts, whether prayed for or not, really be manifested by simply joining my mind with God's? Perhaps it was all random chance and everyone else was right: I was just very, very lucky. After my unexpected decision to write this book, self-doubt sprang forth. What did I know about the process? I didn't even know where to begin. I was urged to start by writing about that first conscious nod to the possibility of a Cosmic Intelligence pulling the strings on this earthly journey when I was nineteen. I liked the idea.

The more I wrote, the more I questioned. What did science have to say about all connecting with consciousness? I was so intrigued that I stopped writing and studied quantum mechanics. While classical science relies on evidence and thereby debunks God, quantum mechanics is conceptual—how subatomic particles interrelate with sound, light, and vibration. In Appendix A, I present a few of the theories that give an idea of how miracles can happen within these realms in our physical world. In Appendix B, I have included examples of paranormal feats performed by enlightened Eastern yogis and Christian mystics, along with excerpts of ancient scriptures from both traditions on sound and light.

My biggest challenge in expressing the ethereal was language. It's hard to define something unseen, let alone God. Everyone has their own distinct idea about the subject. Some people bristle at just the mention of the word *God*. Therefore, when having a conversation about a spiritual notion, it is essential that each person define their conception of it. Once we have this clarity, it is surprising to learn how much more we agree with each other than disagree. To avoid misinterpretation of my use of terms, I have included a glossary to convey their meanings.

Despite my struggles with writing, not once did I consider giving up. As I persevered, difficulties melted away. Signs and people offering help appeared more frequently, confirming that I was on the right path. Any apprehension about the book seeing the light of day dissolved. It didn't matter whether or not it would even get published. It simply needed to be written to hone my faith and deepen my self-awareness. If you are reading this, then know that this book could only have been orchestrated by Divine Intelligence using me as a conduit to bring you a message.

What a privilege it is to walk on this Earth! There is so much love, beauty, and wisdom available to make every one of us humans sublimely happy. I feel that I have found heaven on Earth; however, I do not have a monopoly on grace. I believe without a shadow of doubt that miracles are accessible to everyone. My trusty inner voice says so. The purpose of this book is not to proselytize or provide you with a how-to manual. It's about what has worked for me. You are welcome to adopt the prayers and practices I use, choose from other sources, or be inspired to create your own. But you must first believe that miracles are real. By recognizing coincidence and taking action, your life cannot help but become enriched, too.

CHAPTER 1

The Physics of Miracles

We arrive on planet Earth without an operating manual. Our introduction to this confusing new domain depends on the handbook that our parents assigned to us, inherited from their parents, and then skewed with their own biases—religious or atheist, right- or left-wing, educated or not, rich or poor, tolerant or bigoted, brown, white, red, or yellow skinned. Our primary caregivers' perspectives are our starting point. From here on out, each of us is left to find our own way and formulate a personal set of rules that will serve us best.

This book is about how my own personal instruction manual developed; how I began to recognize that people, places, or things that appeared at the precise moment they were needed were more than coincidences; how I came to understand that auspicious events resulting in loving relationships, healings, the exact amount of money necessary, or simply changes of perception, were guiding messages from the Universe; how these synchronicities I call miracles enriched my life beyond my wildest dreams.

I believe that all of this is available to anyone willing to expand their awareness. Universal Consciousness communicates with us through signs and coincidences, and each one has the potential to benefit us. We just need to grow a set of antennae in order to discover them on our radar screens. If we simply brush a sign off with, "That was *just* a coincidence," we lose an opportunity. The only requirement to begin the quest for miracles is to keep one's mind even a tiny bit open. If you've read this far, you're already on your way.

When I started a small business in the mid-1990s, I sat down with Stephen Covey's book, *The Seven Habits of Highly Effective People*, for some help in creating my organizational mission statement. The first step was to create a personal mission statement identifying my main objective in life. After analyzing my core beliefs and values and visualizing my "uncreated world," I was to develop a set of guidelines that, much like what the Constitution is to the United States, would become the basis of every major life decision I made. For three days I struggled, making endless lists of goals and principles only to end up with a three-word statement: "To be happy." I didn't know exactly what that entailed at the time.

The quest for happiness has recently become an industry. We've learned that excessive personal wealth, better education, bigger houses, cars, and designer clothes do not necessarily make people happier—in fact, depression and anxiety are on the rise. So much so that in April 2016 Harvard received a $21 million grant to establish the Lee Kum Sheung Center for Health and Happiness at the T. H. Chan School of Public Health. It would be much less costly, instead, to turn to children and ask them what makes them happy. They will tell you the truth. I have been collecting responses to this question from children for some time. Here is a verbatim sampling:

- "Being with my family."

- "See family you haven't seen in a while, or getting a toy you really, really, really want."

- "Cuddling with my dad when he comes home from work."

- "It's when you feel good about something, joyful, when you want to dance sometimes."

- "Happiness pretty much means peace. Like the whole world is peaceful and you are so excited."

- "Umm . . . playing happy and playing in the playground and playing with your friends outside. Happy."

- "Having fun and being with my family and friends."

- "Happiness is about being nice and spreading love all around the world."

- "I know what it means! It means you hug everybody and squeeze everybody. And that's all."

I have read shelves of how-to books on self-improvement and achieving happiness, but what the children had to say about being happy gets to the heart of it. It's about human relationships, getting along, play, peace, and love. This is what I wanted in my life. Being happy became my conscious intention.

Much has been written about the "law of attraction," which asserts that positive thoughts become positive things and experiences. Conversely, negative thinking, being in fear of a relationship dissolving or not having enough money, for example, will turn one's fears into reality and sabotage what is desired. I know this to be true, but my view of the law of attraction, as it pertains to cause and effect, is more similar to karma; if your intentions and actions are good, good things will come to you in the future, while ill will and misdeeds will manifest in some degree of suffering. As I learned to let go of my expectations that my good deeds would reward me, positive outcomes increased. It became more and more apparent that, if I lent money that wasn't returned, more money would appear from a completely different source. If the person I helped didn't thank me, I would receive unexpected acknowledgment from someone else.

Some New Age proponents, however, have warped the law of attraction concept to mean that we can have our every desire fulfilled by focusing our intention on it. I have a problem with this. First of all, it doesn't always work. More importantly, it implies that we know what is best for us. We certainly think we do. I sure did. How many times did I focus my intention 110 percent on men I was mad about, jobs I deemed to be ideal, or exciting travel plans, only to have a holy monkey wrench tossed in, keeping the object of my desire out of reach? Baffled and crushed, I would hunker down with a fiercer focus on my target, crafting yet a different approach, when another blow would come out of left field to kill the deal as I bemoaned, "God, why are you doing this to me?"

There were times when it became a good thing that someone or something I had coveted did not materialize. I learned that some of the men who had eluded me after I had set my sights on them had died, lost their minds, or ended up in jail. The firm that had rejected me when I desperately wanted to be part of it went out of business. After missing a plane, I was prevented from staying at a place that was swept away by a landslide during a hurricane. Again and again, I thanked God for the unwelcome obstacle that had kept me from harm's way. Why hadn't I paid attention to those little red flags or that huge, obvious sign that felt as if a cosmic frying pan had come crashing on my head? The need to be in control of the whole show was not working. Why focus on a particular desire that potentially would not serve me when, instead, I could simply ask for what is best and step back? Let go, let God. It was not so easy at first.

Every human being has the potential to have a conscious connection with our Source. Where we are on our spiritual journey depends on how sharpened our inner voice is and how much we have developed our ability to listen to its messages, spot external signs, and take action. After years of discussing coincidence and miracles with people on every rung of the spiritual ladder, I have identified three levels of awareness in which people generally operate. The first level is from the perspective of *wishful thinking*, the second from the perspective of *hope*, and the third from the perspective of *faith*.

To illustrate how one would deal with coincidences at each of these spiritual levels, envision the following scenario. Suppose you have been contemplating a career change. You are considering two divergent paths—get an MBA at the Wharton School of the University of Pennsylvania, or give in to your passion for history and pursue a PhD at a school on the West Coast. The conflicting prospects have kept you from doing the research needed to make the best decision. After boarding a plane to visit a friend in Arizona, you take your seat next to a man you spotted while dining in the same out-of-the-way restaurant the night before. You notice the logo embroidered on his polo shirt, "The Wharton School." The book on his lap, incredibly, is the same obscure novel you looked for everywhere to bring along but couldn't find.

If you operate from the perspective of wishful thinking, you would most likely find yourself befuddled by these seemingly disconnected chance events and, chalking them up to coincidence, proceed to buckle your seatbelt in silence as you continue to wish for help in making the right decision. At the second level, operating from the perspective of hope, you become aware of the triple whammy coincidence as "something meant to be" and wonder if you should give in to the "gut feeling" telling you to strike up a conversation, hoping that you might glean some helpful information. Operating from the perspective of faith, the third level, you wouldn't hesitate for a second knowing that this man was put next to you for a reason, and you would find the first opportunity to engage in conversation that will yield the clarity you need to resolve your dilemma. This level of faith requires practice, but if you have been hovering at level two for a while, noticing signs that pan out, watching your hopes transpire into realities, you will find yourself in a place where faith is a natural state of being.

One of the biggest deterrents when discussing divine or ethereal subjects is language. Unlike the precise vocabulary of science used to describe the laws of nature, language falters when we try to describe the intangible, especially the concept of God. At a seminar I attended on quantum biology, a woman shared that her dog was cured of cancer, crediting quantum biology and higher consciousness. I approached her after the presentation and asked, "Your dog being cured was a miracle. I agree with everything you said. Is there a reason why you never mentioned God?"

"Oh," she shot back, "I would never touch the word God with a ten-foot pole."

"Why not?" I asked, taken aback.

"It turns people off," she explained. "God is out there somewhere, but higher consciousness is everywhere."

"Well," I replied, "your description of higher consciousness is exactly how I define God: in here, out there, in every realm." Had she asked me how I define God instead of assuming, we most likely would have agreed that my definition of God and her interpretation of higher consciousness shared common ground. This is why it's important to qualify the meaning we attribute to the unseen and divine before delving into a discussion.

People's perceptions of God vary depending on how spirituality was introduced to them during childhood, personal experience, and their imagination. In her book, *A God That Could Be Real,* science historian and philosopher Nancy Ellen Abrams serves up a God who emerged out of humanity rather than a God who created it. An atheist who found herself in a recovery program, she observed that people who called on their higher power received marked relief from their addiction issues while she remained miserable. Abrams began pretending to have a higher power. Curiously, each time she did, she, too, found comfort and even joy. Her version of God is contrary to the one she presumes everyone else worships—an old, bearded man with long, white hair sitting on a throne, floating on clouds. While she believes that no scientific concept can be viewed with absolute certainty because the next discovery could render it obsolete, she authoritatively lists exactly what a real God can and cannot be. Her God is confined within the laws of nature, and therefore, His powers are limited in scope.

No, that's ridiculous, Ms. Abrams, I thought. *God is beyond time and space. He is*, I debated her while reading, *omnipotent, omniscient, and omnipresent*. Then, I came upon something remarkable. She described a personal and meaningful relationship with her God. She prayed to Him and received comfort and empowerment. The oneness she felt with Him and the cosmos gave her a sense of duty to care for her fellow humans and the environment. This is exactly what God wants from us! I felt small having judged her. God doesn't care how anyone defines Him, so why should I? Whatever our definition of God is, we only need to acknowledge that there is something bigger than us out there.

You may use whatever term best resounds with you to call your higher power—Divine Consciousness, the Universe, Source, Allah, Infinite Being, Nature, etc. I say all of them interchangeably, but my term of choice is God. I often use words such as miracle, Holy Spirit, and love to describe unseen forces. You may prefer other words to describe the same concepts. Communication, however, is not only about the language we use but also how the listener filters it. Throw in individual biases, and you have a recipe for miscommunication. If we are going to have a conversation about spiritual phenomena, it is critical, therefore, before assuming what the other person means and launch into a dispute, to first clarify terminology and listen respectfully.

My own spiritual journey has brought me to believe that there is one God, one Universal Consciousness. The various religions and philosophies are simply different pathways to this ultimate reality. Each religion, however, proclaims to know who and what the "real" God is, while further differentiation exists among its individual members. Cutting through the rules and canons of the varied belief systems, we find basic teachings common to all— justice, practice, peace, being of service, and loving one another. If more people approached the subject of God with a genuine interest in others' viewpoints, common ground would become evident. Twelve-step recovery programs advocate that members simply accept that there is a higher power, whatever it is, that is greater than us. This is a solid starting point.

In elementary school, I had difficulty reconciling God with the theory of evolution. I was shocked to learn that it took humans millions of years to evolve from apes. I had been taught in Sunday school that God created the Universe and Adam and Eve in seven days. Accepting anything else played into the hands of Satan. I could not, however, reject what has been proven unequivocally by science. Once I accepted that time is relative and a construct to help us humans organize our day, everything fell into place. Nowhere in Genesis do we find that one biblical day equals a human day.

God and science seemed to go hand in hand. Before I began writing this book, my knowledge of science was rudimentary, though my fascination with nature was immense. I was just as dazzled by solar systems and everything that makes up our Universe as I was by the human body with its myriad functions perfectly synchronized from brain headquarters, spectacularly conceived by the collision of an egg and a sperm. I remember in fourth grade listing bodily secretions, amazed at the variety. The assortment of fruits, flowers, trees, mountains, animals, sky colors, and bodies of water there were for us to appreciate left me dazed. Yes, gravity and the speed of light were useful things to know, but through my left-brain lens it seemed as if scientists took all of this beautiful nature, this fantastical world I was part of, and sanitized it into cold little formulas. "Show me the numbers," they said. Nothing outside the laws of nature, their mantra went, could possibly exist, let alone miracles. This made me distrust them. If their pursuit of systematic knowledge was supposed to yield black or white truths, why was there so much disagreement among them?

I was skeptical about science in much the same way scientists I had talked with were dubious about God and miracles. I was advised by many not to attribute my inexplicable experiences to God. One physicist I met at a cocktail party told me that he would have no interest in discussing the nature of miracles, much less in reading a book about them. The idea that God and physics were inextricably tied had germinated in my head after reading Stephen Hawking's book, *A Brief History of Time*, about the workings of the cosmos and how the Universe may have come into existence.

Now, years later, there seems to be a clamor in the quantum world to discover the tiniest particles in existence, the common denominators of everything. We learn of quarks, buckyballs, and Higgs Boson particles. There are some popular quantum physicists who claim that, soon, we will be able to teleport, bilocate, and time travel, feats that enlightened Eastern yogis and Christian mystics have been achieving for thousands of years (see Appendix B: The Physics of Consciousness). If science can talk like this and the laws of nature are tested with each mindboggling discovery, why shouldn't miracles be equally accepted as natural phenomena? Did quantum mechanics actually bolster the probability of the existence of God? At least it demonstrated that the laws of classic science were not so cut and dry (see Appendix A: Consciousness and Quantum Mechanics).

To get me up to speed on quantum and cosmology discoveries in the last two decades, I put my writing on pause and bought Stephen Hawking's latest book, *Grand Design*, co-written with Leonard Mlodinow. It sat next to my favorite reading chair for weeks. I picked it up multiple times only to replace the bookmark and set the book down again. I promised to reward myself with a lobster dinner after I finished reading the first two chapters, yet I could scarcely get through a few pages without feeling it absolutely necessary that I give myself a facial or find old clothes to take to the thrift store. The longer the book went unread, the longer it would take me to resume writing. In desperation, I put out an SOS to the Universe.

Shortly after making my plea, a most fortuitous opportunity presented itself to help me with my dilemma. However, it required me to take action. I received an email from the ICA, the Institute for Contemporary Art, a museum and art gallery that offers cutting-edge contemporary art within walking distance of my home. Though I had attended various exhibitions, I was not a member and not on their mailing list. I asked my neighbors if they had received the email, and only those who were members had. How did they get my email address? It was an announcement for an exhibit of multi-media installations by Jeremy Deller, an influential contemporary British artist. Two of the installations were interactive with museumgoers, and the curator was recruiting volunteers to staff them in four-hour shifts. People were needed to hand out free tea to patrons at "Valerie's Snack Bar," a replica of a Manchester tea shop which was originally conceived as a parade float. For the other installation, a "sitter" was wanted to sit on a black leather sofa against a black matte wall with the words "I (heart) Melancholy" in glossy black letters. I immediately dialed the number to ask if the person who sat on the sofa could be reading. I was told that it was preferred. I blurted out, "Sign me up for ten shifts!"

The material in the book was obtuse, and I had to reread most paragraphs. The forty hours I was held hostage on that sofa was exactly the time I needed to finish it. Hawking and Mlodinow theorize that the Universe originated "out of nothing" and assert their M-theory as the explanation of everything, a unified theory Einstein was hoping to find. It postulates that there are at least eleven dimensions (instead of the four we detect) and many universes parallel to ours, each with its own laws of nature and some of which we could be inhabiting simultaneously. What was most difficult to grasp was that everything seen and unseen in our material world is made up of infinitesimal moving particles. Even more staggering to ponder was that, to our knowledge, Earth is the only planet in our Universe to be perfectly fine-tuned for sustaining human life as we know it.

In *A Brief History of Time*, Hawking includes a reference to God, stating, ". . . if we do discover a complete theory, it should in time be understandable in broad principle by everyone, not just a few scientists. Then we shall all, philosophers, scientists, and just ordinary people, be able to take part in the discussion of the question of why it is that we and the universe exist. If we find the answer to that, it would be the ultimate triumph of human reason—for then we would know the mind of God." But the M-theory in *Great Design* does not bring us closer to know the mind of God. Instead, Hawking and Mlodinow contend, "Spontaneous creation is the reason there is something rather than nothing, why the universe exists, why we exist. It is not necessary to invoke God to light the blue touch paper and set the Universe going." In other words, God is not required—the idea that the Universe(s) sprang up from nothing can be explained by science and does not need to demonstrate divine creation.

Theories about how the universe was created abound. Many physicists believe that the entire Universe existed as an imperceptible dot before exploding all by itself; that this big bang spewed out energy and matter throughout spacetime in no time; and that gravity, simultaneously activated, stabilized the rapid expansion, thereby saving the universe from self-destructing. In a snap, our elegant cosmos was created which would, eons later, provide a perfect place for human existence. Isn't the idea that the universe came into existence by arbitrary self-combustion just as mind-boggling as a Divine Intelligence having created it?

Quantum mechanics hints at how inexplicable events can physically happen in our world. I believe that within the realms of sound, light, and vibration, consciousness resides, where we meet God, and where miracles happen.

I see no difference between miracles and the fantastic phenomena that quantum mechanics claims to be possible. Here is what has worked best for me—how miracles manifested in my life once I learned to listen to coincidence (one of the ways God communicates with us), and to take action; how this, in turn, brought about my absolute faith in the oneness of the Universe and my personal relationship with God; and how I have attained the three-word personal mission statement I wrote long ago, "To be happy." I feel loved, protected, and filled with a happiness I could not have imagined before my awareness evolved. I call this state of being "Grace." I thank God for it every day and wish the same for you.

Before the age of nineteen, I didn't have a clue . . .

CHAPTER 2

The Dream

I began experiencing existential rumblings at the beginning of my junior year in college. I was grappling with two issues in particular. My mother had a law of celibacy until marriage, and I had gone along with it. Now I was questioning the viability of her policy. I also started feeling insecure and expected to have the approval of everyone. It seemed only logical that if I was a nice and helpful person, I should be liked and accepted by all. Yet someone inevitably would come along who did not *see me that way*, leaving me befuddled. I felt a constant hum of internal turmoil and began questioning everything. Although I was flourishing in college life, there seemed to be something insular and superficial about it. An inner voice was indicating there was a bigger picture that I was part of.

I shared a one-bedroom apartment close to campus with my roommate, Christine. We furnished it with a futon we bought at a thrift store, jade plants, and Japanese art posters. The bunk beds were from Christine's childhood. She slept on the top bunk and I on the bottom.

Christine was a psychology major. She lacked creativity but made up for it by quickly assessing and compiling articles and authoritatively quoting from them as if they were her own. She could knock out comprehensiv papers in rapid-fire succession. A man magnet, she went through guys at a similar pace. Some of the ones who didn't click with her tuned in to me. Clinging to my virginity was becoming tougher.

While my conflicting feelings about sex had me in a tizzy, I met Rob. At a reception after a lecture, his piercing blue eyes penetrated through me from across the room, rendering me immobile. He was twenty-seven, already married and divorced, and finishing his PhD dissertation in physics. No matter that he was a reclusive introvert—not my type—I was spellbound. It was the first time I felt I was with a real "man." My mother's indoctrination of abstinence and what my body/heart/mind was blasting at me were diametrically opposed. What if I never got married? What then? Seriously, was I supposed to die a virgin?

My struggles felt unsolvable. One night as I tried to go to sleep, unable to reconcile the emotional havoc, I was overcome with a wave of isolation and began to cry.

The voice from the top bunk was clipped. "Is something wrong?"

"I feel alone."

"That's ridiculous," Christine coolly shot out. "You're at a major university; there are tons of activities you can participate in."

"It's not that I'm lonely. I'm just feeling . . . alone."

Clearly perplexed, the psychology major continued spewing advice in her best professional tone. "You can do so many things—you can join a club or be a tutor or do yoga . . ." Her utter cluelessness was just amusing enough to take the edge off my anxiety and allow me to fall asleep. I began dreaming:

> *I find myself alone, wearing a white wedding dress and veil on a stage in a large, dimly lit auditorium filled with people. A spotlight is on me, and I notice that I am inside a glass box the size of a phone booth. I touch the sides and decide it is plexiglass. No matter that there is no*

groom, I feel elated that so many people have come to see me. Another spotlight shines to my right, and three girls I recognize from my past enter the stage from behind the curtain. Void of expression, they take their places diagonally between me and the audience, face me, and curtsy. They are wearing pink and green Indian saris with a black print. Three more girls enter and do the same thing. I realize I had had a falling out with each of them at different times in my life. Two more trios of my "enemies" follow. I wonder if they are supposed to be my bridesmaids. One girl hisses at me. This doesn't faze me. What matters is that they are now here, and I forgive their past transgressions. Once all twelve girls have taken their places, the lights turn up, as if the show had ended.

We are now at a reception hall. A woman carrying a clipboard and wearing a navy coat and thick, round-framed glasses, waves as she directs guests to form a receiving line. One by one, friends and acquaintances I have known since childhood file by without turning their heads. One out of every ten or so "well-wishers" turns to look at me without expression. I try not to let their lack of affect dampen my gratitude that so many people are here for me. I am overjoyed after my best friend from childhood and another longtime family friend smile as they walk past. Anxiety begins to grip me as each familiar face appears—will this one walk right past me? Turn and give me a blank look? Smile? I keep telling myself what matters most is that they cared enough to come. As my apprehension mounts, I look down and see that I am still in my wedding dress but, to my horror, I am lying in a black coffin. It's my funeral.

I woke up at two in the morning in a cold sweat gasping for air, terrified, certain the dream was forecasting my imminent death. Was I going to be hit by a bus? Had I already contracted some incurable disease? I leapt out of bed and threw on whatever I was wearing the day before. I needed somebody to talk to—someone who understood me. Now.

At the time, a serial rapist was active on a daily basis on and around campus. Worried parents sent highlighted news clippings urging vigilance. Nothing was going to deter me from walking the ten blocks to Rob's house. The light in his window signaled he was still up as usual, writing. He answered the door and greeted me with a Buddha-like smile. He sat me down on the sofa next to him. With his blue eyes transfixed on mine, he listened to me relate my dream as if the task at hand were the single most important priority in life. I told him that in real life, the idea that someone I knew would walk past me without acknowledging me would be devastating.

"But in the dream, I didn't feel a bit of resentment toward those who walked by without turning their heads to look at me, not even toward the girl who hissed at me," I said, surprised. "I just felt grateful for their presence." I then disclosed how distressing it was to find out someone didn't like me before getting to know me.

"Why would someone who decides they don't like you without knowing you matter to you?" Rob asked gently.

"Wow," was all I could say. The question jarred me. Why would I care what others thought of me if they didn't know me? Or even after they got to know me?

"It doesn't seem important anymore," I murmured in astonishment as another thought dawned on me. "There will always be somebody who doesn't like me, just as there are people who rub me the wrong way. Some chemicals don't mix. What is important are my friends."

One realization followed another. "Now I can be myself and not have to worry about pleasing anyone!" I felt exhilarated. Free. "But what about the coffin?"

Holding my gaze, Rob said, "The dream has nothing to do with physical death. It just means that a part of your self that wasn't working for you anymore has died. The box you were in on stage was plexiglass, and that says to me that what has been discarded was artificial. It's being replaced with a more authentic part of your self." I knew he was speaking the truth. I felt changed.

Rob got up, went to his desk, and returned holding several sheets of paper. They were poems he had written about the struggle I was having with my sexual self that longed to break through. I listened to him read them in awe. His words eloquently expressed exactly what I was feeling and brought me clarity. There was not a doubt in my mind that he was the one who would carry me through that unknown threshold of sensuality's door. I also knew this was not the right time.

I left Rob's place as the new day was dawning with my head spinning. The walk home gave me time to process. A walking cocktail of emotions, I felt different from the agitated young woman who set off in the middle of the night needing answers. My inner knowingness had safely led me to the appropriate person. It was as if a champagne cork popped from the depths of my being, freeing me from the need to please others. My life was not going to be lived according to other people's rulebooks any longer. I alone was responsible for my own happiness. Rob's poetry also had lit a flame in my core. I felt exhilarated about what lay ahead. I returned to find the psych major sound asleep on the top bunk, oblivious to my departure or my transformation.

Rob invited me over for dinner the following Saturday night. I dressed carefully. I walked, or rather floated, over to his place with a sense of certainty that had not been there before—knowing that I was choosing what was right for me, no longer having to conform to somebody else's criteria. Rob welcomed me with an embrace that was different from anything I had experienced, as if our cells were dancing together. The aroma of Indian food wafting from his small kitchen intoxicated me. There were candles everywhere. The Erik Satie album was mesmerizing. Rob poured two glasses of wine that perfectly complemented curries and chutneys. After dinner, without lifting his eyes from mine, he touched the small of my back and led me into the candlelit bedroom where I entered a glorious new dimension of womanhood, a part of me I knew was there.

Start to finish, my relationship with Rob lasted just four months. The more time I had spent with him, the more our differences became evident. At that time in my life, spending hours solely discussing consciousness raising, German philosophers, and the mysteries of the Universe in hermetic seclusion was not my cup of tea. He certainly did not blend with my crowd. It no longer mattered that he was an amazing, mystical lover. The relationship dissolved naturally, and I never saw him again. Two ships on divergent cosmic paths collided at just the right moment. Our brief communion could not have been more timely or meaningful in providing me with what I needed for my physical, emotional, intellectual, and spiritual growth.

The synchronicity of events that had influenced such a drastic shift of perception was not lost on me. I had been feeling solitary while steeped in existential soul-searching, trying to reconcile my sexual feelings with my upbringing and to resolve my issues about how others regarded me. Why was it that, at this pivotal time, a jarring dream that made no sense to me drove me to venture out in the middle of the night and seek guidance from someone who had only recently appeared on my radar screen, rather than from a close friend? It was as if Rob were an alien from outer space who had landed on earth specifically assigned to help steer me through the muck, find clarity, and enter another level of awareness. Mission accomplished.

Most important, I had discovered an inner voice that had guided me correctly with a dream and another human being. Luckily I ignored neither. It was as if my cries for help and healing were heard by some mega-force and my supplications sublimely answered. Was it all one big coincidence?

It felt as though I had tripped on a secret that had not entirely revealed itself. What did come through, though, was loud and clear—I had to start paying close attention to what came my way. I felt downright fortunate with my newfound perspective. Anxiety was replaced with gratitude—for my friends, family, childhood, everything. I remembered my mother telling me how she and my father almost didn't see each other again after they first met. I came that close to not making it here on Earth! Now I was grateful for my very life.

My soon-to-be parents on their wedding day, fourteen days after being introduced and my mother's initial rejection of her suitor.

My birth created a sensation. It fulfilled my mother's lifelong dream of having a child; for my father, a bachelor until he was fifty-seven, sudden parenthood filled him with awe. I was the center of their universe for two and a half years, until I learned of the bizarre notion that I would have to share their adoration with a baby brother.

After living in Dearborn, Michigan, during my first seven years without one relative nearby, moving to Greece instantly exposed me to a legion of extended family and a magical childhood. Here we all are at Easter, roasting whole lambs on spits.

Pictured here summering in Loutraki, Greece are my mother, brother George, Thio (uncle) Gregory, and my Thia (aunt) Angeliki, whose cunning in bringing my parents together I am eternally grateful for.

Having settled in Portland, Oregon, this is one of the scads of family photos my father insisted on taking after church on the Sundays my mother convinced him to join us.

After having funded my college education for ten years, during which time I changed majors twice, my parents were justifiably thrilled when I finally received my diploma.

Buckminster Fuller and me in his office in 1979 at the Science Center, Philadelphia.

Photograph by Daniel Perry

After three serious relationships, it was while living with my extravagantly artistic friends, Michelle (center) and Alice, that I embarked on a decade of glorious singlehood and party-going, here at a Painted Bride fundraiser in 1985.

Frank in 1994, a year after we met when, finally, he asked me out.

With Heidi Hopkins, one of my immensely talented assistants, in 1995 at the salon of my dress designing business, Sophia Demas Couture.

Photograph by Gregory Tobias

My ecstatic mother leading me, Frank, and my brother in a Greek line dance at our wedding reception while friends and family enthusiastically followed along whether they knew the steps or not.

Wearing one of my millinery creations at one of Michelle's evocative soirees in her organically over-the-top Victorian parlor.

Inspecting the rubble at the place we were supposed to spend our honeymoon in Mexico while thanking God for the obstacles that kept us from the hurricane's destruction.

Frank's wedding band, crushed by a part of our heavy concrete fountain that fell on his hand. The band not only miraculously saved his hand, it was one of three events that together rescued our marriage from the brink of divorce.

Having dreamt of seeing Hagia Sophia in Istanbul since I was in the second grade, I am pictured here on my sixtieth birthday, the day I walked into that awe-inspiring structure seen here lit up in the background.

With my dear friend Pushpa in Shillong, India, we are attending an event featuring the Shillong Chamber Choir, with which she is closely associated.

During our visit to Kaziranga National Park in Assam with Pushpa as our guide, we rode on an elephant to catch a glimpse of the fabled one-horned rhinoceros. One of the baby elephants took a liking to me, and here we are petting each other.

Frank and I being blessed by a Brahmin monk at the Galta Ji Monkey Temple near Jaipur.

It was the pyramids in Egypt that ignited the celebratory bucket-list trip for my sixtieth birthday. Here, we are next to our camels. Heeding travel warnings due to political unrest, tourists were avoiding Egypt, so we practically had the whole place to ourselves!

Visiting holy sites in Israel capped off our two-month pilgrimage. Here, a group of Christians are being baptized in the Jordan River at the location where Jesus had been baptized by St. John the Baptist. Not pictured are the two heavily-armed Israeli soldiers standing guard.

Also in my sixtieth year, after Hayal came into our lives (thanks to Fr. Stephen, pictured here) and asked if she could call me "Mom," I had every reason to celebrate Mother's Day.

It was when Hayal was baptized and took the name Eleni that I experienced the miracle of motherhood. Right after the ritual, my friend Mary snapped this grainy photo of Eleni and me, in which a ball of light hovers over each of our heads, and which I would refer to as our halos. It was my friend Angelique, however, who saw the angel with a scepter looking down upon us. Amazingly, the face is that of my mother's.

On December 20, 2014, through adult adoption, Eleni became our legal daughter, and her name, Eleni Demas, became official!

Despite my aversion to the idea of writing a book, circumstances once again forced my hand. Fortunately, friends and family offered their homes in beautiful settings that made the job palatable. It doesn't get better than this: on the veranda of my friend Charlotte's villa on the Greek island of Astypalaia, overlooking the Aegean Sea.

CHAPTER 3

Getting Here

If there is one person I owe my existence to, it's my Thia (Aunt) Angeliki.

My father, Ioannis Athanasios Demas, immigrated to the United States from Greece in 1909, all by himself, when he was just sixteen years old. Promptly upon arriving at Ellis Island, he changed his name to John. He hailed from Manesi, a dirt-poor village near the city of Nafplion in the Peloponnese, where his mother and four younger siblings lived without a source of income. His father had come to America a few years before to find work and support the family, but instead, he became a drunk and squandered his money.

As the oldest child, my father-to-be took seriously the responsibility of providing for the family, working hard at his cousin Gregory's diner in New York City and sending money home. An adventurous spirit, John soon got antsy and migrated out West by hopping on freight trains with other immigrants. The expanding network of railroads wove along the Pacific Coast, where new towns were being established, furthering prosperity. Short and solid, John took advantage of the boom and laid down train tracks. After getting wind of the rapidly growing Ford Motor Company, he headed to

Dearborn, Michigan, where he built automobiles on the assembly line at the Rouge Plant.

Anna Karida, my future mother, was an embroidery designer in Argos, Greece, also near Nafplion. Known for her natural beauty, she had once been engaged to a man through an arranged introduction. Upon finding out that her fiancé's father had taken part in a murder, Anna's brother, fearing that disgrace would be brought upon the family, broke off the engagement. Heartbroken, Anna became deeply religious and devoted herself to taking care of her elderly mother.

Both John and Gregory did well for themselves. Gregory's diner prospered, and he married a young woman of such beauty that artists were clamoring to paint her portrait. John, now a US citizen, was self-taught on the ins and outs of the stock market. Ford was paying good wages, and he was able to save money, stowed away under the mattress. National Cash Register (NCR), one of America's earliest tech stocks, which he had been following, introduced the first electric-powered cash register in 1906 and in 1926 joined the New York Stock Exchange with the largest public stock offering to date. The crash of 1929 was swift. Having amassed $10,000 in cash—a huge sum at the time—John put all his eggs in one basket and acquired NCR at the drop. It was the beginning of a successful sideline as a stock investor.

Gregory's wife died during childbirth. In the midst of his grief, he returned to Greece, where he opened what was to become the premier *kafenion* (café) in Argos, located across the central church square. Just before Mussolini invaded Greece in World War II, Gregory married Angeliki. Though plain-looking, she was smart and savvy with a wickedly dry sense of humor. She became pregnant with twins during the German occupation, but, tragically, they were stillborn. On top of the *kafenion*, the couple built a house with red-painted columns reminiscent of the Palace of Knossos, and turned the large terrace into a roof garden. There, they remained childless but happy.

Still a bachelor at fifty-seven, John had stopped supporting his mother and siblings. They had become prosperous landowners with the money he had steadily been sending them, amassing olive, orange, and apricot orchards and tobacco fields. In 1950, he made a trip back to the "old country." He had not seen his mother, three brothers, and sister since leaving for America forty-one years earlier. He was welcomed as if royalty had descended on the village. John spent most of his stay with Gregory and Angeliki, who decided that John needed a wife. Angeliki had just the woman in mind—Anna the embroidery designer. She had learned that Anna's mother had recently died and that Anna, who lived quietly by herself at the age of thirty-eight, was destined to be a spinster. John, who had given no thought to marriage, reluctantly agreed to meet her.

Embroidered tablecloths, runners, and linens were essential items in every young woman's hope chest. Under the guise of commissioning an embroidery for her niece, Angeliki visited Anna to check things out. She found her home to be tidy and was particularly impressed with the spotless outhouse. Anna was interrogated about what she liked to cook, if she wanted children, and what she did in her spare time. Anna passed the interview with flying colors. When Angeliki brought up the prospect of being introduced to John and Anna agreed, Angeliki lost no time inviting her to her home for coffee and pastry.

Not only had John never married, but he had not, to anyone's knowledge, ever had a romantic relationship with a woman. He was instantly smitten with Anna. The set-up, however, had flustered him, and he sat up in his chair stiffly in silence. As he got up and took a step, he tripped on the rug and almost fell. That was the last straw for Anna. Taking his awkwardness as a sign of mental imbalance, she nixed the match. Had it not been for Angeliki's certainty of the union's potential, my presence on Earth would have been foiled by a momentary loss of footing! Angeliki had a bird's eye view of the church square and was familiar with Anna's church-going patterns. Undeterred, she arranged for the three of them to "accidentally" run into Anna after evening church services. John was telling a story and having a good laugh when Angeliki called out to Anna to join them and made John repeat it. This time, John, ruggedly handsome, exerted confidence and took the lead. Anna responded with a lighthearted giggle. Gregory announced that they were all going out for grilled fish by the seaside and hailed a taxi.

That night, Anna returned to her house and, in her own words, "felt my heart flutter." She wrote John's name on back of an icon of the Virgin Mary and prayed for guidance; if this was supposed to happen, let it be. She woke up with an overwhelming desire to see him again. Any and all doubt had vanished. John and Anna were married two weeks later in an intimate church ceremony with Anna carrying a bouquet of flowers her friends had collected from their gardens.

What else but blind love, trust in God, and divine intervention would make someone leave the impossibly blue skies of Greece for Dearborn, and Ford's smokestacks spewing smoke the color of charcoal? John flew back to the states to begin Anna's immigration process. After three months of bureaucracy, John met her as she stepped off the plane in New York. Before heading for their new home, John and Anna visited her two older sisters, Bessie and Katina, both of whom had immigrated to Massachusetts as mail-order brides to marry nice Greek men. It was the first time the sisters had seen Anna since she was a teenager.

Dearborn, a suburb of Detroit, was at the time inhabited by Ford's white employees. Anna found the two-bedroom, first-floor duplex apartment John had rented to be stark. After furnishing it and settling in, John returned to work on the assembly line, and Anna, finding out she was pregnant, stayed home embroidering curtains and knitting baby clothes. She embraced the Annunciation Greek Orthodox Church, which was central to the Greektown section of Detroit, and began making friends. One of them, Vasso, who happened to live just a few blocks away with her husband, Niko, became Anna's closest friend. Nine months after John and Anna's marriage, I arrived on the scene.

My birth was a really big deal. My mother had dreamt of having children her whole life while my father found the whole idea to be in the realm of science fiction. My being born a girl, pink, and hairy at nine pounds frightened him at first. But this quickly gave way to pride and jubilation, and he began photographing my every move. My mother lavished her full attention on me, teaching me songs, prayers, and the Greek alphabet regardless of my inability to speak. The constant attention began taking its toll, and I started to show symptoms of perfectionism. While washing dishes, my mother happened to peer into the dining room, where, at eight months, I struggled to stand up by grabbing onto a table leg. As I let go to take my first step, she ran in screaming with glee. Having been caught practicing, I promptly plopped down, refusing her pleas to try one more time. Two months later, as my parents sat in the living room, I paraded in one door and out the other showing off my achievement.

Much to my parents' mounting alarm, at almost two-and-a-half I hadn't spoken a word. I chose, instead, to communicate through hand signals. The doctor told them that nothing was wrong with me—I just wasn't ready. One Sunday after church, we were sitting at an ice cream parlor, and I was enjoying my ice cream cone. Having finished his, my father said, "Okay, Anna, let's go." I then delivered my first utterance, a perfectly formed Greek sentence: "First, I will finish my ice cream, and then we'll go." Shocked, my father bellowed, "Did you hear that, Anna?" I will never know if he was expressing delight that I spoke or dismay at a sign of defiance toward authority, which he would never be able to deal with very well in the future.

A lot of power came with being the center of the universe. Water had to be the perfect temperature, or I would refuse it. I loved the smell of cigar smoke and demanded that I accompany my father down to the base-ment—his cave—where, much to my mother's objections, he smoked after dinner. This is also where every year he would make wine, climbing into the laundry sink and stomping on the grapes with his bare feet. Believing there were special natural vitamins in his red wine, he began giving me a teaspoonful when I was a month old. Later, I was up to a shot glassful and refused to eat meat without it. There were only two magazines, *Life* and *Harper's Bazaar*, that I would allow my mother to leaf through, showing me photographs and pointing out fashion trends while patiently coaxing me to eat my vegetables. All-in-all, life was good.

I started hearing references about a "baby," and I knew full well that people weren't talking about me. After a little pep talk on my mother's lap, I put two and two together. All this propaganda about how a baby brother or sister was going to add to the quality of my life meant only one thing: that I would have to share my empire. I was right. My brother George was born a preemie and arrived home with a big head on a tiny body. My father must have expected him to arrive with biceps and moustache because he was at a loss of what to do with him. It was my mother's attention I was afraid of losing. She had taken on the caring for the new family addition with the resolve of a hen with glazed-over eyes as she incubates her eggs. It was clear from here on out that Georgie was going to be a thorn in my side, and I had better accept it.

My parents were emerging as two distinctly different personalities with contrasting parenting styles. My mother was constantly kissing, stroking, and hugging me. She would talk to me about fashion and her life in Greece as if I were one of her friends. She cheered on my delight in drawing "ladies' dresses." I was particularly enthralled with brides and painstakingly drew elaborate gowns on the plain, white inserts that came with her nylon stockings, which she would cheerfully tape on the refrigerator. She told me that the dresses I drew were far more beautiful than those in the magazines. Her favorite subject by far was religion. I regularly heard about how much the Virgin Mary protected us, that little Jesus was all about love, and to have faith in God without question. When I was four, I asked her if stars got closer together the farther they were from Earth, forming a solid mass of light, or if they grew apart until there was total darkness. Visibly shaken, my mother told me that little Jesus didn't want us asking questions about the cosmos, and I should merely accept how God had created it. It was the only time, ever, that I did not believe her. I knew that the Jesus I had come to know would welcome anything I had to ask and that He would want me to have the answer.

My father expressed affection by pinching, tickling, throwing me in the air, and swinging me around the room. He would orate about the toxicity of white sugar, the importance of money attained through hard work, and the horrors of communism. Every day, he gave us a stock market report. I soon understood that a jolly Daddy meant that the stock market was up, while one with a low patience threshold guaranteed that it was down. Having only completed the second grade, he considered education to be the key to everything. He would regularly describe what it was like growing up poor in Manesi and being forced to tend sheep in the cold, dark night, afraid and hungry, when he was only seven. This would be topped off with, "How would you like to live without food, electricity, television, or toys and go to the bathroom in an outhouse where you have to use leaves instead of toilet paper?" This, we were assured, was what lay in store for us if we did not do well in school.

I had to accept the fact very early on that my father made up stories, and to know the truth I had to go my mother. On my fourth birthday, Thia Vasso came over to babysit my brother, and my mother took me on the bus to go shopping at Hudson's in downtown Detroit. Until then, I had never seen a black person. Here, they were everywhere. I was transfixed.

Apparently, I was still processing what I had seen after we came home. I was sitting across from my father at the kitchen table while he was reading the newspaper and my mother was preparing dinner.

"Daddy, why are there black people?" I asked.

From behind the paper he responded, "Because they eat black olives."

"You eat black olives; why aren't you black?"

The paper came crashing onto the table, my father's face frozen in disbelief that I had questioned him. His arm shot out, and, much as a pitcher uses the windup to psych out the batter, he swung it around, bellowing, "They eat bushels and bushels of black olives!" I remember staring back, my cheeks burning with indignation that he would expect me to buy his story, but I said nothing. For the first time, I understood my mother's silence at these novel pronouncements and remained silent.

After dinner and birthday cake, my father went down to the basement with his cigar. Sitting at the table with me, my mother said softly, "Sophia, you asked why there are black people. What if God had only made roses? Instead, God made gardenias, lilies, carnations, and jasmine, a myriad of different flowers, all beautiful. He did the same thing with people. One is not more beautiful than the other. He just made different people." I just knew she was telling me the truth.

This abundant attention and encouragement came at a price: my parents' overprotectiveness. I was not allowed to climb a jungle gym because I might fall and break my leg. I couldn't hula hoop because I would hurt my back. I couldn't play in the foot-high fountain with the other kids because I would drown. Walking through the park, holding my father's hand, I stopped to watch a little girl fearlessly whirl her body around a bar, the biggest no-no of all. While my parents were laying the groundwork for love of learning, they were, unbeknownst to them, planting seeds of my seeking independence.

The first time I remember experiencing real fear was after learning that my mother had to stay in the hospital for "tests." I knew that very sick people went to the hospital and that many died there. The thought of losing my mother threatened my very existence. Both my mother's sisters came to help take care of us. The happiness I felt when my mother finally came home, thin but smiling, overwhelmed me. She told me that she prayed on the way to the hospital that it would not be serious, and she immediately heard a clear soft voice telling her, "Don't worry, it's nothing." The voice had been right. The doctors found nothing wrong with her, and her symptoms disappeared.

The next jolt to my universe was kindergarten. Not only was it the beginning of my very important formal education, but it was also my initiation into American life. Up until that point, I was under the impression that we were special because we were Greek, and everything civilized came from Greece. "Americans" on the other hand, ate from cans and boxes and were poisoning themselves with white sugar. I discovered that I was saddled with parents who were different from those of the other kids—parents who were from the old country and a generation older than the other moms and dads. No one else in school had the same name as mine, and I fantasized being a Debbie, Sharon, or Wanda. I wore handmade clothes other people thought were beautiful, while the other girls wore store-bought dresses that I was jealous of. I brought sandwiches made with homemade whole wheat bread and craved what was in the other lunch boxes—bologna or peanut butter and jelly sandwiches on Wonder bread accompanied with M&Ms, Twinkies, and cupcakes. The world no longer revolved around me simply because I existed. There were blonde girls who I thought were cuter than me. I did not get the lead role. I thought I was a shoo-in as Mother Goose in the school play, but instead was cast as the spoon that ran away with the plate in the Hey Diddle Diddle skit. How could life possibly get more humiliating?

To continue having the constant approval I was accustomed to receiving at home, I decided that I had to excel in everything, especially the English language. I was the only kindergartener who could read, and on parent-teacher day, I read from *The Cat in the Hat* out loud. I loved school, especially art. My obsession with drawing fashion figures had given me a boost. In second grade, I won a fifty-dollar savings bond for me and a color TV for my school after my drawing won first place in a statewide Michigan art contest. We had to draw what we wanted to be when we grew up, and I drew myself as an art teacher in a classroom with my students. My mother had brainwashed me with the idea. She could not fathom how any woman could make a respectable living in art other than by teaching it, while Georgie, of course, would become a doctor. The recognition of my artwork gave me a heady sense of achievement. I learned that artists were grownups who did nothing else but paint. That's what I wanted to do, but every time I brought it up, I was told to take my head out of the clouds.

According to plan, my father retired from Ford, and we moved to Argos, Greece. I was seven, smack in the middle of second grade, and Georgie was four and a half. The transition into my new world, the old country, was glorious. My mother's brother, Thio Demetri, had four daughters ranging in ages from one to seven, and instantly I had an extended family and playmates. My mother had so thoroughly described her life before coming to America—her house and garden, the church square, and the cast of characters of her youth—that it felt as though I had always lived there. Greeks revered America for the assistance provided during World War II, and we were regarded somewhat as celebrities. Kids at the public school hounded and chased me. My oldest cousin, Georgia, and her friends tried to shield me. Fed up, my parents placed me in a private school where English was taught, lest I forget it. I excelled in my newfound interests: math and writing essays and poetry in Greek. I was finding my footing.

What most fascinated me was life in Manesi, the village of my father's birth, which was inhabited by another slew of relatives. I now had a grandmother, my father's mother, who wore black, floor-length dresses. My aunts wore headscarves, and everyone spoke among themselves in Albanian. During the tobacco harvest, I was allowed to thread the large leaves on long pins, which were put out in the sun to dry. The cured tobacco gave off a wonderful woodsy aroma of citrus and juniper berries. My three male cousins were in their teens and taught me how to shoot a rifle. We had contests shooting at tin cans, and I would feel delight at their consternation when I won. Although my uncles had built their houses within the past decade, electricity and running water were yet to arrive. We had to go to the outhouse, and if you forgot to bring the toilet paper, there were leaves. My father had told the truth about that one!

My mother was in her element and could not have been happier. She had many friends who did not hide their elation in having her back. We often exchanged visits with them. I was always included in the discussion and made to feel that my opinion mattered. I liked all my mother's friends but loved no one more than Thia Angeliki. We would visit her two and three times a week, and sometimes, I would go all by myself. At each visit, the woman who had bet the farm on my parents' successful marriage told me a story she would pull out of her "story bag." She would tell the best jokes as we dunked our biscotti in Greek coffee. I could ask her anything, and I knew that she would tell me the truth.

I asked her if she thought Jesus minded if we had questions about the stars and why we were here on Earth. She said that not only did he want us to ask questions but he would also help us find the answers. "Sometimes," Thia Angeliki explained, "the answer comes when you are silent." She told me that it was okay that people like my mother took the Bible literally, but that I didn't have to. "Jesus taught in parables, painting mental pictures that made it easier for us to understand His message." I asked her what He meant when He said that it was easier for a camel to pass through an eye of a needle than for a rich man to go to heaven. She asked me what I thought it meant. I said that some rich people cared more about their money than about the poor. "See!" she exclaimed, her eyes twinkling, "That is an excellent interpretation!" I was sure that if Thia Angeliki had grown up in America she would have been on the Supreme Court.

The Bay of Pigs invasion on April 17, 1961 dropped a bomb on my magical childhood and our idyllic existence. President Kennedy had reluctantly approved the CIA's secret plan to invade Cuba by bombing Fidel Castro's small air force and sending in specially trained infantrymen, a plan started by his predecessor, President Eisenhower. Castro, however, found out about it and moved his planes to safety. Ground fighters were killed or taken prisoner. The Cold War was overheating, and my father feared retribution from Nikita Khrushchev, the leader of the Soviet Union. He convinced himself that if the USSR won, Khrushchev would take over Greece and put missiles there to counter the ones the United States had placed in Turkey. My father announced that we would be leaving for America in two days. When I asked him where in America, he answered, "I don't know yet." It was surreal. We needed to pack our belongings, make travel plans, and bid farewell to family and friends. The worst part was witnessing my mother's despair. That night, behind closed doors, I heard my parents arguing and my mother crying. Gripped by insecurity, I knew that nothing was going to change my father's mind.

A flurry of activity ensued. Everyone appeared to be in a state of shock. The only person who was levelheaded, like an anchor that keeps a boat from drifting into a stormy sea, was Thia Angeliki. Relatives, the handyman, even the laundress pitched in, packing our belongings for storage until we could send for them. Throughout the day, one by one, my mother's friends came to say goodbye amid hugs and tears. My brother and I went to school to break the news. The time came to say goodbye to my cousins, but it wasn't until Thia Angeliki hugged me tight that I cried.

At the Port of Piraeus, we embarked on the ocean liner *Saturnia*, bound for New York with four suitcases, one for each of us. My father had decided that we were going to live somewhere on the West Coast and had prepared a list of twenty-one cities where he had worked or visited in his youth. During the entire crossing, he stared at the piece of paper. Every so often, in an "aha" moment, he would bang his fist on the table and cross off a city on the list. When we arrived at the port in New York, three cities remained: Portland, San Francisco, and Los Angeles. After eleven days at sea, the three of us sat in the terminal and stared at him, I on my little blue suitcase, waiting for him to make his decision. All of a sudden, pointing to a poster of Oregon with the "O" depicting a bright sun, he bellowed, "We're going to Portland, Oregon!"

"Where's that?" my mother asked.

"It's above California," he informed us and then lied, "It only rains there seventeen days a year."

After spending the night in a hotel, we boarded a train for the three-day cross-country trip. My father deemed it important that we understand the vastness of America. When we complained of being tired, he told us stories of the "old days" when he crisscrossed the country, catching rides atop boxcars, "in the wind, the cold, and the rain with only a quarter in my pocket." My mother stayed mostly silent as she stared out the window.

We emerged from the train in Portland amid a torrential downpour. That was when my mother had her meltdown. "Where on Earth did you bring us? Where did you bring us . . . ?" she repeated, wailing, while tears streamed down her face along with the raindrops. There was no consoling her. Finally, my father offered something that seemed to work. "Listen, Anna, we'll rent a furnished apartment, and I'll go to California for ten days to see if it's better there."

My parents found an apartment across from the Maroutsos family in downtown Portland. They were one of the many contacts that friends and relatives had provided us. Our two families formed an instant bond, and

Betty Maroutsos became my best friend. As soon as my mother and Mrs. Maroutsos forged their friendship, my father took off on the California scouting mission he had promised my mother. He returned exactly ten days later. "Los Angeles was too flat, and San Francisco was too hilly," he declared. "We're staying here." My mother sighed a resigned acceptance. I had the distinct feeling that my father had made up the trip to California and, instead, had gone off fishing somewhere to recharge and give us time to acclimate. I was allowed to attend Shattuck School at the tail end of fifth grade. I loved the diversity of kids. It was the first time I had Jewish classmates, and Henry, an African American, became my protector.

My father had great disdain for credit cards and debt. He paid cash for everything, including the house we moved into the following year in Laurelhurst, a neighborhood close to downtown. The house met the main requirements that it have good schools and be near the bus stop and within walking distance of the Greek Orthodox church. I was enrolled in the sixth grade at the Laurelhurst Grade School. This was an entirely different environment. The students were all white. The girls came to class wearing lipstick and nylon stockings while I was still in anklets. Every day they wore different, perfectly matched outfits. My meager wardrobe was mixed and matched, as my mother felt it unnecessary to have more than four or five changes of clothes. Makeup and nylons were strictly forbidden.

There was a hierarchy of popular girls, and I was at the bottom of the heap. I had never been called a nerd before. I became depressed and longed for our life in Greece. Without any support from my parents in the socialization arena, I realized that I was solely responsible for my own self-improvement. I read every teen fashion magazine I could get my hands on. My mother had taught me how to sew, and home ec became my favorite class. If my parents were not going to buy the clothes I needed, I would make them myself.

Attempting to mirror the other girls' clothes with my hair in a flip and nylons that I would sneak to school, I began to regain my confidence. I was considered "funny" and began making friends. My enthusiasm for school returned, and I was noticed by my teachers. When I was in eighth grade, my seventy-year-old father learned how to drive and bought his first car. Nothing but a Ford would do. He wanted a Thunderbird, but it wouldn't fit in the garage, so he bought a copper-colored Comet with cash. Having a car made me feel "American."

While my goal in grade school was to fit in with everyone else, US Grant High School, with more than 3,000 students, gave me a platform on which to experiment with my individuality. I hated that I had to wear glasses. I took the wire-rimmed ones that my father had worn in the 1920s, now made cool by John Lennon, and had them filled with my prescription. I was the first one in my school to wear clogs that I bought at the orthopedic shoe store that sold sturdy, old lady shoes. Soon, more girls were heard clopping down the halls in clogs. I was regarded as "artsy." Girls who were good in math were considered nerdy. After taking the required algebra class my freshman year, I abandoned math for art and creative writing. There was a network of tight cliques, and I found my place in a circle of good friends.

I still had to deal with the strict rules my parents expected me to adhere to. Dating was forbidden until I graduated from high school. There were stories circulating at school that my father had a shotgun. The restriction had made me boy crazy and put my mother at her wit's end. "Why can't you be like Betty?" she bemoaned, referring to my straight-laced Greek friend. My mother became ultra-vigilant. Once in my sophomore year, she figured out that I had lied about my whereabouts to go out on a double date, and I was grounded from going anywhere by myself for one year to the day. However, my parents were losing the battle to control my attire. Never had I seen my father's face get redder than when I appeared in my first mini dress that laced up an open back before going to a party. "Anna, look at this!" he hollered. "Your daughter is going out in her underwear!"

The next time my father got that mad was in my senior year when I announced that I wanted to be a cheerleader. "Forget about it if you think you're going to advertise your legs to the world," he yelled. "Not my daughter!" I went on a hunger strike. After my refusal to eat three consecutive meals (at home), my mother frantically begged for his mercy until he finally relented. I tried out and made it on the rally squad.

I was chomping at the bit to go away to college and run my own show. Most of my friends were going to the University of Oregon, and I wanted to go with them. My parents emphatically refused. I pled my case with my list of pros but was struck down. We fought and screamed. Finally, we struck a deal. I could transfer to the U of O after spending my first two years living at home and attending Portland State College.

When I entered Portland State College in 1969 as an art education major, there were protests everywhere. The war in Vietnam raged on, and students staged peace demonstrations. I witnessed students standing in the park directly in front of the school, arms interlocked in solidarity, being clubbed by the riot squad. The Black Panthers, a revolutionary black nationalist organization first formed to counter police brutality in neighborhoods, were expanding across the country, protesting against racism while being unfairly branded as terrorists by FBI Director J. Edgar Hoover. Women of all ages, tired of male oppression, took their voices to the streets. And then there were the hippies, the "flower children," who rebelled against what they viewed as a controlling "establishment." They rejected middle-class values of the "bourgeoisie" while advocating psychedelics, peace, and the if-it-feels-good-then-do-it attitude of the free-love movement. I had friends in all of these groups. There were enough Greeks at PSC to form the Delphi Club, aimed at promoting Greek culture and an excuse to come together to have lamb roasts, drink, dance, and discuss politics.

It was my ethics class that had the most profound impact on me. I had blindly accepted that only the New and Old Testaments of the Bible gave instructions on how to be a good person. I vacillated about the Jesus story, particularly the resurrection and the idea that our salvation depended on our belief in Him. It seemed unfair that good people all over the world who had not been exposed to Christianity would go to hell. Now, I was learning that ethics and morality had been hotly debated topics among atheists hundreds of years before Jesus walked on Earth! If there were just as many female saints as male, why were all the church canons written by men? To subjugate women, of course; to keep us silent, pregnant, and oppressed while they wielded money and power!

I became disillusioned with Christianity, finding it hypocritical that the Church had taken people's land and money to build grandiose cathedrals when Jesus was all about humility and embracing the poor and disenfranchised. I agreed with Karl Marx that religion is the opiate of the masses, and my poor mother had drunk that Kool-Aid. Logic overruled my belief that Jesus was the Son of God. My mother had taught me to "talk" to Jesus and "take His hand" whenever I felt sadness or anguish. I could still do that with God. I concluded that Jesus was a very wise teacher who also condoned socialistic concepts, something I could never have brought up at home.

At the end of the summer of my sophomore year, without a spiritual bone in my body, I was off to the University of Oregon. My independence, at last!

CHAPTER 4

Meeting Bucky

The U of O campus in Eugene, two hours south of Portland, was a progressive oasis in the middle of proud redneck country. In 1971, Eugene was a collision course of long-haired, tie-dyed-clad hippies, preppies, Hare Krishnas, New Agers, cool professors, and gun-toting, deer-hunting loggers. It was a hotbed for intellectual discussions and new ways to break out of conventional norms.

The life-changing breakthrough I had experienced after my freaky dream that Rob so eloquently interpreted had me seeing the world out of a different lens. No longer content to be living life out of someone else's playbook, I was ready to peel off what was no longer working for me and create my own reality. Losing my virginity in such a mystical way confirmed my resolve. I was one of the last of my friends to "do it," and some had half-jokingly wondered if the sex would turn me into some kind of nymphomaniac. Just the opposite. The experience that had deeply touched me on so many levels had raised the bar. I wasn't interested in having arbitrary sex with any Joe Blow. I knew what was possible, and I knew that I would just know when it was supposed to happen again.

My art education track and I were not a good fit. I went into the program thinking that it was an opportunity to explore different art mediums but discovered that the creative juices were not always flowing for my 8 a.m. painting class. Just as I would get into it, it was time to pack up and switch gears to sculpture, silk screening, jewelry making, or photography. Art was supposed to be expressed without restrictions, and turning my creativity on and off according to some school schedule felt mechanical. With only six credit hours left to complete along with a teaching internship, which I dreaded, I had to stick it out and graduate. One night, I had a dream that was brief and to the point:

> *The doorbell rings. I open the door, and the mailman hands me an enve-*
> *lope. I tear it open, and as soon as I realize that it's my official teaching*
> *certificate, the thought kicks me in the gut—I don't want to be a teacher.*
> *I toss it in a blue, plastic waste paper basket.*

I woke up with a jolt. I didn't need anyone to help me interpret this one. It was as if the decision had been made for me—I was not going to teach, and I would continue drawing and painting regardless of my profession. I lay in bed contemplating different career paths. Presenting arguments in court as a criminal attorney seemed exciting, but there were all those cases to memorize, and what if an innocent person went to prison because of me? Skin behavior—rashes, sweat, zits, wrinkles—had always fascinated me. As a dermatologist I could treat weird skin diseases, but that meant medical school and dissecting cadavers, so that was out.

My mind floated to the summer between my junior and senior years in high school spent in Greece with my family. There was a French team of archeologists digging in the ancient theater of Argos. I loved hanging around watching them carefully extract, dust off, and organize artifacts. In fact, it had been thrilling. That's it! I would become an archeologist. That day, I marched down to the registrar's office, and because there was no formal archeology department, I changed my major to art history.

When I excitedly announced my new field of study to my parents, my father had a meltdown. How could I do anything as stupid so close to graduation? He threatened to cut me off financially. I argued that since I had completed all of my basic requirements, it would take no more than two extra terms. He then launched into the life-threatening dangers the profession of archeology posed to women. I held my ground. He relented, and we made a deal—I would pay for any additional classes beyond the two terms. I threw myself into ancient art history, studying the Greeks, Romans, and Etruscans.

Toward the end of my first term in my new major, the department awarded me the scholarship I had applied for to study with a top Etruscologist the following summer in Perugia, Italy. As much as my father disapproved of my changing majors, this impressed him enough to give me his blessings and financial support.

The art history department at the U of O was unaware or did not convey to me that the esteemed Etruscologist did not speak English and that his lectures were in Italian. When I arrived in Perugia, my Italian vocabulary consisted of pizza, *arrivederci*, and *ciao*. I took language courses and discovered that all things Italian—art, fashion, food, opera, and the people—zinged my senses.

What had the most profound impact on me was the architecture. I tuned in to how designers manipulated space to evoke different sensations. Coming upon a large, open piazza felt more dramatic after walking down narrow winding streets. The ornateness of Renaissance churches aroused awe, while sleek, modern, minimalist interiors projected a Zen-like quality. I rented a spacious room and shared the tiny bathroom that doubled as a shower stall with a Japanese girl.

My landlady was heavily into Rococo, and my room had an elaborate chandelier and a massively carved bed. Umberto, who lived with his mother on the top floor, had transformed their apartment into a *2001 Space Odyssey* disco with black lights and moving lava lamp images projected onto a blank wall. Discovering these contrasts of the very old mixed with the new was invigorating.

While in Perugia, I learned of a spectacular art school in Firenze, L'Universita Internazionale dell'Arte. It had opened only a few years before in response to the disastrous 1966 Arno River flooding that had damaged thousands of masterpieces and manuscripts. The focus was art restoration, but the school also offered classes in painting, drawing, art history, film, and industrial design. The idea of studying art and art history in such a beautiful, historic city was overpowering. I called my parents to tell them why I needed to stay an additional three months. They demanded I come straight home. I reminded my mother that it was she who taught me that only I could decide what was best for me, and here was an opportunity to put her preaching into practice. Reluctantly, they agreed to wire not one penny more than four hundred dollars. I was jubilant even though the money would only provide for my living expenses but not tuition. At the end of my course work, I hitchhiked to Firenze with an American girl I met outside the American Express office.

Firenze looked as if the Renaissance paintings I had studied in art history class had come alive. I could not have dreamed up an educational facility or atmosphere more conducive to study art. On a hill just above Villa il Ventaglio, a sprawling park overlooking the city, stood the refurbished Villa San Paolo and San Paolino, replete with many of the original antique furnishings. The faculty was top-notch, and there was a revolving door of world-renowned artists, film directors, and historians coming to lecture. The seats in the auditorium were equipped with phone sets for instantaneous English translation like the ones at the UN. This was school? How was I going to come up with the tuition? The Super 8mm movie camera I had brought with me gave me an idea. In return for free tuition, I would propose to shoot a film to promote the school in the States. I made an appointment with the director to make the pitch.

I was led into *il direttore*'s office and was surprised at how tiny he was. His desk was on a raised dais where he sat on a chair that looked like a throne. He gestured toward a very low contemporary armchair into which I sank even lower. Clearly, the setup was designed to intimidate. I told him about my promo film idea and explained how it would be distributed to art departments in major universities in the States. I would need to attend classes for no more than three months to get a good feel for the curriculum, and since I would not finish the semester, I should not have to pay. Incredibly, he agreed to let me sit in on four classes. I took painting and art history, which were taught by Louisa Beccherucci, past director of the Uffizi Gallery. Federico Fellini came to my film class to discuss *8 ½*, and we previewed *Cries and Whispers* with Ingmar Bergman himself before the film came out. In my industrial design class, we had ongoing dialogues with Italy's leading designers, who also critiqued our work. My project was one of six selected to be exhibited at the Pitti Palace. Could I have been dreaming all of this? Although I did film some footage of the school grounds and classrooms, I never saw *il direttore* again; he seemed to have forgotten about me.

I roomed with two of my classmates, Jacqueline from Belgium and Erika from Switzerland, in a three-bedroom apartment. The living room had a fresco on the ceiling. Going into my third month, I had to face the reality that my funds were drying up, and I could not afford the rent. I desperately wanted to finish my projects, but asking my parents for more money was not an option. Another classmate, Rod, who lived with six guys—mostly American—offered to share his room with me, and gallantly created a divider of storage boxes between us.

It was a vibrant, heady time. One of my new roommates, Ward, was a passionate student of architecture. We would stay up until dawn smoking too many Gauloises cigarettes while solving the world's problems.

Thanksgiving caught us off guard. Finding a turkey in Italy was problematic; it had to be ordered a month in advance. I opted to stuff three chickens instead. Since there was no room in the fridge, I waited to buy them on Thanksgiving Day. I went to the market early in the morning only to find everything closed. It was a Virgin Mary holiday. We all pooled together whatever food we had, and I stuffed green peppers with eggplant, bread, and cheese, proudly presenting them on a platter in the shape of roast turkey.

One night in the midst of an existential discussion, Ward asked me if I could spend a half hour with anyone dead or alive, who would I choose. I probably said Thomas Jefferson, but that's irrelevant. I asked whom he would choose. He said Buckminster Fuller. I had heard the name and that he had invented the geodesic dome. I wanted to know why, of all the humans who have walked the Earth, Ward would pick someone so obscure. Ward looked at me as if I had said that I had never heard of Santa Claus. He went to his room, returned with a thin book entitled, *No More Secondhand God*, and handed it to me. I took it to bed and read it all the way through. It was an astonishing thirty-page poem. I had never seen words used like that before. Some of them seemed to be made up. Some were strung out into very long, stream-of-consciousness sentences.

The book touched a deep, spiritual chord. I had resisted accepting God as an enthroned, white-haired despot whom we were supposed to love and, at the same time, be in fear of lest He send us to boil in oil in hell. Here I was presented with a dynamic God, one who had created everything with love energy. I felt as if I were having a dialogue with the author. Yes, God is energy, and energy is everywhere—in every single one of us. All of it resonated with me. Who exactly was this R. Buckminster Fuller? It would have been impossible to fathom at the time how that exchange with Ward would impact my future.

With just enough lira to get me to the airport, it was time to say *arrivederci, Italia*. As soon as I arrived back in the States just before winter term of 1973, I read *Operating Manual for Spaceship Earth*, Buckminster Fuller's book that mapped out his evolutionary journey. I was blown away by this man's genius, world perspective, and compassion for his fellow humans. He had designed a streamlined three-wheeled car that could pivot on a dime, which he claimed could reach 128 mph with its flat-top V8 engine, and a round house constructed of strong, lightweight aluminum left over from World War II to help reduce homelessness. He proposed a two-mile long geodesic glass dome covering lower Manhattan to regulate climate, conserve energy, and reduce pollution. Fuller was about saving humanity by using available resources and new technology economically and efficiently. He predicted a day when we would transmit and retrieve information instantly on handheld devices. I could not stop talking about him with anyone who would listen, or not. Why wasn't this American Leonardo da Vinci on the tip of everyone's tongue?

Back in school after Christmas break, I saw the flyer. Dr. R. Buckminster Fuller was coming to speak at Erb Memorial Hall on campus and give a separate lecture in the architecture department. It seemed unreal that someone I had hardly known anything about just months before had not only become my hero, but now I was going to see and hear him in person.

My friend Mark, who was president of the student union, dropped by my apartment. He was one of the few people who would enthusiastically discuss with me minute information about my newfound idol.

As soon as I opened the door, he said, "Guess who's coming to speak this Tuesday?"

"Buckminster Fuller!" I could hardly contain my excitement.

"I'm picking him and his wife up from the airport in Portland. Do you want to come with me?"

I stood dumbfounded.

"One guy offered me a hundred bucks to ride with me," he continued, "but I know how much he means to you."

"Are you kidding, Mark? I would love to! Thank you, thank you, thank you!" I said, unable to find better words to sufficiently express my gratitude. I couldn't concentrate on anything but the fact that I would be in the same car with Buckminster Fuller all the way back from Portland. How could I be so lucky!

I woke up very early Tuesday morning to a light snowfall. There were predictions, however, of significant accumulation, a rough after-work commute, and canceled flights. I refused to entertain the thought that their flight might be canceled. Mark called to say that we should set out on the two-hour drive to Portland as soon as possible to beat the heavy snow.

At the airport I waited in the car while Mark went to meet our esteemed guests. It was hard to fathom that I was about to meet the man I had only recently come to so greatly admire. Until Mark asked me to come along with him, I would have never considered it to be in the realm of possibility.

Mark beamed as he escorted the smiling couple. Neither one could have been taller than five feet four. Buckminster Fuller looked quite preppy wearing a blue blazer, button-down shirt, and striped tie. He was bald, and his glasses were so thick that they magnified his eyes unnaturally. His wife wore her snow-white hair in a bun, and her eyes were an intense sky blue. He climbed in the front seat, and his wife settled in next to me in the back. As Mark began making formal introductions, Dr. Fuller looked back at me, interjecting, "That's Anne, and you can call me Bucky."

The snow was thick, and the four hours it took to drive back to Eugene afforded us the time to get well acquainted. I was delighted at how natural it felt. At one point in the middle of a sentence, Bucky turned around and said, "Darlin', I need to take a nap," and as soon as his head nestled back on the headrest, he fell asleep. Noticing my surprise, Anne said, "He does this all the time." After a ten-minute snooze, he cheerfully picked up where he had left off. Even though I called Anne by her first name, I could only address him as Dr. Fuller.

By the time we arrived on campus, I had fallen in love with the couple. Bucky invited me to accompany them to the day's scheduled events. I was not prepared for the honor or the thrill. It was standing room only at both lectures. Bucky lectured for hours, speaking in robot-like staccato, running sentences together, circuitously painting concepts with his unique use of words, then stopping for effect. He spoke the way he wrote. He relished students' inquisitiveness and animatedly answered their questions. While students stood around to meet him after the lectures, Anne and I were having cozy conversations about their life together. She told me that normally she did not accompany her husband on his non-stop lecture tours around the globe, but she had come with him on this one because it was her birthday. They were both seventy-seven.

I made arrangements with Mark and his girlfriend, Jeannette, to take Bucky and Anne out for her birthday later that night at Farrell's Ice Cream Parlour. As the entire wait-staff brought her cake and ice cream with a lit candle and sang "Happy Birthday," I floated in a state of grace. It just could not get better than this.

But it did. As we were leaving the restaurant, Bucky took me aside and said, "Darlin', Anne and I have taken a shine to you, and we want to ask you if you would travel with us." I could only stare at him, speechless. "Talk it over with your parents, and let me know," he added as he placed his card in my hand. Overwhelmed, I was unable to fully process his proposal or the reality of it. As we said our goodbyes and hugged and kissed, I knew that my parents would never allow me to quit school and travel with Anne and

Bucky. We had forged a real friendship, and I also knew that we would be in each other's company again.

As I lay in bed that night, my mind kept replaying the fortuitous events that had culminated in my meeting Buckminster Fuller. Had I unconsciously manifested it? What if I hadn't changed my major and gone to Italy? What if Ward had never brought up his name or shown me the book? Was it just luck that Mark not only shared my interest in Bucky but had been in a position to invite me to ride along with him to the airport, spurning others' offers of money? Could it be that the mental conversation I had had with Bucky about his conceptualization of God while I was reading *No More Secondhand God*, which opened my mind to Him, had something to do with it? What else could explain the forces that brought us together and the instantaneous connection between us?

A new desire burst forth—to study architecture. It encompassed all of my interests—my love of buildings, art, history, psychology, and improving people's lives. Meeting Bucky had confirmed it. I fell asleep thanking my lucky stars.

CHAPTER 5

Finding a Path to a Career and the Way to a Greek Island

Clearly, I had found my passion. Architecture was my calling. Just one year before, I had not even considered studying art in Italy, let alone tuition free for six months. Buckminster Fuller was an obscure name until Ward introduced me to his work. Never in my wildest dreams could I have imagined that not only would I meet him, but that we would now be corresponding. I was emboldened with a sense that anything is possible. No obstacle was going to stop me from my newfound destiny if I could help it.

There was the issue of breaking the news to my father. I asked him to sit down, told him my decision, and braced myself for him to throw a fit. Instead he looked at me with an expression peculiarly void of affect.

"What happened to your passion for archeology?" he asked matter-of-factly.

"It's still there, but architecture incorporates that and every other interest I have—design, history, human nature . . ."

His eyes squinted as he interrupted, "Are you saying that you are not going to graduate when you are supposed to and that I'll be paying for college until God knows when?"

"Yes, but think about it: when I'm done, I'll be designing buildings! I thought you would be really happy about it," I lied.

"Ha! I'm happy if you're happy, but it's not coming out of my pocket!" He meant it.

"Fine, I'll do it by myself," I said resolutely. Deep down, I couldn't blame him, but being cut off financially only fortified my determination.

I decided to first take a break from school and move back home to save money. Working in an architect's office as a girl Friday seemed like a good idea. Armed with a portfolio of my artwork, I landed a job as a gofer at a firm in a Portland suburb. The setting was beautiful—a quintessential Pacific Northwest all-wood building encircled with outdoor decks nestled amidst tall firs. Most of my time was spent in the print room breathing ammonia fumes while printing architectural drawings. I learned how to draft while my responsibilities grew. One young architect, Ron, took a special interest in me and my enthusiasm about how buildings are designed. He would meticulously explain details of his projects while sketching little diagrams. He was dashing with longish, dark hair and hazel eyes, and soon, I looked forward to his witty banter. Every so often at lunchtime, he would saunter off into the woods playing his flute snake-charmer style. It worked. Ron and I began dating.

At the time, University of Oregon's architecture department was rated third in the country and offered a five-year Bachelor of Architecture professional degree. It was daunting to learn that only ten out of hundreds of change-of-major applicants were accepted into the program annually. My experience at the architectural firm certainly would be a boost, but I also felt the need to get to know professors who would attest to my abilities. In the fall I quit my job and moved back to Eugene, enrolling in three general architecture courses offered to students outside the program while working as a part-time hostess in a popular restaurant. Ron and I visited each other every weekend. Our relationship had blossomed into true love. My first.

I treasured my friendship with Bucky and Anne Fuller. Bucky informed me that he would again be visiting the U of O as a guest lecturer and asked me to lunch at the Eugene Hotel. When I told him about the steep competition in getting accepted into the program, he whipped out his Mont Blanc fountain pen and on his paper placemat began drawing a series of triangles that turned into a geodesic sphere. Next to it he began by writing, "Dear Bob," addressing it to Bob Harris, the dean of the department, who had once been his student. Awestruck, I was witnessing Buckminster Fuller writing me a letter of recommendation.

At a party, I met a professor of architecture and a Grecophile who went by the name of Raffaello. He told me that he and George, the chair of the ceramics department who was of Greek descent, had been talking about offering a combined art and architecture summer course on the Greek island of Spetses, but the problem was that neither of them spoke Greek. I could think of nothing more wonderful. I told him that, contingent on being accepted to the program, I would love to join the group and be their interpreter. That, he said excitedly, would solve the language issue.

With shining letters of recommendation from my professors, I moved back home. I put all my efforts into the application process and waitressed as much as I could. The packet was sent out and uncertainty crept in. My entire future was at stake, let alone the prospect of starting my formal architecture training on a Greek Island. Not only was the group holding a spot for me, but the full tuition would be waived in exchange for my translating services. The logistics, however, were tricky. The acceptance letters were due to be sent out by April 1, and the deadline for registering for the course was April 4. Would I know if I was accepted in time? I put out an SOS to the Universe, beseeching a miracle. I decided that all my actions henceforth would be taken as if I had already been accepted. Ron and I made plans to meet in Athens after my course was over.

Every week, a group comprising twelve art and twelve architecture students met with Raffaello and George to discuss particulars of the trip, which was now to begin in Copenhagen, touring social housing projects. I attended the meetings when I could, making the two-hour drive each way and staying overnight with my friend Linda, a fourth-year architecture student. She lived in one of three, tiny, one-bedroom cabins in back of the large main house where I used to live.

After one of the meetings in mid-March, Linda and I made our usual plan to meet at her design studio and go out to dinner. As we were walking down the hall, another student stopped to greet her and began relating what had just occurred at the department's admissions committee meeting. He was one of six students who, along with six professors, were in the process of selecting the change-of-major applicants. They had spent two hours discussing the fate of a controversial student whose transcript consisted of mostly A's and F's and no-passes. It appeared that she excelled in the courses that interested her without officially dropping the ones that didn't. I had been suspended for doing that—could I be standing face to face with someone who had a hand in my fate? I felt like a fly on the wall as he described how all six students and three faculty members were in favor of her, two had concerns, and one was gung-ho against her. In a heated exchange, one of the students had challenged the professor who vehemently opposed the applicant, accusing him of being threatened by the possibility that she would find his class boring and quit attending. Linda's friend then stuck his face smack in front of hers and said, "And this chick had a frickin' reference letter from Buckminster Fuller written on a frickin' placemat!"

I felt a kick in my solar plexus—he was talking about me. "So, did she get in?" I asked, trying to sound blasé.

"Hell yeah!"

Standing there in blissful anonymity, I felt utter elation. "Linda, excuse me, I'm going to stop in the bathroom," I said hurriedly, trying to avoid any possible last-minute introductions.

"Oh, I'm coming, too," she said as she waved goodbye to her friend. "I'm so sorry I didn't introduce you; he was talking so fast. His name is . . ."

"Linda! Didn't you get it? He was talking about me! I'm in!" I whooped. "First I have to stop at a pay phone and call Ron. You and I are going to a restaurant that serves champagne, my treat!"

The Universe had answered my pleas with an improbable coincidence. In one fell swoop I was made aware that my short- and long-term goals were materializing. Summer study on a Greek island and an architectural career were now a certainty. I had two weeks to buy the ticket, register, and get my things in order—not just for the trip, but also for transitioning back to being a full-time student in the fall, this time without financial assistance from my father. With financial aid and a part-time job, I was determined to make it work.

Ron was thrilled to learn that we were going to meet in Greece for real. When the acceptance letter arrived, he took me out to my favorite Northern Italian restaurant to celebrate and pledged his love and support.

I began to prepare for the trip in earnest. Anticipating delectable Greek food—fresh fish, traditionally prepared dishes, and butter-and-honey-laden desserts—I made two skirts and two pairs of pants with expandable, drawstring waistbands. Ron and I bought our tickets and set a date to meet in Athens, spend two weeks in Spetses and mainland Greece, and fly home together. My acceptance letter came the day before the deadline to register. Mary, a beautiful, blue-eyed blonde with a sunny smile, lilting laugh, and quick-witted humor, who was one of the art students in the group and lived on campus, offered to register for me.

After standing in a long line toward the end of the day, Mary encountered a glitch. She was told that the library fees I had incurred had to be paid before I could be registered. She had tried calling several times, but I wasn't home. My mother, with her limited English, kept telling her to call back later and hanging up. In a mad dash, Mary found another student in the group to front the money and registered me in the nick of time, indebting me to both of them.

Ron drove me to the airport, and we met up with the rest of the group at the gate. When it was time to board, he kissed me and gave me a card I was not supposed to open until the plane took off. From my seat, I could see Ron watching the plane from the terminal. I opened the card. Like the others he had given me to express what was in his heart, he had painted it with watercolors.

Once in the air, I went over to where Mary sat to tell her how grateful I was for all the hoops she had gone through for me. I sat in the empty seat next to her, and we began talking as if we had been friends forever. Her boyfriend was coming to meet her at the same time as Ron. She related her phone conversations with my mother, hysterically imitating her Greek accent. I told her about my expandable skirts and pants and described the foodie experiences awaiting us—tiny fried smelts with cold beer, moussaka, pastitsio, lamb souvlaki grilled over coals, kataifi, and loukoumades—my favorite—deep-fried dough balls with soft centers, slathered with honey and cinnamon . . .

"Um," Mary cut me off, "I'm really not into food that much."

My heart sank. How could someone so lively not be into food? She probably came from one of those American families my mother always talked about who ate out of cans and boxes. How could I be so wrong about having so much in common with her? I returned to my seat.

Having arrived in Spetses, the group was divided into three villas. Mary was in mine. She soon became my hearty eating companion, starting out the day with a heavenly breakfast of feta cheese and tomato omelets with crispy fried potatoes, thick Greek yogurt, and honey for a midmorning snack, lunches of dilled garlic meatballs and peasant salads with crusty bread dunked in the juice, and afternoon coffee with ice cream. Dinner was always a spread of traditional Greek dishes washed down with Greek wine followed with a baklava or kataifi and a big, solid chocolate bar on the way home. We did this every single day. We became inseparable, confiding in each other all aspects of our lives and hopes for the future. We decided to take eleven days between the end of our course and our boyfriends' arrivals to visit my relatives and a few nearby islands.

There were classes, of course. We'd meet for full-day drawing marathons and fired clay pots in pit fire kilns we made by digging holes in the ground. My first of ten required studio projects was to design a small house, adhering to the island's historic committee's strict vernacular exterior tradition and given artistic license with the interior. It seemed unreal that I was finishing my first term studying architecture on a Greek island accruing eighteen credit hours.

Mary and I each gained twenty-five pounds in two months. We wondered how our boyfriends would react. We made a plan. After visiting my relatives for a few days and having homemade meals, finishing everything on our plate lest they be offended, we ate only yogurt with canned peaches and pears, a diet I had read about in a magazine. Only once did we stray from our regimen. Walking past a bakery, I caught a glimpse of large, puffy cinnamon-and-sugar-covered donuts. We shared one with our coffee. Our days were spent walking on beaches, swimming, and going to the bathroom. We both lost eleven pounds in ten days.

Back in Athens, Mary and I parted, she to meet her boyfriend and me to spend the night catching up with Eileen, my friend from Portland who lived in an Athens suburb with her Greek husband. The next day was my long-awaited rendezvous with Ron. We were to meet at noon outside the American Express office where tourists cashed traveler's checks and picked up their mail. Eileen dropped me off early. I couldn't wait to see Ron. It was hard to believe that in a couple of hours we would be in each other's arms.

After picking up my mail, I found a table at the outdoor café right next to the office and, happy to be alone with my thoughts, ordered a Nescafe, the Greeks' interpretation of American coffee. Two Austrian guys sitting at a nearby table, having noticed my Fodor's guide in English and me speaking fluent Greek with the waiter, introduced themselves, eager to engage in travel talk. I told them how much I was anticipating meeting my boyfriend, whom I had not seen or talked with in more than two months. The waiter brought the coffee, and I took the opportunity to read my mail. As I looked up, someone who looked like Ron except for a bizarre haircut was walking toward the American Express office.

"Ron! Ron?" I stood up and yelled. Frozen in his tracks, he stared in my direction. Realizing it was me, he broke into a run. In the midst of hugs and kisses he asked, "What are you doing here today?"

"We were supposed to meet today. At noon," I replied, baffled.

"I thought we were meeting tomorrow," he said, equally mystified. "I came by today to cash some checks."

"What happened to your hair?" I asked, staring.

"I was visiting my father in Miami and went to a Cuban barber who could barely speak English. I tried to tell him in my high school Spanish to cut it short in the front and longer in the back, but he got it backwards." We laughed until we cried. "Well, look at you!" he said with a wide grin, looking me up and down.

"Well?"

"I love it!" he said enthusiastically, "You look so . . . healthy!"

"I know, you're talking about my tan. This," I said, pointing to my hips, "is after losing ten pounds. You'd better hurry up and go before the office closes, and come back!" As Ron took off running, it dawned on me how we had met by chance. Had he waited until the next day, there would have been no way to communicate with each other. I turned around to the Austrians and told them about the remarkable happenstance.

I reflected on the events that had given me the courage to find the path of my heart and not the one that my mother had chosen for me. Against substantial odds, I was accepted into the architecture program, which had put me on a glorious Greek island studying art and design. Had I not taken action and offered to be the group's interpreter, would Raffaello and George still be kicking the can down the road about what a great idea that would be? And what about Linda's friend on the admissions committee? What were the chances of me being present while he unwittingly disclosed the controversy around my application? Again, it was because I had spoken up and surreptitiously asked about the applicant's fate that I found out I had been accepted and was able to prepare for the trip.

Now, here in Athens, I was about to spend two, glittery weeks in Greece with the man I loved. I was overcome with gratitude. I closed my eyes to keep in the tears. Just then, Ron kissed me on the forehead, and we embraced, not needing to verbalize how lucky we were.

The waiter approached the table with two glasses of cognac. I told him that we hadn't ordered them.

"They are from us," one of the Austrian guys shouted. "We have just witnessed the power of love."

CHAPTER 6

The Choice

There was barely any time to transition from the deep blue Mediterranean sky to Eugene's gray clouds and relentless rain. Linda was leaving to study in Japan for a term, and I sublet her little, pine-paneled cabin until the one across from hers became available. Mary and I were joined at the hip. I procured grants and loans, got a work-study job designing and drafting stage sets in the theater arts department, and waitressed one night a week. I had never studied or worked this hard in my life, nor with such intensity of purpose.

Of the ten design studios required for graduation, students could only take two per school year. Design studios offered off campus, such as the one in Greece, however, were allowed in addition to the two-per-year limit. Since I was paying for tuition and living expenses myself, and with one studio under my belt, I vowed to blaze through and finish within three years.

Two required classes, Structures, involving heavy-duty math, and Environmental Control Systems (ECS), the design of plumbing/heating/ electrical systems, each spanned two terms and culminated in a formal review where student presentations were showcased and critiqued by professors. First-year students were advised not to take both classes concurrently because of their high difficulty and time consumption. My accelerated graduation plan did not allow for this option. Each group of two or three students was required to select an existing building, analyze one of its structural components, and design appropriate electrical, plumbing, heating, and cooling systems. I partnered with Rebecca for the structural analysis, and Skip, Mary's new boyfriend, joined us for the ECS part. I was diving in the deep end without knowing how to swim.

Male students far outnumbered females, and some of the mostly male faculty were patronizing toward the women. Rebecca and I chose a pole structure and took on the challenge of analyzing a joint with five intersecting stresses. After presenting our proposal to our two professors, we were told that it was going to be too difficult and were advised to choose something "less complicated." Were we not there to learn? We argued that this building had been built and that someone had figured out the joint loads, so why not give us the chance to analyze them? The men shared knowing smiles and approved our proposal.

We quickly learned that they were not kidding—it was tough. Between learning a whole new discipline with its own language and trying to hold on to two jobs, I made fewer trips home, and Ron, a most patient tutor, visited more frequently. I developed a twitch in my left eye when the weekly quizzes were passed out in Structures class. My mother began to worry about me and slipped money into the bags of food she sent down with Ron, whom she solidly regarded as her future son-in-law.

As the end of the second term approached, so did the joint Structures and ECS review. Ron was bringing my parents. Everyone was pulling all-nighters drawing, hand-printing, gluing, and coloring presentation boards. In the final three days I had slept less than a total of four hours. At four in the morning on the day of the presentation, as I was cutting out shading paper on the light table, I glanced out the window onto the highway and began hallucinating that I was taking off in an airplane. I was feeling the increase in speed and altitude when a flight attendant placed food in front of me. When she came into focus, I realized it was Mary. She was bringing Skip and me breakfast. Clearly, it was time to wrap it up. I went to my apartment and set the alarm clock for two hours.

It was show time. The shared excitement was palpable as we taped up our boards to the walls. Everyone had cleaned up nicely. The room was soon packed with students, professors, and guests. Reviewers moved from one group of presenters to another as our instructors proudly stood aside. Out of the corner of my eye, I saw Ron and my parents walk in. I waved. My father glowed as they walked over to me. Having only completed second grade, he viewed education as holy, college as church, and professors as high priests. As I was trying to explain the project to him, my two professors approached us. In front of my father, the Structures instructor extended his hand toward me, saying, "Put it here. You did a great job. Congratulations!" They had my father's full attention. God could not have choreographed it better. As I was introducing my father to them, his chest puffed up more with every handshake. After they left, he announced that the money spigot was back on again.

The rest of my time in architecture school went as I had mapped out. I was able to take three more off-campus design studios that helped me reach my goal of graduating in less than three years at the end of the winter term of 1979. One of them took place in London. That summer was miserably hot, and I was cooped up with my fellow U of O classmates on the eleventh floor of the dorm at the Royal Polytechnic (now the University of Westminster), across the street from Madame Tussauds Wax Museum. Everything was beige and gray, including the food, except for the pink breakfast sausages that looked like human fingers. The boring, bland, boiled British cuisine of the time drove me to my summer's only real cultural experience;

I became a regular at an Indian restaurant by Oxford Circle that served an array of fragrant, delicious, vegetarian dishes.

Academically, London was a success. Classes were held at the Architectural Association. It had a bar where you could get a cognac to accompany your afternoon tea. The excessive heat and few opportunities to interact with Londoners outside the pubs allowed me to devote more time to my research on distinguished nineteenth-century English architect Sir John Soane, a neo-classicist who had been influential in the post-modern movement. The English have some great buildings, and we spent a lot of time in air-conditioned buses touring fine examples of Norman, Gothic, Baroque, Palladian, and, thanks to the general philhellenism of the mid-eighteenth century (the Brits have yet to return the Elgin Marbles to Greece), Greek Neo-Classical gems. The program could not have ended soon enough for me.

Upon my return, Ron and I spent a few days together at his place. Whenever I came to Portland, I would first surreptitiously stay with him before going home to my parents, fueling my mother's delusion that I was saving myself for marriage. Although there had not been a formal marriage proposal, Ron assumed we would be getting married as soon as I graduated. My mother regarded a June wedding as a given. Every time Ron would talk about the children we were going to have, I would sweep the notion under the rug, but somehow, I was going along with the program.

Linda, who had extended her stay in Japan for more than a year to work as a hostess at a nightclub, had returned to Eugene and was living with her mother. She inexplicably dropped out of school and began exhibiting odd behavior. When we were together, she would blankly look through me. Our mutual friend, Jan, made the same observation. Linda had porcelain skin, green eyes, and a long, lush mane of dark hair, which she was very proud of. One day, she unexpectedly showed up at a meeting I was attending on campus with short, jagged hair she had cut herself. She told me that she had given away all of her jewelry because she didn't want to be attached to things. This put Jan and me on edge. We were in constant contact with Mrs. Barris, Linda's mother, who felt helpless. Linda's diagnosis of manic depression, now known as bipolar disorder, provided some relief in having an explanation, but Linda refused to take her Lithium.

Winter term, finally. All I needed was one more design studio and a physical education class to fulfill my graduation requirements. I had expected the sprint to the finish line to be a cakewalk, but I started feeling anxious. It was more than Linda's mental illness or my impending wedding that was the source of my apprehension. I began questioning whether I had compromised my education by barreling through in three years instead of five. I sat in on any class I could. My design studio professor pulled me aside to ask if everything was okay. I told him about the misgivings I had about stunting my education. He said that experience in the workplace is the best education. That made me breathe a little easier.

Three weeks before my last design review, the phone rang way too early in the morning for comfort. Not wanting to, I answered it. It was Mrs. Barris. My heart sank. Her voice was matter of fact—Linda had walked in front of a speeding train and was killed instantly. "Oh no!" was all I could repeat as I tried to imagine Linda's anguish. A once vibrant girl had become utterly despondent, and now, just like that, she was gone. After the funeral, Linda's friends were invited to Mrs. Barris' house for refreshments. Only "happy talk" was allowed. Jan and I huddled together at one end of the couch while Mrs. Barris snapped pictures of everyone, desperately preserving memories of her daughter's college years.

Linda's suicide touched my core. It made me ruminate about my own mortality. I had a vivid mental image, more like a daydream. I was dying alone, not surrounded with loved ones the way it's supposed to be. I visualized two selves, a "dying" me who was full of regrets comforted by a "tending" me. The notion was jarring. By now I had learned that any provocative thought or dream I had required me to pay attention. The meaning that came to mind was simple yet profound—at the end of the day, there was no other person whom I could depend on 100 percent to take care of me to my dying breath than my own self. I promised myself that I would do whatever I could in this lifetime so that the dying me would never leave with regrets or unfulfilled longing. At that moment I understood that only I was responsible for my own happiness. My anxiety lifted, and I felt an unexpected love for myself.

The long-anticipated graduation had finally arrived. For my father, it was as important as the wedding was to my mother. I was the first person on his side of the family to even attend college. When my name was called, I felt a wave of pride. I had overridden the aspirations others had for me to pursue my own heart's desire, despite the initial financial hardship. The second wave that followed was one of intense gratitude. I thanked God for the people dearest to me, whose love and support had made this achievement possible. I was bursting with joy as I was handed my diploma. I felt like a bucking bronco just out of the gate, ready to express my creativity and design beautiful buildings.

I already had an entry-level position lined up in a reputable, mid-sized architectural firm in Portland. Ron couldn't have been happier that our long-distance commute was over, and we began house hunting. No one was more elated than my mother. My marriage to Ron would bring her long-awaited peace of mind. Every time she came after me for a wedding guest list, I felt a tightening in my gut.

My mother's stress over planning the wedding annoyed me. What was the big deal? The church was a given. You decide on a dress, a place to have the reception, the music, and the menu. Almost immediately after I sat down to do the guest list, I got a stomachache followed by a fluttering sensation in my lower digestive tract I hadn't felt since my bout with colitis when I was ten. Mother made me chamomile tea, but the cramping continued into the night. As I began working on the list again a few days later, a pain even more severe had me doubled over. My mother accused me of being dramatic. A huge fight ensued. The third time it happened she insisted I see the doctor.

The office visit was a short one. I related my history with colitis and how the current symptoms had followed my attempts to compile a wedding guest list. The doctor reached for his prescription pad and scrawled on the paper while consulting his rolodex. He tore it off and handed it to me. On it were the names of three psychiatrists. A little voice within told me that I did not need a psychiatrist and that my body was trying to tell me something.

I had to take matters into my own hands. I needed alone time to process what was going on, and I decided that a road trip all by myself would be the treatment vehicle. There was no need to fast track a wedding. I was aware of the backlash I was going to face, but my mental state was at stake. Predictably, my mother came unglued. Clutching her hands, she alternated between lamenting my certain insanity and invoking God's mercy. Ron just stood there frozen, trying to understand. Surprisingly, despite his deep affection for Ron, it was my father, who had dodged marriage until his late fifties, who empathized with me. My request to postpone my new job for another month was approved, and the wedding was postponed until September.

I purchased a one-month Amtrak rail pass and planned my trip according to where I had friends I could visit—San Francisco, Los Angeles, Boise, and Philadelphia, where Bucky and Anne Fuller lived, and where they had invited me to stay with them. Ron was quiet as he drove me to the train station. He walked me to the train, handed me the lunch he had packed, and kissed me goodbye. He did not wait for the train to leave. It made my heart hurt. I could feel his deflation.

I was on my way—my own way! The steady sound of the train as it meandered through majestic mountain ranges and expansive plains was nurturing. My concept of time and space blurred. Borders became arbitrary, and rules about when you ate or slept did not apply. Opening the lunch bag, I was moved by Ron's aesthetic. He had individually wrapped everything Japanese style, including a love note tied into a scroll.

My senses were on high alert, and my thoughts ping-ponged all over the place. I took out my black-bound journal and wrote down everything I felt. Somehow I knew this trip was going to provide me with answers and that everything was going to work out for the best. My faith was gelling.

Visiting old and new friends I had met over the years made me reflect on the organic nature of human connections—some develop into deep friendships that go on forever, others go into remission, and then there are those that wither and die for lack of nurturing. I considered Bucky and Ann to be one of my most treasured friendships and couldn't wait to see them again.

The train arrived in Philadelphia in the afternoon. I picked up a bouquet of flowers and took a cab to Bucky and Anne's condo at the Society Hill Towers, where Anne greeted me with a warm embrace. Bucky was due to arrive from Texas late that night. I knew Anne hated to cook, so I went down to the market to buy ingredients for Greek avgolemono soup. She swooned over it during dinner as if there were no gift that could have pleased her more. It was late, and exhaustion had caught up with me, but I had to stay up and see Bucky. Exuding energy as he strode into the room, no one would have guessed that he was in his mid-eighties.

After breakfast, Bucky and I drove to his office at the University City Science Center. The first thing I noticed upon entering was a long, meandering Chinese dragon kite hung from the ceiling. The space was packed with a colorful mix of artifacts from different cultures. There were Balinese paintings, African masks, and Japanese figurines mixed in with geodesic spheres and tensegrity structures of all sizes. Bucky showed me his Dymaxion Chronofile, a chronological filing system he had developed that included every piece of correspondence, drawing, photograph, and document he had ever received, and copies of everything that had been sent out. He introduced me to his administrative assistant, Shirley, who towered over both of us, and took me around to meet his staff of about half a dozen researchers, designers, and archivists. The environment could not have been more invigorating.

Heading back to spend the afternoon with Anne, I took the bus to I. M. Pei's contemporary towers in old Philadelphia. Over coffee, Anne told me stories of her life with Bucky. Their union epitomized unconditional love and acceptance between two very different, independent people. I told her about my relationship with Ron, my shrinking away from the idea of having children, and the turmoil I was experiencing about my impending wedding. She told me that marriage and babies were not for everyone. She said that our most important responsibility was to be true to ourselves.

As the three of us sat and talked in the living room after dinner, Bucky asked me what I wanted for my future. I thought back to my design professor's advice about how work experience is the best education. I told Bucky that I saw architecture as an adventure and wanted to take the next couple of years learning outside the box. He then asked if I would come to Philadelphia and work with him. I was in utter disbelief. I blurted out something about how I was supposed to be getting married. He told me it was an open-ended offer. "Wow," I said before going to my room, "you have just given me a lot to think about."

I went to bed more conflicted than I have ever been in my life. The idea of working with Bucky in such a stimulating environment had me zinging, unable to fall asleep. Many times I had wondered how exciting it would have been had I accepted Bucky's invitation to travel with him and Anne the first day we met. What had kept me from doing so were my studies. What was standing in the way now was marriage. Once again, I swept the idea under the rug. After Anne and I said our goodbyes the next morning,

Bucky drove me to the train station. As he saw me off, he repeated, "It's an open-ended offer."

Next stop was New York City, where I was going to stay with my friend Tracey, a classmate who had graduated the year before and now worked at I. M. Pei's office in Manhattan. It was Saturday, and after a tour of her workplace, we walked around as I breathed in the energy of a city like no other. We ended up at the Plaza Hotel, where I had the most expensive strawberry shortcake I had ever eaten while a duo played the piano and violin.

Tracey and I talked and sipped wine into the night until we could no longer keep our eyes open. It was before seven in the morning when I woke up with a jolt, surprisingly clear-headed. A message came directly from my solar plexus. I jumped out of bed and woke Tracey up. I had to tell her that I was not getting married in September. I was going to work with Buckminster Fuller.

I ditched the Amtrak ticket and got on the first plane I could for home. I no longer needed time to think on a train. All traces of guilt, fear, and self-doubt were lifted. Watching the clouds float by, I kept replaying my exchange with Bucky. When he had asked me about my future, I had told him I wanted an adventure, and he had just offered me a grand one. I loved Ron, but he had to realize that this warranted putting off the wedding a while longer. This was my life, and as Anne had said, I had to be true to myself.

Back home, I announced my plans as soon as I could. I would take six months to have this experience of a lifetime and re-postpone the wedding to some time the following year. As expected, my mother took the news as if it were a dirge. My father told me to trust in God. After a momentary silence, Ron said, "Who am I to keep you from working with Buckminster Fuller?" I hugged him with all of my might and heart.

I had to put all my ducks in a row. I targeted my move for early September of 1979. I wrote to Bucky that I would happily accept his offer, and Shirley and I negotiated a salary. Janet, one of my future coworkers, and her husband, Peter, offered to rent me a room in their apartment. I was set to go!

I arrived in Philadelphia with two suitcases for my planned six-month stint at Buckminster Fuller's office. My coworkers, all from various fields of expertise, quickly made me feel part of the group. I joined the design department, made up of Rob and Chris, two brilliant MIT graduates who, in my first week on the job, inundated me with a comprehensive orientation to Bucky's book, *Synergetics*. Bucky regarded words as tools to convey the precise meaning of a concept, and if he couldn't find the appropriate word, he'd invent one. By Friday afternoon, I had a headache. I left work early and walked to Center City, where I found a second job to balance the mental concentration required at the office—waitressing a Saturday lunch shift.

I never took one moment for granted. Bucky, who identified himself as a "global citizen," tirelessly traveled and lectured around the world. He considered his staff his family, and after visiting a particularly exotic place, he would bring us thoughtfully selected gifts. The office was run democratically, regardless of everyone's educational level or position. We all took turns answering the phone. Calls came in daily from the likes of Indira Gandhi, Isamu Noguchi, Woody Allen, John Cage, and Merce Cunningham. I tried to call him "Bucky" like everyone else, but my conditioning only allowed me to continue to address him as "Dr. Fuller."

For all of his generosity of spirit, Bucky felt he had proprietary rights. One time I came to work wearing a T-shirt with Mies van de Rohe's face screened on it with his famous quote, "Less is more." My phone rang. Shirley called to tell me that Bucky wanted to see me in his office. He sat me down and proceeded to give me a fifteen-minute lecture about how he had come up with "more with less," meant to signify more shelter with less material, which van de Rohe stole and reworded to express a banal aesthetic. I never wore the shirt to the office again.

By far my most challenging assignment was to design the interior of the "Fly's Eye," a thirty-six-foot diameter sphere that looked like a fly's eye. So much for designing beautiful buildings. Conceived to house a family of four, it was Bucky's response to the world's lack of affordable shelter. I came up with a design that looked like a handheld mixer with a bed on top, a service core in the middle, and the rest left open. Bucky insisted that all our work be drawn in ink. I had to draw the twenty-sided space-frame floor system in perspective, deriving the intersecting points using trigonometry. He asked for the drawings to be sent to him while he was in California, and he called me as soon as he received them. "No, Darlin'!" he said excitedly. "I want an inside-outside, Japanese feel, circus space." Click, he hung up. Bucky loved sailing. I pictured a sailboat with the furniture in the floor accessed through trapdoors and a pulley system. The floor had to be completely recalculated. After I handed Bucky the revised drawings and he closely inspected them, he looked up at me and grinned like an impish child who had finally gotten the toy he wanted.

Philadelphia marked the beginning of the end of my relationship with Ron, one of the most wonderful men I have ever known. I loved him, but I realized that marriage and babies were not for me, at least not then. I had been going along with the plan that would have made everyone else happy. I was operating in denial in order to protect the hearts of people dearest to me. I believe that both Ron and I were saved from potential heartache. Had we married and started the family he so yearned for, he most likely would have been stuck with a wife embittered over her clipped wings and would have been the resentful mother of his children. Instead, we were both freed so that each of us could have our deep-seated desires fulfilled—me working with my mentor in Philadelphia, eventually making it my permanent home, and Ron marrying a lovely, loving young woman who could not have been a better mother to their two amazingly gifted children.

The choice I made did not result from consciously deliberating the pros and cons of marriage; it sprang up from the depths of my being. My inner voice knew what my soul craved, and it alerted me, first with uneasiness and then with full-blown anxiety. I wasn't listening. It took a body-shaking gastrointestinal attack for me to pay attention. I thanked my inner voice for that. It had earned my trust, much like an acquaintance who keeps giving good advice over and over again until one day you recognize her as a trusted confidant. I thanked God for bringing Bucky into my life. I can't think of anything else that could have made Ron more accepting of my leaving.

So, where do I direct my boundless gratitude for these fortuitous outcomes, God or my inner voice? I was slowly learning that it's all one ball of wax.

CHAPTER 7

Please

One of my favorite subjects for discussion is God. I'm interested to know how others conceptualize Him, whether they have developed a personal relationship with Him, and to what degree. I especially like to talk about God with self-described atheists. I'm intrigued by how many of them know for certain that nothing more exists than what meets the eye and that when we die, poof, we transition into nothingness. What fascinates me the most are atheists who believe in miracles, even mysticism, but do not believe that God has anything to do with them. They explain away paranormal phenomena due to the power of the mind, a surge of adrenaline, or hiccups of nature. My close friend and neighbor, Mary, an avowed atheist, who is also an editor of this book, believes that every one of my miracles happened, attributing them not to God but to quantum. I have told her that it is perfectly fine for her to call Him Quantum, and I call Him God.

"You are not the only one who has a direct phone line to God," Mary likes to declare. I keep agreeing with her. My experiences have solidified my faith that God—who resides in the realms of sound, light, and vibration where miracles happen—can be accessed by anyone. I believe everyone has the potential to communicate with Divine Consciousness. Many people who believe in a Higher Power have told me that having a personal relationship with it is out of reach. From my perspective, if you have ever put out a vibe to the Universe—seeking healing or safety—if you have ever felt intensely grateful for a desire fulfilled and expressed your gratitude into thin air, you have made contact with God. If you have ever experienced an uncanny coincidence, God has communicated with you. Even within the same religion, there are differing concepts of who or what God is. Although I refer to God as He because it is customary, mine has no gender. In the Bible, when Jesus invokes God as my "Father," he is referring to his creator. If I were truly made in God's image, then He is female. I doubt it.

With every "please" and "thank you" we are, at least passively, praying. Prayer is one of the tools with which we communicate with God. What makes it potent is the emotion behind it. It is utterly natural to ask the Universe for what we want or need. The question is, do we know if what we want is what's best for us? My mission is not to proselytize for prayer or try to convince you of what I believe. My job is to tell you how it has worked for me. The amazing results of prayer with emotion are exemplified by the following two healings:

One morning, I had woken up with my left eye swollen shut. It was goopy, crusty, and itchy. After rinsing it several times, I was able to open it, and by bedtime what was left was a pinkish, pulpy lump on my eyelid. It persisted for several days, and I went to see my ophthalmologist. He diagnosed it to be a chalazion, a cyst caused by a blocked oil gland, and recommended lancing it. After that fun procedure, the lump diminished considerably, only to reappear a few days later even more pronounced. At my follow-up visit the doctor recommended a steroid injection. Against all my misgivings, I reluctantly agreed. Instead of dissipating, the spongy lump morphed into a smaller hard mass in the shape of a kidney bean, which caused annoyance every time I blinked. The doctor said that he could repeat either procedure or leave it be until at some point in time, it might decalcify on its own. At my friend's urging, I went to her ophthalmologist for a second opinion. His prognosis was the same. I decided to take the Wu Wei route, the Taoist concept of conscious non-action.

About eight months after the bump first appeared, on Great Wednesday during Holy Week before Easter, I went to church to participate in the Sacrament of Holy Unction, when one is anointed with blessed oil by the priest and appeals are made for forgiveness and the healing of body, mind, and spirit. I had loved this ritual ever since I was little. My mother had insisted that during this sacrament Jesus was physically present but invisible to us, and that if I dabbed some of the oil on a hurt, it would heal. As I took my place in line, I wholeheartedly said a prayer for my eyelid to heal. Immediately, I began to feel a high degree of anticipation, a kind of vibrational energy. The closer I approached, the stronger the vibration pulsated throughout my body. I had never experienced anything like this before. After I was anointed, I dabbed the oil on my eyelid. The sensation I experienced next is difficult to express. For lack of better language, I've described it as if a thousand angels were taking turns hugging me.

I wanted to bolt from the church. I felt the physical structure too constricting but forced myself to return to the pew. My friend Voula, who was in the choir, was going to give me a ride home. The thought of being cooped up in a car suddenly felt unbearably claustrophobic. As soon as the service was over, I ran up to tell her that I was walking home. She was adamant that under no circumstance was I going to walk fifteen blocks at ten at night through a questionable Philly neighborhood. "Trust me," I told her, "nothing is going to happen to me."

I floated home in a state of grace, unable to keep from smiling. I had experienced communion with a loving, healing energy. When I reached my apartment, I was overcome with a wave of sleepiness and went straight to bed. The first sensation I was aware of when I woke up the next morning was the absence of irritation when I blinked. I looked in the mirror, and, astonishingly, in place of the mass on my eyelid was a slight pink spot. I quickly got dressed and briskly walked to work, searching for a rational explanation. As soon as I walked in the door, I bee-lined to a mirror. Any physical trace of the mass had vanished.

Another healing was also spontaneous. When Aida became my client, we immediately hit it off. Charming, vivacious, and always meticulously dressed in haute couture, we shared a passion for good design. She was a Christian from the Middle East and was also raised by a deeply religious mother. We had similar upbringings. We became fast friends. I soon learned the reason Aida, her husband—an international businessman—and their three children had moved to Philadelphia several years earlier. Salina, her oldest daughter, had been diagnosed with cancer at the age of thirteen, and the family had sought treatment at the Children's Hospital of Pennsylvania, where at the age of twenty-six, she continued to be monitored by a team of doctors. Depending on the blood count numbers, Aida would vacillate between hope and despair.

Salina courageously persevered in living as normal a life as possible, pursuing a master's degree in architecture. Though the cancer was in remission, years of chemotherapy had scarred her lungs, preventing her from walking long distances or climbing stairs. She presented her thesis connected to an oxygen tank. Living with the threat of death from a young age had imbued Salina with a Buddha-like detachment and an acceptance of whatever faced her, good or bad, with a grace that inspired everyone around her.

One morning as soon as I answered the phone and realized it was Aida, I knew something was terribly wrong. In a leaden voice, she told me that Salina's tumor had returned, and a new mass had been detected at the base of the spine.

"No!" I cried. "What are they proposing to do now?"

"They're bringing in the big guns," Aida replied, resigned.

Weren't these the same guns that had caused scarring in her lungs? *No! No! No!* resounded from the depths of my being.

The following Sunday in church, I lit a candle preparing to ask the Virgin Mary for her intercession in Salina's healing, something I had seen my mother do countless times. At the last second I implored my mother instead, "Mama, as a mother, you know what Aida is going through—do something up there, do something!"

Aida called the next morning practically hyperventilating. "The radiologist just called from the hospital. He told me, 'Aida, I don't know how to tell you this, but I am staring at the PET scan, and the masses that were there before are gone.' He said, 'In my profession, this is considered a miracle.'" In tears I thanked my mother, the Virgin Mary, baby Jesus, angels, and the Universe.

After Salina's team of doctors studied the scan and concurred that the cancer had disappeared, they jointly recommended she undergo a second bone marrow transplant to ensure that every last cancer cell was annihilated. Another bone marrow transplant? Can't they leave a miracle alone? The doctors did what they knew was best. It was unsettling to watch Salina with her Mona Lisa smile have her immune system be brought down to zero, but the exhilarating news was that she had been cured! After her recovery, Salina was declared cancer free, and she began living her life to the fullest.

It's nice to have explanations, but does it really matter what physically happened to make a hard lump on an eyelid spontaneously disappear or a metastasized cancer that showed up in a PET scan vanish? Would it have made a difference whether my entreaty was addressed to my mother or the Virgin Mary? Would it have been less significant if my devotional offering were a stone instead of a candle? Was my prayer more powerful than Aida's daily prayers?

No to all of the above. Perhaps the disappearance of the lump on my eyelid and Salina's cancer could be explained on a quantum level, but I don't need to know the mechanics of it. What I do know is that I directed my emotional appeal for an intercession to my mother, someone I could put a face to. Devotionally lighting a candle, something I did since childhood, helped focus my intention. I believe that my heartfelt intention, Aida's ardent prayers, and my mother's intercession forged together to transcend the laws of nature in a place where Divine Consciousness takes over and where miracles naturally happen. Prayer is one way to take us there. Here is my take on the who, what, where, when, which, and how aspects of prayer:

What prayer is: I have identified four components to prayer—intention, emotion, faith, and inner stillness. Prayer is a way of asking God to honor my will either directly or through an intercessor. It is as if I were baking a cake with Him. I bring the ingredients of intention, emotion, faith, and stillness to the table with an open heart and let God do the cooking. What about my unanswered prayers? As my faith grew, so did my acceptance that there was always a reason—either what I prayed for was not in my best interest or there was a lesson I needed to learn. Not getting the Lamborghini I might have asked for may have saved me from a fiery death. After countless times of thanking God for the obstacle that kept me from the object of my desire only to save me from certain disaster, I've learned to be less specific for what I pray for. My practice is to end my prayer with, "whatever is best." Prayer is most powerful when we pray for others. Not only do our hearts commune with God, but we also connect with the heart of the one prayed for. This results in our own healing.

Why pray: Prayer and meditation are potent vehicles by which we connect with Universal Consciousness, God, to ask that our desire be granted, be it health, protection, or abundance. In this elevated state of consciousness, there is no intellectualizing about God. Here, my heart and mind meet Him, and I become flooded with high-frequency emotions such as love and compassion. It is in this realm that miracles are triggered. There is no law of attraction more fruitful than uniting my mind with God's to achieve what is best for me, especially when I'm not sure exactly what that is.

When and where to pray: Individually, you can pray anytime, anywhere. A special place and time of day can also be appropriated for prayer and meditation to acknowledge their value as a regular part of life. An altar can be created with meaningful symbols, and the senses can be incorporated by lighting candles, burning incense, chanting, listening to music, or playing singing bowls. There is something powerful about communal prayer and meditation, whether in church on Sunday, the mosque on Friday, synagogue on the Sabbath, or at the Buddhist or Hindu temple. When people come together to hear ancient scriptures or silently place their intention on a collective outcome, it produces a collective cohesiveness. If indeed God is everywhere and in every one of us, by connecting with our fellow humans, we also connect with Him. A family holding hands at the dinner table before a meal, giving thanks, and praying for each other's good health is an opportunity for all to feel as one body.

How to pray: When I set out to understand how prayer is utilized by major religions, I expected to find deep divides. I was surprised to learn that followers of the major religions prayed alike, whether together out loud or in silence, by singing or chanting, or meditatively in solitude. From my experience, it doesn't matter how you pray as long as it comes from the heart.

There is a profound similarity in the way the scriptures of each religion beautifully express the purpose of connecting with God, Allah, Consciousness, or the various manifestations of the Formless Divine. Whatever you call it, there is one reality. Yet, how people should pray has been the root of dissent and divisiveness, even within each religion, pitting Jew against Jew, Muslim against Muslim, and the various flavors of Christianity against one another. Prayer is personal, and debating the correct way to pray is as ludicrous as arguing whether French, Italian, or Chinese cuisine is best.

Dr. Andrew Newburg, a radiologist at the University of Pennsylvania, studied the brain activity of Tibetan Buddhist monks during meditation and Franciscan nuns during prayer, using images taken with single photon emission computed tomography (SPECT). Both groups showed increased activity in the frontal lobe indicating heightened concentration and a decrease of activity in the parietal lobe, which aligns one's bearings within three-dimensional space, leading to a transcendence of the self from the physical world to somewhere else. While the Buddhist monks reported oneness with Universal Consciousness and the Christian nuns described communing with God, both sets of scans showed that everyone had gone to the same place!

To whom should we pray: You can either pray directly to God or to countless other entities—saints, prophets, divinities, or dead relatives—to act as intercessors and pray for you. Or, you can pray to nothing in particular. It helps to have a face to pray to. Muslims and Jews worship only God. Christians worship the Father, Son, and Holy Spirit, considered to be One. Many Christians stop there. Eastern Orthodox Christians and Catholics sanction a rich roster of saints to pray to (not to be confused with worship) and also pray to the Virgin Mary, considered to be above the saints. Saints are looked upon to protect a country, as St. Patrick is the patron saint of Ireland, or a specific group, as St. Brendan the Navigator is looked upon to safeguard sailors. Certain saints are looked upon to fulfill certain needs. Catholic friends of mine swear that by burying a figurine of St. Joseph upside down in the yard of a house up for sale, the property will sell for a hefty price in a timely manner. They insist that lost objects are found by praying to St. Anthony. It is ironic that a history of animosity between followers of Judaism, Christianity, and Islam are based partly on disagreements about whom one should or should not pray to, when all three religions claim to be descendants of Abraham and regard Jerusalem as holy ground.

Many westerners mistakenly believe that Hindus pray to many gods. In fact, Hindus believe in one Ultimate Being who has many different manifestations seen as deities and that the most fitting deity can be selected for a desired outcome. Ganesh, for example, is the face of God who removes obstacles, while Saraswati, who represents God's knowledge, would be prayed to by a student wishing to pass an exam or by one seeking understanding. This richly personalized prayer system allows one to place intention on a face of one of God's limitless attributes. Many Buddhists, on the other hand, will tell you that they don't believe in God. They seek to unite with Universal Consciousness and attain enlightenment through the practice of meditation and loving kindness. Transformation is considered to be the miracle. They may not conceptualize God, but from my perspective, they connect with what I consider to be God's nature.

All prayers work: I have been collecting prayers and writings from all major religions and other sources that praise, beseech, and give thanks to God, or simply provide guidance. The poems of Rumi, exalting his devotion and love for God, stir passion in me. When I hear, "Let us lift up our hearts; let us give thanks unto the Lord," during the Orthodox Liturgy, I feel my heart fill up and rise. If a prayer resounds in me, I keep it. The following are my go-to prayers that have literally worked miracles for me. I recite the first three every morning:

The Lord's Prayer

When his disciples asked Jesus how they should pray, He responded with what is known as the Lord's Prayer, which includes words and meaning from traditional Jewish prayers such as the Kaddish, the Shemoneh Esreh, and other scriptures. I maintain that this prayer is universal. Anyone can benefit from it regardless of their religion. It invokes our Creator, who resides in all realms (in Greek it is "heavens"), whom we call on by His holy name, allowing us to have a personal relationship with Him. We beseech His kingdom of peace and love. We ask that our will align with His so that we may experience heaven on Earth. We pray for spiritual nourishment. We implore His forgiveness to free us from guilt, as we free others who wronged us from their guilt. We appeal for His help to avoid succumbing to the ego (in Greek it is literally "the sly one" or deceiver), whose aim is to separate us, and to return us to our true purpose and nature—to connect and love one another. It is the perfect prayer.

Jesus related the prayer in Aramaic, the language most Jews spoke at the time. It was first written in the Bible, however, in Greek, the language I learned from my mother. One day, as I was having my lunch on a park bench, I noticed a thin, paperback book next to me entitled *Who Told You That You Were Naked? Freedom From Judgment, Guilt, and Fear of Punishment* by John Jacob Raub, a Trappist monk. I leafed through it to find that it was about the powerful benefits of forgiveness. It brought to mind the line in the Lord's Prayer, "Forgive us our trespasses as we forgive those who trespass against us." That is when I realized that the word "forgive" was not in the Greek version. The more I compared it with the Greek, the more nuances I found to be missing in the English translation.

Several years later, I fell upon a translation in Aramaic. Ostensibly translated from Greek, the word "heavens" was interpreted as "sound, light, and vibration," which I found to be exceptionally inspiring. With the counsel of Fr. Demetrios Constantelos, an eminent theologian and Greek scholar, I retranslated the prayer from Greek to English, incorporating phrasing from the Aramaic version in order to restore the essential meaning that had been lost in translation:

Our Creator, who resides in sound, light, and vibration,
Holy be your name.
May your kingdom come,
May your will be done,
On earth as it is in the Heavens.
Give us today our essential sustenance,
And free us from our offenses
As we free those who offend us,
And let us not surrender to temptation,
But rid us from the deceiver that keeps us from our true purpose.

Prayer from A Course In Miracles (pg. 28)

This is one of the most powerful prayers I have encountered. It affirms my purpose—to be helpful to my fellow humans; that I represent God as best I can, that I have faith that I will be divinely guided, that I know I am not apart from God, and that I allow God to work through me so I can help heal and be healed:

I am here only to be truly helpful.
I am here to represent Him who has sent me.
I do not have to worry about what to say or what
   to do, because He Who sent me will direct me.
I am content to be wherever
He wishes, knowing
He goes there with me.
I will be healed as I let Him teach me to heal.

Intercessory Prayer

This definitively Christian prayer is at the very end of the Orthodox Liturgy. It asks that the intercessory prayers and blessings of our departed ancestors be heard:

> *Through the prayers of our Holy Fathers and Mothers,*
> *Lord Jesus, Son of God, have mercy on us and save us.*

Namaste

This comes from a greeting used in India and South Asia. It is accompanied by the gesture of palms together at the heart in prayer pose and a slight bow of the head. More of an affirmation than a prayer, this is particularly helpful when in the company of someone you find problematic, even despicable. It helps me to see that we are all children of God. The translation I have adopted is as follows:

> *The divine light in me sees the divine light in you.*

There is an abundance of beautifully-worded prayers from every tradition. If you are inspired, compose your own prayer that is meaningful to you, or just close your eyes and pitch a plea as it comes to mind.

Some people doubt the power of prayer. The questions I am most often asked are about unanswered prayers. I can attest that there were times when not having my prayer answered had saved me from negative, even perilous, situations. If two people have cancer and both are prayed for, why does one die and the other get cured? That is not for me to answer. What I do know to be true is that bad things that happen to good people can bring about a change of perception that takes them to a higher level of consciousness. Loss and other disastrous events do provide opportunities for transformation. I know several people who have lost an adult child. All but one have described a profound shift in their worldview as their grief process slowly made room for acceptance, even peace. The one who still carries the weight of grief close to his heart seems perpetually victimized and angry. This is Earth, not paradise. We have every reason to hone our intention, intensify our belief, and practice being in stillness so that we can ask for what is best and receive our due inheritance.

Stillness takes practice. Our busy minds, filled with doubts and fears about the past and future, are the main reason we miss the answer to our prayers, even if it is right under our noses. We must be forever vigilant with our awareness—if we drop the ball, we'll miss the miracle because we won't hear the message. One of the aims of yoga is to bring our attention to the here and now, harness the stillness within through meditation, and focus on the breath. It is in this stillness where one can connect with Universal Consciousness, the source of all knowing, and find perfect guidance we call intuition. The same goes with prayer.

In his book, *Listening to God's Whispers*, Fr. Domenic Rossi expresses this stillness perfectly: "The point here is very simple: in order to listen, one has to enter into the other's world—even if that other is just a houseplant—which means temporarily stepping out of one's own 'world,' or outside one's own fixed agenda. Listening to God is basically an art of listening in the silence—in the silence that comes from discarding not only daily distractions, but also the distraction and obstacle of a mind so set in its own ways that it could not possibly be open to the thoughts of another."

Fr. Domenic believes that we are continuously given signs from God to guide us to our true purpose by actively listening in stillness. With practice, we will more and more recognize and receive the message. In his book, he recounts how signs and events led him to help homeless and mentally ill men and women in Philadelphia, where he is the founder and CEO of the Bethesda Project, one the most successful agencies of its kind. He also relates one of my favorite stories—despite many profound revelations in his life, his ego and lack of awareness nearly cost him a meaningful lesson.

In 1977, Fr. Domenic felt inspired to visit the Basilica of Our Lady of Guadalupe in Mexico City. The first night there, he had a vivid dream of being in a huge church where the Virgin Mary, standing directly in front of him, directed her gaze toward a group of people in the church who appeared to be poor and downtrodden. He took this as a direct message to turn his attention away from himself and direct it to the needy. After visiting the Basilica, Fr. Domenic stumbled on the old church of St. Francis of Assisi where, upon entering, he noticed a large mural depicting St. Francis, a proponent of the poor who had gone through his own transformation, kneeling and looking up to the heavens. In back of him stood a beggar leaning on his crutch, staring at him. Fr. Domenic interpreted the beggar to represent the love of Christ. Meditating on the mural, his dream of the Virgin Mary was brought to mind. Then came the revelation—his purpose of traveling to Mexico was to receive divine instruction. He, too, would find a closer connection with God by turning his attention to the downtrodden

A few years later, while studying in Italy, Fr. Domenic visited the village where his mother was born. There, he experienced another epiphany. A woman asked him to come to her house to pray over her eighty-four-year-old ailing mother, who was in constant pain. The woman led him to a room where the old lady, propped up in a chair, was unable to move and moaned, "help," over and over. Filled with compassion, Fr. Domenic prayed for her suffering to end. As he bent down to kiss her cheek, he saw that her face, contorted with pain, was the same as the beggar's in the mural of St. Francis. At that moment, he saw Christ's face in agony, literally directing him to help others. The idea instantly crystallized—Christ makes himself one with us because of our brokenness. If Christ is one with the beggar, and we help a beggar, our fellow human, we are in communion with Christ.

More than twenty-five years later, Fr. Domenic was visiting the Vatican Museum in Rome with two friends. Overwhelmed with the volume of religious and ancient art treasures, a tapestry depicting Christ breaking bread with two of his disciples after the Resurrection stood out to him. The disciples had just recognized it was Christ as He broke the bread, and they remembered Him breaking bread at the Last Supper when He told them, "Take and eat. This is my body broken for you." The epiphany hit Fr. Domenic like a thunderbolt. Until that moment, the connection between Christ's broken body symbolized by the bread and our human brokenness had eluded him. He realized that Christ was not only inviting us to take Holy Communion, but also to enter into a deeper communion with the Christ who is mystically present in the brokenness of the beggar and of all humanity.

Fr. Domenic couldn't wait to share his newfound revelations with his companions over lunch. They were seated at an outdoor table, and as soon as the food orders were placed, Fr. Domenic began relating the connection he had made between the broken bread of the Eucharist with our brokenness. Not only can we be in relationship with Christ by taking Holy Communion, he explained, but His essence can be found in every broken person, and every time we have the opportunity to help a beggar, we are communing with Christ. As Fr. Domenic went on with his story, a woman was going from table to table begging. When she came to his table asking for bread, Fr. Domenic was so engrossed in expounding his epiphany that he gestured to her to go away. The beggar went to the next table where there were two young women. Entirely self-absorbed, he watched as one of the women tore off a slice of bread and gave it to the beggar woman. It wasn't until the other woman reached for the bread basket and gave her the entire loaf that the cosmic frying pan came crashing onto his head.

Fr. Domenic was mortified. The woman had not asked for money but for bread. Bread! It was the ultimate irony. He was so busy pontificating about the breaking of the bread and Christ in the guise of a beggar that he shooed away his opportunity to commune with Him. In front of his audience, Fr. Domenic experienced his own brokenness.

I had the opportunity to meet with Fr. Domenic. I told him of the impact his insights had on me, especially the story about the beggar woman. He talked about the insidious power the ego wields on us, so much so that his chatter had made him disobey a direct order he had received from the Virgin Mary in a dream, to take the attention off himself and give it to those who have no one to attend to them. His lack of stillness had caused him to miss the opportunity. I wondered out loud how someone as astute as he could have had such a lapse of consciousness. Grinning from ear to ear, Fr. Domenic responded, "I believe God didn't want me to recognize the beggar in that moment so that I could be profoundly humbled and write about it." It made me want to write about it, too.

Studies show prayer works. Some people need proof, so now science has a finger in the pie. Many studies conducted in controlled settings have produced evidence that intercessory prayer has a positive effect on healing. Dr. Larry Dossey has reviewed studies on prayer and has analyzed their detractors. From his commentary in "Prayer and Medical Science,"[1] Dr. Dossey suggests that critics who dismiss the healing effects of prayer do so from a position of befuddlement rather than from ignorance. Their scientific training in hard facts simply does not allow them to wrap their heads around the evidence. He points out, however, there is agreement within the scientific community that "only about 15 percent of medical interventions are supported by solid scientific evidence," many of which are practiced simply because they have traditionally worked, and that "much, if not most, of contemporary practice still lacks a scientific foundation." Dr. Dossey

1   Dossey, L. (2000). Prayer and medical science. *Archives of Internal Medicine, 160*(12), 1735–1738.

theorizes that possibly a double standard is being applied to prayer research by requiring greater levels of proof than are demanded of conventional therapies.

In the face of empirical evidence that intercessory prayer works, critics have nonetheless expressed concern that conducting prayer studies in hospitals may jeopardize a hospital's reputation, despite the fact that nearly 80 percent of Americans believe in the power of prayer. In one study, 75 percent of hospitalized patients polled believed that their physicians should be concerned about their spiritual beliefs. Dr. Dossey counters that "it is more likely that the widespread application of prayer will enhance the reputation of healing institutions." This is not far-fetched, since, in the same study, half of the patients indicated their preference that their physicians not only pray for them, but pray with them. Why can't a physician prescribe, along with medicine and rest, prayer or meditation? The medical field needs to acknowledge that prayer does work for some people and makes sense to many.

Dr. Dossey points out there is no consensus among scientists as to what forces govern consciousness. They persevere to prove what yogis have known for thousands of years: that consciousness is real. So far, no one knows how it works in the brain. Since prayer occurs in the realm of consciousness, it cannot be measured. What can be measured is what prayer manifests. When dealing with matters of faith, however, there will always be questions that cannot be answered. It is therefore courageous that some physicians risk their reputations in attempting to prove the efficacy of prayer in healing.

Religion, however, is based on faith, not proof. People with faith who have experienced spontaneous healing and other miraculous events do not need explanations. Prayer does work, and it works miracles. It certainly has worked for me. It's as easy as saying "please" with emotion, intention, faith, and stillness. As each leap of faith brings about a miracle, the miracle reinforces our faith until we transcend praying and become living prayer; we transcend performing kind acts and become loving kindness. Then, worries disappear. If a prayer goes unanswered, even if it brings suffering, we know that ultimately it is for our own good. This is what it means to be in an unceasing, personal relationship with God, whatever your concept of God is. That is the goal.

CHAPTER 8

Thank You

Expressing gratitude is the easiest way to connect with God because emotion is built in. It is the highest form of prayer.

One of the first things we are taught to say as little children is thank you. That doesn't mean, however, that we've been practicing gratitude all our lives. We are gladdened when we receive a gift or an unexpected bundle of money, when we are reunited with an old friend we haven't seen in years and pick up where we left off, or when we learn that a loved one was cured of a disease. But do we pause to deeply appreciate the gift? The ever-busy mind bombarded with internal and external stimuli soon turns its attention capriciously to the next thing. If we can be still and say thank you for the joy we feel, the potential for receiving more gifts is exponential.

The simple act of expressing gratitude launches a cosmic dynamic that brings about more reasons to be grateful. The surest way to stop these benefits from manifesting is getting stuck by feeling deprivation or obligation. If we're in a constant state of perceived lack, how can our hearts open to gratitude? We have nothing, we do nothing, we are nothing, and down the rabbit hole we go. What we can do is practice changing our perception.

The power of gratitude will take over if we give it from the heart, not out of obligation.

It's easy to feel and express gratitude when our prayer is answered or a desire fulfilled, especially a big one, and we are bursting with joy. There is another form of gratitude that takes us to a place of pure bliss, nirvana, or what I refer to as a state of grace. We feel it when we unexpectedly receive exactly what we need that we didn't consciously ask for. It is a moment of profound connection with another human, an animal, or nature that leaves us changed forever. It can happen as one beholds a breathtaking scene, a fantastical coincidence, or the beneficent kindness of a total stranger. The feeling is described best by first-time mothers after bonding with their newborn. Pure love. One feels oneness with the Universe, Divine Consciousness, God. As with prayer, gratitude also comprises three components—attention (rather than intention), faith, and inner stillness. If we're not attentive, the opportunity for transformation is lost.

Researchers have not only conducted studies on prayer and meditation, finding them to be beneficial, they have also jumped on the gratitude bandwagon. A study conducted in England[2] found that gratitude leads to lower stress and depression and higher levels of social support. One of its conclusions states:

". . . Increasing gratitude is a legitimate goal of therapy. Potentially, giving people the skills to increase their gratitude may be as beneficial as such cognitive behavioral life skills as challenging negative beliefs."

Robert Emmons, a professor of psychology at UC Davis and an expert on gratitude, acknowledges that gratitude has long been espoused by other disciplines to be essential to personal fulfillment and spiritual growth:

"Gratitude heals, energizes, and transforms lives . . . Scientists are late-

---

2   Wood, A. M., Maltby, J., Gillett, R., Linley, P. A., & Joseph, S. (2008). The role of gratitude in the development of social support, stress, and depression. *Journal of Research in Personality, 42*(4), 854–871.

comers to the concept of gratitude. Religions and philosophies have long embraced gratitude as an indispensable manifestation of virtue, and an integral component of health, wholeness, and well-being."

Researchers have made gratitude sound like a wonder drug! As Dr. Larry Dossey had suggested that doctors prescribe prayer to their patients, perhaps they should also recommend gratitude.

When we express deep gratitude, we are elevated spiritually, and this opens us to having a change of perception, a miracle. I will relate three transformational experiences and the accompanying, essentially indescribable emotions. Two events that occurred over twenty years apart had three things in common—a homeless person, a twenty-dollar bill, and timing. Both took place a few days before Christmas. The third took place when I was alone on the morning of my fiftieth birthday.

My first experience happened after I left Buckminster Fuller's office. Working with him was one of my life's highlights; the pay, however, negligible. Meeting famous people and working on theoretical projects was stimulating, but it was time to get some architectural experience and design real buildings.

The recession had hit the building industry hard, and with unemployment over 8 percent, architectural jobs were scarce. I decided to pursue work in the field anyway and moved into Michelle's spectacular house, where my friend Alice had lived for years.

Michelle was the ultimate California hippy chick. An artist, she had transformed a four-story West Philadelphia Victorian twin into an intoxicating, organic sanctuary with rich tapestries, blue glass orbs, stained glass windows, crystal prisms, and erotic art. Her magical, lush garden was a sensual backdrop for her themed summer parties. Alice, Michelle, and I would have powwows around the large, carved, wooden table in the kitchen surrounded by antique china cabinets, solving world problems and discussing our favorite subject—men. This terrarium-like environment provided me with the support I needed as I searched for my career footing and grieved my father's death.

I went after every vague job lead I got wind of. With my limited architectural experience, I was willing to consider anything even remotely associated with the field. After answering an ad for a draftsperson listed by an electrical engineer, I was called in for an interview.

I found the address to be on a modest three-story row house near 13th and Pine. The door was answered by an enormous man with thick glasses and plushy, purple lips who introduced himself as Ray. My interview with Ray, the engineer, consisted of presenting my portfolio while he stared at me intently. In his thick Romanian accent, he explained that he had survived the recession because virtually all of his work was contracted with the Navy. He stressed that in these hard times, all he could pay me was a pittance. I took the job anyway. It was going to be a placeholder until the economy turned around.

Ray lived on the third floor. The first floor, used for storage, shipping, and receiving, was also where the unheated employee bathroom was located. The office on the second floor was beige and dreary. I shared it with two coworkers. Yian, also from Romania, was a brilliant, young architect who spoke very little English and was paid slightly more than me. Married with two children, he also cleaned Ray's rental properties. Bill, a registered architect in his late seventies, made just a little more than Yian to stamp the drawings. Like the Lion, Scarecrow, and Tin Man in the *Wizard of Oz*, each of us had a handicap—Bill's was age, Yian's was language, and mine was inexperience. Ray was taking undue advantage of all three of us.

The situation got worse. Ray always had on the same bloodied khaki hunting vest he wore on his African safaris. Every day, he would huff and puff as he clonked up the stairs and made his way over to my desk, infiltrating my personal space with the same query, "What are you working on now, my little chicken of the sea?" I told myself that time gaining construction document experience was currency, and each day added to my career bank account.

Since I was planning to fly out to Portland for an event in January, I had decided not to go home that Christmas, the first one I would spend away from my family. My friends Jane and George invited me to their annual Christmas dinner with all of George's Greek relatives, which brought me some consolation. Always a sumptuous feast, I was asked to bring potatoes au gratin.

Our office holiday lunch party was held the Friday before Christmas at Ray's apartment. Ray made his specialty, a chicken roasted in a brown paper bag, which we ate under the menagerie of two dozen taxidermy animal heads mounted on the walls. For our Christmas "bonus" he let us go home early after lunch. Ray took me aside and gave me a heart-shaped box carved out of cinnabar, leaving me with a cloying feeling that made me want to walk the two miles to home.

It was a crisp, balmy afternoon. My work environment was depressing, but unlike my coworkers, there was light at the end of my tunnel. I was going to miss Christmas with my family. I began to feel sorry for myself. Thoughts changed to lack of finances. The twenty-eight dollars in my wallet had to last me until the 1st, when I would receive my paycheck. Could I make it without borrowing? As I walked up Walnut Street, I made a mental shopping list of ingredients for the potatoes au gratin. I needed about twenty more dollars than what I had. Gloominess took over. Just as I reached Rittenhouse Square feeling poor, the homeless man who regularly begged at the corner jumped in front of me with an ear-to-ear grin. With his head cocked to one side inches from my face, instead of asking for money, he bellowed, "Merry Christmas, ma'am!" Startled and annoyed, I mustered a mumbled, "Merry Christmas" back and crossed the street.

What just happened here? A homeless man without a roof over his head wished me Merry Christmas without asking for anything in return. I was on my way to a beautiful home I shared with my wonderful friends. I would spend Christmas at my dear friends' house with a crowd of warm people, endless platters of Greek food, and my favorite dish, Jane's delectable chestnut pate en croute. Soon, I would be in Portland with my loving family and more great friends. All this richness, and I was walking down the street boo-hoo-hooing over what I lacked! A homeless person who scrounged for food from the trash had spontaneously tried to cheer me up from a cloud of doom I had created. The irony stung. What an ungrateful twit I was!

Walking toward the Walnut Street bridge, counting my blessings and feeling lucky, I was overcome by an indescribable realization. The homeless man had cracked open the portal of my heart just enough to allow the Holy Spirit to enter and permeate my being with gratitude. With tears streaming down my face, I felt genuine love for the man. I crossed the bridge with a new level of consciousness. It was the first time I had considered happiness without material things.

Dusk began to settle, bringing the Christmas lights to life. I felt vibrantly alive. I was noticing every little thing. Less than a block away from home, the evening breeze picked up as an eddy of leaves swirled at my feet. All of them were twirling but one. It was stuck to the sidewalk. For some reason I bent down to look at it. It was not a leaf but a neatly-folded twenty-dollar bill. I might as well have found twenty thousand dollars. Clutching it to my chest, I ran the rest of the way, sobbing.

My change of heart and shift of perception, from what-I-don't-have to tears of gratitude, could have easily eluded me had I ignored the homeless man. Thankfully, the juxtaposition of his life to mine had grabbed my full attention. The Universe no doubt was teaching me a lesson and, mesmerized by the leaves, stillness allowed me to spot the money, exactly the amount I needed.

Years later, working elsewhere, another event occurred involving a homeless person that changed my mind from self-absorption to profound gratitude. Again, a few days before Christmas on a cold but dazzling morning, I had gotten off to a late start but still felt compelled to walk to work. I was cutting it close. Myrna, my friend and coworker, had prepared her annual holiday breakfast for the staff, and I wanted to be there on time.

Clicking along in my high-heeled boots, all I could think about was my day's agenda. Though distracted, I noticed an odd figure up ahead. As I got closer, an old, homeless woman came into focus. She could have been one of the wretched poor from the cast of *Les Miserables*. She was slight and had matted hair. Her face and the long, ragged, greenish coat she was wearing were caked with dirt. Now squarely on my radar, she was dragging three, large, yellow, heavy-duty trash bags one at a time. Struggling, she pulled one bag several feet to meet the other, then dragged the third one to the other two. As I was about to pass her, the woman turned to me with a twinkle in her eye and in a sweet voice said, "Can you help me, dearie?"

The interruption flustered me. "Sorry, I can't. I'm late for a meeting." I didn't have time to help her, but something made me ask, "What do you want me to do?"

"Would you take this bag over to the corner?" She pointed to a spot a third of a block away.

Now I was going to be late for sure. But, she was old and looked tired.

"Okay," I said. Bending down to grab a bag, I was inundated with the stench of urine. I dragged the dirty, yellow, plastic trash bag filled with who-knows-what down the sidewalk, wondering about lice. It was very heavy. Where could she be going? I left the bag at the corner and glanced back. Exhausted, the old woman was leaning on a concrete ledge with the two bags at her feet. I marched back.

"I'll help you with another one."

"Thank you, dearie," she said wearily. Just as I got a good grip, a well-dressed lady approached and, gesturing to the other bag, said, "I saw you take the bag over there. Can I help with this one?" as though she were asking my permission. "Thank you," I nodded. It was surreal, the two of us in high heels dragging these large, heavy, plastic bags along the concrete. We placed the bags together and shared a smile before the lady left, crossing the street. I looked behind me. The old woman was slowly walking toward me. I went back to meet her and pulled out my wallet. There were two bills, a one and a twenty. A wave of compassion overcame me. I was on my way to a holiday breakfast, and what did this woman have to eat? "Merry Christmas to you!" I said, placing the twenty in her hand.

The woman stared down at the money and, looking up at me as light emanated from her big, glistening, blue eyes, softly said, "I love you." The warmth that surged throughout my body was indescribable. Spontaneously, we fell into an embrace for what seemed like an eternity. The urine odor didn't matter, nor did the possibility of lice, nor being late for breakfast. All that mattered was what was happening in the moment. There were no boundaries between us. We came from worlds apart, but there was no separation. It went beyond simply connecting with another human being—I felt united with everything, and in that oneness, I felt God's presence. As we let go of each other, tears streaming down my face, I felt as if my heart were going to burst. Once again, language fails to convey the sensation of being in a state of grace.

I hurried the rest of the way to work, crying. The love energy that had overwhelmed me would not go away. It felt like I was getting blessed over and over again. I couldn't stop thinking of the old woman and her shining, grateful eyes as she clutched the money to her chest. Without judgment, both of us had communed in a holy instant of gratitude. What could have caused her to end up in this condition? Why didn't I take her home and clean her up?

When I got to work, my coworker, Eve, came over to ask me what was the matter. Wiping away my tears, I tried to explain what I had just experienced as best I could. When I told her my idea of going back and taking the woman to my house, Eve staunchly objected. She advised to get the woman's permission and call a homeless shelter. I walked the few blocks back to where I had left her. There was not a trace of her. Could she have been an angel who appeared to teach me a lesson about loving a fellow human without judgment or condemnation?

After the breakfast, I took the rest of the day off. I was too busy processing my experience to concentrate on work. The urgency of my mind's chatter had lost all importance. Once again, a shift in my perception resulted in grace and gratitude. This time it took an old homeless woman dragging giant heavy bags to grab my attention. With utter faith, I believe that her profession of love opened up my mind and heart, allowing the Holy Spirit in to do His trick—transform a stranger, whom I initially felt disgust for, into an angel who showed me true love. It was in the stillness of the embrace that I was transformed. This was the miracle.

Several years later I was attending weekly classes on ancient Jewish texts taught by an Orthodox rabbi. During one class, the rabbi talked about mitzvahs, the good deeds one does for others. He said that there are basically eight levels of charities, ranging from giving out of obligation to giving from the heart, which in turn divinely transforms the giver. Level eight was reserved only for mystics. I recalled my experience with the homeless woman with the bags. The rabbi's message was that good deeds count when given cheerily, but this had not been the case. Initially I had felt repulsed. I had been focused on arriving on time to a holiday breakfast while she had nothing to eat. My behavior made me feel small.

After class, I approached the rabbi and asked if I could speak to him. The rabbi motioned me to an armchair, took a seat directly across from me, and began stroking his long, salt-and-pepper beard while listening intently. After relating my experience, I asked him if helping the woman even counted as a mitzvah, as I did it grudgingly. "Level seven!" he declared.

I leaned forward in amazement. "Level seven?"

"Level seven," he said conclusively.

"But I was not cheery when I agreed to help her carry the bag. I was annoyed, and how she smelled disgusted me. She forced me to help her," I countered.

The rabbi explained that the mitzvah would not have counted only if I had ignored her. Had I unwillingly helped her and then walked away, it would be considered the lowest of the mitzvahs. Giving her the twenty dollars and wishing her well elevated my mitzvah level. The key, he said, was setting my ego aside so that we could merge as one on the same level. It was this transcendence to a place where I, the giver, became spiritually filled with love and gratitude that brought it up to mitzvah level seven. I felt as if I had hit the spiritual jackpot!

The two experiences, which took place years apart just before Christmas and involving a homeless person and a twenty-dollar bill, had something else in common—gratitude. In each, my transformation was the miracle.

The third story I will relate illustrates how brilliantly creative God's response can be when we communicate with Him by expressing our gratitude in nature. Every year a few days before my birthday, I become self-reflective about the people, places, and things I am grateful for. As my fiftieth approached, I sensed my inner voice telling me to go off somewhere by myself and hear wise words. The few workshops I had attended at the Omega Institute in Rhinebeck, New York had been rejuvenating. From time to time, I would receive notices offering special programs. I paid no attention to one pamphlet that kept popping up from under the piles on my desk. A month before my birthday, the Omega pamphlet resurfaced. This time it got my attention. A three-day conference billed, "Eleven Shamans from the Four Corners of the Earth," was to take place on the weekend of my birthday. It was too good to be true. I immediately called to register. Soon thereafter, the terrorist attacks on 9/11 shook the world, and I needed wise words more than ever.

The Omega Institute, situated on 195 acres of beautiful grounds with its own Long Pond Lake in the Hudson Valley, is peppered with white cottages and a Victorian main house where meals are served. Omega's environment is restorative. The mid-October weekend I would be there was also the peak time to see the change of foliage into brilliant fall colors.

The shamans who had convened from all parts of the world had a collective message—the Earth cannot be sustained if we humans continue to abuse it. As one shaman from the Brazilian rainforest declared, "If we do not stop destroying the lungs of Mother Earth, she will expel us the way a dog shakes off fleas." It was clearly communicated that, regardless the culture, most people desire the same thing—to coexist with peace and love. On the eve of my birthday, I withdrew to my room right after dinner. At seven the next morning, a Q'ero shaman from a remote part of the Peruvian Andes would be performing a Despacho ceremony to help release negativity, and I needed time to reflect.

It was still dark when I awoke. Fifty years on the planet! I was lying in bed listening to the cicadas when a wave of claustrophobia hit me. For no apparent reason, I felt an urge to be outside. I threw on whatever I was wearing the day before and started out on a walk. Dawn was breaking. As I walked by the mirror-like lake, I was entranced by the beauty surrounding me. Words of wisdom I had already received had exceeded my expectations, and I thanked God for the pamphlet. Soon, I was thanking God for everything.

Feeling intensely grateful for my fifty years of life, I came upon a clearing. There, in an arc, were the most beautiful, tall trees I had ever seen. The diffused light painted each one a different matte color—magenta, gold, copper, bronze, purple, scarlet, bright yellow. I stood in awe for a few minutes then whispered, "Oh God, it doesn't get better than this." Instantly, something remarkable happened. It was as if God said, "Oh yeah? Watch this!" Light streamed down through the clouds at the exact second a breeze hit the trees. The colors spontaneously exploded in an electric fireworks display as if suddenly plugged into a celestial socket. The leaves twinkled and rustled in a melodious hum. Were they singing "Happy Birthday" to me?

God and I were conversing while He was presenting me with a cosmic sound and light show! I didn't bother to wipe away tears as I whispered back, "Thank you." The extraordinary sensation I experienced was immediate. I felt boundless, ceasing to be the audience. The energy of love, nature, and I were one in the here and now. Time stood still as I floated in that space of grace. Then, just as I noticed it was daylight, the trees resumed their stillness. I was back but not the same. I had been given a sublime assurance that I was deeply loved.

As I reached the group gathered around the Q'ero Medicine Wheel, I had been downloaded with new information—I, too, was sound, light, and vibration. We all are. Everything is. I was neither saint nor shaman, yet what I experienced was divine, holy, and transcendental. I had not been sitting cross-legged chanting Om, nor had I been praying in church. I was rooted in the midst of trees. With utter certainty I knew that this oneness is available anywhere, to anyone who taps into gratitude—the state of being where the more you give, the more you get.

All you have to do is remember to say thank you.

CHAPTER 9

Discovering *A Course in Miracles* and Changing Course

My career in architecture lasted just over ten years. I never got the opportunity to design the beautiful building that I had dreamed about. Working with Buckminster Fuller and his team on the *Fly's Eye*, a visionary cost-effective answer to the world's shelter problem, had led me toward challenging solution-based design. My last stint in architecture was in the life sciences division of a large firm designing biotechnology laboratories. There were eight architects and 150 engineers. Creating spatial sequences to reduce germ populations to 100 microbes per cubic meter at the location where, say, syringes were packaged, felt like I was solving logic puzzles. I loved the autonomy—seeing the design process through to the end without anyone breathing down my neck.

My workplace, with rows of aging, mismatched beige and gray steel desks, could not have been further from beauty. My boss was pressuring me to accept a "promotion" as a project manager, with added administrative duties. This made me question my role there. Rather than quit, I took a three-month leave of absence to figure out my next professional move. It was also an opportunity to visit friends and family in Portland and make some necessary repairs to my mother's house.

Despite perpetual cloudy skies and consecutive rainy days, I loved Portland. I still considered it home. My mother and I shared a deep, emotional bond, and I delighted in discussing everything with her during our four-in-the-afternoon "coffee time"—except for one sticky topic. She could not comprehend why I didn't want a husband or children. After three long-term relationships with outstanding men that ended after they started pushing marriage, I was enjoying a robust single life, and my mother hated it. As soon as she would bring up how I needed to find a "good boy," settle down, and have a baby, I would change the subject to God. It never failed to work.

Lee, one of my Portland friends, would periodically see a psychic. Everything the psychic had told her had come true. I was impressed. A few days before leaving to return to Philadelphia, I decided that I wanted to see the psychic and called Lee to ask for the phone number. After several minutes, Lee came back on the phone sounding exasperated. "This is so weird. I can't find her card anywhere. It must be at work. I'll call you tomorrow." She called the next morning, befuddled as to how the card had disappeared. I pressed her for the location. After all, she had been there many times. Lee could not recall. She said that the psychic's first name was Peggy and vaguely recollected that her office was somewhere between 28th and 38th on Division Street, that the building was blue, and that the sign in front began with the word "Sun."

I jumped in my father's 1965 bronze-colored Ford Comet. Even though my mother didn't drive, she insisted on keeping it in the garage after he died, where it sat good as new with the original plastic protector on the back seat. Without an address or phone number, I set out to find the psychic. I drove up and down Division looking for the markers Lee had plucked from her blurry memory. I found a sign with "Sun Lee" on it, but it was a

Chinese restaurant. There was a blue building but no sign in front. I pulled over anyway. The blue building was an apartment complex with no Peggy on any of the mailboxes. Disheartened and returning to my car, I noticed that I had parked in front of a bookstore with a sign that read *A Course in Miracles,* and all of the books in the window had the same title. I went in to check it out. There were banners on the walls with quotes. I approached the only person there, a young, bookish-looking guy. "What's *A Course in Miracles?*" I asked. Without saying a word, he handed me a pamphlet.

On the plane back to Philadelphia, after I had read my magazine and put it back in my bag, I saw the pamphlet. Leafing through it, I found myself resonating with its message and began to pay attention. *A Course in Miracles* teaches that everything negative is rooted in fear, and the only antidote to fear is love. *Check, I go along with that,* I thought. It stated that all emotional pain can be healed when you forgive yourself and others. *Check.* Heaven was defined as a "condition" we experience here on Earth after having been healed with love, which unites us with God through the Holy Spirit. *Check.*

The concepts presented were striking chords, ringing true. Some were more difficult to grasp than others—how the world we see is not real but made up of our individual perceptions; and how God, who we are one with, is Love and the only truth. The ego, which resides in the illusory world, promotes separation. This explained to me how stubbornly holding on to our opinions and refusing to consider another viewpoint results in disagreements, even wars. The Holy Spirit, the word of God here on Earth, seeks oneness. It waits to be invited in to heal us by helping us forgive, love, and connect with our fellow humans.

Everything I was reading validated what my mother had taught me about love and the teachings of Jesus. The concept that we are all one with God is a fundamental doctrine of Christian Orthodoxy. I had studied Hinduism and found a similar belief about the nondual nature of Divine

Consciousness that was extolled by the Hindu school of philosophy, Advaita Vedanta. When I read that the *Course* had not been authored but was channeled, or "scribed," by a woman through Jesus Christ, I felt a wall go up, but kept on reading. The unconventional manner in which the book purportedly came to be—the people involved, timing, and circumstance—fascinated me. I learned that the scribe, Helen Schucman, was not only part Jewish and an atheist, but also a clinical psychologist and professor of medical psychology at Columbia University's College of Physicians and Surgeons. How clever of God to pick an atheist to channel the "Christ Mind." A woman, no less!

I just knew there was something to this. Why would an esteemed academic risk her reputation to have something so utterly metaphysical published? I empathized with Schucman, who felt bewildered at the spiritual content of what was being dictated to her. She accepted her assignment as her mission nonetheless. It took her seven years to transcribe what the "voice" was telling her, culminating in 1,200 pages of text.

My biggest takeaway was how the book defined a "miracle." The pamphlet explained that it is more than divine intervention that cures an ailment in the body; it is the healing of the mind. It is the "aha" moment when our perspective shifts from me-me-me to higher frequency emotions—empathy, compassion, and love. When we break away from the clutches of the ego, which seeks to keep us in fear and isolated from each other, and we make the shift to loving kindness, we experience a miracle. I couldn't wait to read the book.

I found *A Course in Miracles* in the Transformation/New Age section of the bookstore. I picked up the soft-cover tome and flipped through it. It reminded me of the Bible. The pages were super thin, and every paragraph was numbered. Not for me. I put the book down and left.

My friend, Michael, an interior designer who had just been offered a position in a corporate design firm, was frantically finishing his freelance projects. One of them was a store that would be renting high-end evenin-gwear to women—the equivalent of what men had been doing for years, renting tuxedos. One Night Stand was the brainchild of his friend, Amy, a stylish young woman who had worked as an accessory buyer for Phila-delphia's most famous fashion establishment. The dressing room needed curtains, and Michael asked me to select the fabric and if I knew anyone who could sew them. "I'll sew them!" I said without giving it a second thought. My mother had taught me to sew clothes for my dolls when I was six. Later in high school, I perfected my sewing skills so that I could wear trendy clothes, which I otherwise could not afford.

Amy had connections with New York's top fashion houses—Halston, Chanel, Armani, Carolina Herrera, Oscar de la Renta, Terry Mueller, Gucci, Pucci, and a few younger designers in the mix. We immediately hit it off. She needed an assistant to help with customers and do basic alterations, and I needed a job until I figured out my new direction. In the meantime, I would be surrounded by beauty. I gave my notice at the architectural firm.

We opened the store in September of 1989, and the timing could not have been better. Along with the affluence of the Ronald Reagan years and a skyrocketing stock market came a profusion of black-tie parties that continued as the economy began to wane and the recession crept in. Amy's business was booming, and even women who could afford the gowns at full retail price rented at a fraction of the cost. I witnessed self-esteem levels rise within minutes. Dressing for an evening occasion gave a woman dramatic license to explore a hidden aspect of her personality without spending an arm and a leg. I loved helping women feel good about themselves with a store full of evening clothes as my toolbox.

Being a fashion designer had been one of my childhood fantasies. I began sketching dresses as soon as I could hold a pencil. The creative process wasn't that much different from architecture—just as the site and usage criteria determined the design of a building, a woman's personality and body shape dictated the clothing that would enhance her assets. The more I observed the effect that beautiful clothes had on women, the more I wanted to design them.

A friend who was a successful entrepreneur came in to see the store. Growing up with a father in the "rag" business, he scrutinized and critiqued each garment. Abruptly, he asked, "What are you doing here peddling other people's rags when you can be selling your own designs?" I took his belief in me as a confirmation.

When the Clinton administration took over, along with the new president's stance against "a Gilded Age of greed and selfishness," came a taming of excess. Fashion turned its back on ostentation, and black-tie affairs fizzled. And so did One Night Stand. Our fashion store party had lasted four and a half years.

Just before we closed the shop, a beautiful, young woman came in and tried on a black, strapless gown with a beaded-lace bodice and full tulle skirt. It fit perfectly. She said that she was getting married and asked if it came in white. I told her that, unfortunately, it only came in black. Clearly crestfallen, the woman said that it was exactly the dress she had envisioned. We continued chatting while she was changing in the dressing room. Her name was Elaine, she was a model, and of Greek descent. I told her that I also was Greek-American, had sewed since childhood, and offered to make any alterations her wedding dress might need. Elaine stuck her head out between the curtains. "Will you make my wedding dress?" she asked. "I just want the exact same dress in white." I was speechless. It was a no-brainer. I only had to copy it. The words just came out, "I would love to make your dress." She emerged from the dressing room in her underwear and hugged me. We agreed that she would pay me the same price as the retail cost of the dress, and I promised her that hers would be even more beautiful. I took the gown home and made the pattern. And thus, my dress designing business began.

Running a business during a period of economic austerity would require me to be on a tight budget and take a one-toehold-at-a-time approach until I built up my clientele. Starting out by working at home, I would also do alterations, slash spending, and save every dime. I imposed a moratorium on buying artwork and clothes. Thank God I had amassed a classic quality wardrobe that would see me through, though I would allow myself a delicious pair of shoes now and then. Elaine's wedding dress would be finished before the store's closure, when I would be eligible for unemployment benefits until I got on my feet.

I considered it my extreme good fortune to live on the entire fourth floor of a brownstone row house on Delancey Place, one of Philadelphia's best streets, for remarkably low rent. Mrs. Ward, my landlady, who was in her mid-eighties and lived alone on the second floor, had never raised my rent in the several years I lived there. I created a workspace in the bedroom and would use the living room for consultations and fittings. Working on Elaine's wedding dress, I felt like a pastry chef whipping up lace, tulle, and pearls. Elaine's mother had died, and she was planning the wedding by herself. My role extended beyond dressmaker, more that of a confidante. After each fitting we would sit down with tea and cookies and discuss wedding preparations. As promised, the finished gown with its hand-appliquéd lace, pearls outlining the strapless neckline, and a frothy tulle skirt, was more beautiful than the one Elaine had tried on in the store. It made her look ethereal.

My next clients were my friends. Meg wanted a gown to wear to the Academy of Music Ball. An all-American blonde with a perfectly proportioned figure, she dressed conservatively. I wanted to see her razzle-dazzle and talked her into "sumptuousness." I scoured 4th Street, otherwise known as Fabric Row, but nothing took my breath away. Amy suggested I contact her friend Gloria, a local accessory designer, whose bags and delectably hand-painted shawls we had carried in the store. Gloria had a substantial collection of luxurious fabrics, and I made an appointment with her to see them.

Upon visiting her studio, Gloria led me into her storeroom where there was row upon row of the most opulent bolts of fabric I had ever seen: an array of colors, patterns, and textures—lush velvets, extravagant brocades, and silks from translucent chiffon and organza, to rich peau de soie and taffeta. I chose several samples to show Meg, but my heart was set on a magnificent silk brocade of vibrant red and fuchsia flowers. It was nothing she was used to, but I knew I could convince her.

Gloria was all that is Italian. She generated a natural sensuality that spilled into her surroundings with hand-painted silk panels on the walls and pillows in luxurious fabrics strewn about. She invited me to sit down. Every time Gloria came into our store, she had a different hair color. Strawberry blonde that day, Gloria reminded me of Gina Lollobrigida. She spoke in thickly accented English with Italian grammar and bounced from topic to topic—fashion, food, business, men, the human condition—regularly interjecting a throaty laugh. We found that we had a lot in common. As the discussion turned to spirituality, she tossed out words and phrases that were eerily familiar. She spoke of fear being the opposite of love, the ego and the Holy Spirit, and how the world is not real but an illusion. "Are you familiar with *A Course in Miracles*? I asked.

"*Sì, sì!* I have been a student for eight months!" she exclaimed as her eyes widened. "How did you know?"

I told her about trying to find the psychic but, instead, had unwittingly walked into the tiny bookstore where I stumbled onto the *Course*.

"They say you only learrrrn about it when you arrrre rrrready!" she proclaimed as she protractedly rolled her r's.

Gloria extolled the teachings of the *Course*. It was comprised of three parts, one of which consisted of 365 lessons, one for every day of the year. She implored me to buy the book and immediately begin with the lessons.

"Even if it doesn't make sense to you, you must continue doing them." Gloria showed me flash cards of quotes from the *Course* that she kept in her desk drawer to help her crystallize the concepts. She wanted my assurance that I was going to buy the book. I said I would, but I didn't. Gloria and I became friends, and she gave me the book for my birthday. I placed it on the bottom shelf of my nightstand.

One Night Stand quietly closed, and I was formally unemployed. Meg's two-piece gown turned out magnificently. The red and fuchsia brocade coatdress, with a low-scooped neckline and three-quarter sleeves, divided into four panels that fell below the knee. Underneath, a floor-length skirt, yards of fuchsia silk chiffon, peeped through the panels, swishing in waves as she moved. Word of my work had gotten out, and my phone began to ring more frequently.

Although my apartment was working out well for me, the three flights of stairs to the fourth floor were not ideal for my clients. I had to start looking for studio space. My vision was a French salon. I needed a reception desk or table, chairs, rug, cutting table, industrial sewing machine, serger, shelving, lighting, drapes, and a dressing room. It felt overwhelming. I had designed a logo, and my business cards were waiting to be ordered. First, I needed an address.

Waking up one night, unable to go back to sleep, I began assessing my financial situation, making a mental list of the dreaded expenses that far exceeded the income. Liquidating some of my stocks seemed inevitable. I went over my stock portfolio in my head, evaluating which ones to sell. Anxiety set in. I told myself that front-end expenses were part of doing business, but my thoughts quickly spiraled down from bad to worse. *I'm forty-three years old*, I thought, *and I have nothing; I have no husband* (even though I didn't want one), *or children* (which I had no longing for), *I don't own a car or a home, I have no steady income, and no experience running a business.* The anxiety mounted. My stocks represented security for my future, and this business was a vortex that was going to suck up all of my money. Within minutes I visualized myself as a bag lady on a street corner with meager belongings stuffed in a shopping cart.

As the imminent panic attack was about to hit, a voice inside me ordered, "Turn on the light and find something to read!" I sprang up, turned on the lamp, and looked around for anything. My heart was banging against my chest. I saw *A Course in Miracles* at the bottom of my nightstand. Grabbing it, I sat up and opened it randomly. I began reading at the top of the left page. It said that lack was not part of my life, that everything was available to me to ensure my happiness. It enumerated everything that enriched my life—not only the timely coincidences that had brought about exactly what I needed, but the love from my family and friends that had sustained me. The wisdom emanating from the page made me feel exceedingly fortunate. When I felt tears fall on my chest, I instantly grasped that any book that can transform a bona fide panic attack into gratitude after less than a third of a page deserved my full attention. I pledged that I would read this book no matter what and complete a lesson every day.

Via forces and a will beyond my own, and by listening to my inner voice, my career path had veered in a completely new direction. Designing "shelters" for the body allowed my creative juices to flow again and realize the fruits of my labor much quicker than the time it took to complete a building. A custom-designed dress not only enhanced a woman's positive features and hid the not-so ideal, it also allowed me to tap into her psyche and prod her to explore different aspects of her personality and fantasies. The way each client lit up after donning the finished gown was proof. I was helping women feel sexy and confident!

From the time I stumbled onto the tiny storefront in Portland and was given a pamphlet on the *Course*, to the moment when I was truly ready to actually crack open the book was approximately a year and eight months. How many times did the cosmic frying pan have to hit me on the head while I continued to stubbornly resist reading it? It took an anxiety episode to make me pay attention.

Reflecting on the *Course*'s definition of a miracle—a change of perception from fear to love—I realized that that was exactly what had happened to me after opening the book to a random but unbelievably relevant page. The profound shift from acute anxiety to intense feelings of love and gratitude was a miracle brought about by a book about miracles! All of my fears about money ceased.

I felt a powerful inner knowingness that I was being taken care of. I couldn't wait to find the perfect place for my studio and launch Sophia Demas Couture.

CHAPTER 10

The Brooder

My fears were replaced with a fire burning in my belly. I was eager to dive right in, but something told me that first I had some things to learn about running a business. I followed Stephen Covey's advice in *The 7 Habits of Highly Effective People* and created personal and business mission statements to help identify my goals. I determined that my life's purpose was to be happy and helpful, and my professional objective was to grow a successful dress designing business and help women feel good about themselves. The Wharton School at the University of Pennsylvania offered a program to help entrepreneurs incubate their business. Those chosen to participate attended a weekly class and were assigned an MBA student as a business coach. My application was approved, and my designated coach was Monica, a lovely young woman of Indian descent who was a marketing whiz. Our weekly meetings were somewhere between brainstorming powwows and mental health therapy sessions.

My list of requirements for a workspace was ambitious. Retail space was financially prohibitive, so I was looking for a first-floor, one-bedroom apartment with a window to the street near pricy Rittenhouse Square. The bedroom would be turned into a workroom and had to be large enough to accommodate two workstations, a cutting table, and a dressing room. The living room, which would be used for consultations, had to evoke European elegance. The discouraging part was my budget for rent—$550 per month was as high as I could go. Undaunted, I set out on my search for a space I was determined to turn into a French atelier.

After weeks of looking at cramped and characterless spaces, I was waiting to meet a rental agent in front of a stately three-story, somewhat neglected Victorian Gothic Revival stone building with two-story bay and pointed arched windows. The agent led me through the entryway lit by a bare, fluorescent bulb. He opened the first door into a room that looked like a wedding cake. Light poured in through an enormous bay window revealing a symphony of white, decorative plasterwork. The high ceiling was adorned with raised plaster botanical motifs and rimmed by an egg-and-dart cornice. Beneath the cornice was a bas-relief border of flowered scrolls embroidering the perimeter. Opposite the door was a columned mantel with dentil moldings. The floors were wood parquet with a contrasting border. A wide opening revealed another spacious room that could be closed off with a pair of paneled doors. That room had a Tudor theme with exposed wooden beams, wainscoting, and a huge mantel that looked like the entrance to a castle. A dated five-foot-long kitchen unit was tacked onto the back wall, but who cared? All of this for $425, including heat!

Surpassing my fantasy for old-world charm, I had found a veritable Victorian theme park! Giddy, I wrote out a check for the security deposit and took measurements. It was the end of November, and I figured that I could have the space ready by February and a formal opening as early as March. By the time I left, I had the salon's interior designed and furnished, from the brocade drapes and the pattern of the tufted Chinese rug to the exact paint color of the consultation room—the subtle pink hue inside a conch shell.

Three mornings a week, I religiously worked out at the gym. Once a theater, the vast room had molded ceilings with chandeliers and was lined with exercise machines. The stage was for stretching. Not a morning person, I avoided socializing. Rather than use the communal coat rack, I hung my coat on a hook in the utility closet. Shortly after I had joined the gym the year before, I noticed an artsy-looking man barreling through the main room toward the locker rooms in the back, as if on a mission. He had great shoulders. His thick, disheveled hair was longer than chin length, and he had a salt-and-pepper beard. He wore the same exact style of clogs I did. I decided that he must be the brooding intellectual type in the midst of resolving an issue of his latest creative endeavor. He became my fantasy cool guy.

The brooder also kept to himself. One morning I went up on the stage where he was stretching and made what I thought to be a witty remark. I found his flat, one-syllable response to be mournful and dismissive, as if I had intruded on his deep contemplation. I turned and went back to my usual morning solitude. Though the brooder appeared to be perpetually preoccupied, I would often catch him unabashedly staring at me. Shortly after our nanosecond interlude, I arrived at the gym and found a man's Australian oilskin drover coat hanging on one of the hooks in *my* closet. I hung my coat next to it, feeling encroached upon. From then on, the caped coat always hung in the closet. After one of my workouts, I was putting on my coat when the brooder entered. The coat belonged to him. He said hello. I said hi back. This became our sole communication.

A year later, the brooder still intrigued me, but I was too busy readying my salon to wonder about his state of mind. Days before I was to leave for Portland for Christmas, on my way to the Stairmaster at the gym, I passed by Don on the treadmill. He stopped me to invite me to his firm's annual holiday party. Don was a partner at Friday Architects and Planners, where I had interviewed for a job during the recession. The party was a Philadelphia institution, jam-packed with artsy types. As I began exercising, the brooder got onto the machine next to me. "How do you know Don?" he asked.

"I've known Don for years. How do you know Don?"

"He's my partner."

I knew that Don and his wife, Arlene, were partners in the firm. I had attended the holiday party in previous years but had never noticed the brooder. So, he was an architect, a creative type, just as I had pegged him. "I'm Sophia."

"I'm Frank." He was a man of a few words.

"Well then," I chirped, "I guess I'll see you tonight at the party."

"See you," he said, got off the machine, and left. It was the most we had ever spoken to each other.

That night I had plans to go out with my friend Tanya. She was an engineer at the firm where I had designed biotech labs. Tanya was Russian and looked and talked like Natasha Fatale from *The Adventures of Rocky and Bullwinkle*. We agreed to stop by the Friday party before going out to dinner.

The firm was known for its whimsy. Every Christmas, a stylized depiction of an animal hung on each of the nine columns between the windows. This year they were green turtles. Revelers filled the long, narrow office space shoulder to shoulder. Making our way through the crowd, I spotted Frank. His long, thick hair was now in a ponytail. He had on a white poet's shirt, and his red-framed glasses hung on a string around his neck. When he finally noticed me, it was the first time I saw him genuinely smile. He came over, greeted us, and led us to one of the tables laden with food and drinks. He poured each of us a glass of wine, and we chitchatted. I told him we had dinner reservations, and as he walked us out I said, "It was nice to see you in your milieu."

"It's always nice to see you at the gym," he replied.

I felt more than an affinity for Frank—I felt a spark. I couldn't wait to call my friend Jane the next morning and tell her what happened with the guy from the gym.

"Frank Mallas, the architect?" she asked, surprised. "George knows him. Let me talk to him, and I'll call you right back." It's nice to have good friends with an inside track. Jane called back to report, "George likes him; he thinks he has a brilliant mind but said that he comes across a little like a stevedore. He seemed surprised that you are attracted to him." A stevedore with a brilliant creative mind? Just my type!

I returned from Portland and looked forward to the gym and seeing Frank. We had established an unmistakable connection, and I was excited to pick up where we had left off. This was not to be the case. Frank reverted to never saying more than hi as he continued to hang up his coat next to mine.

One morning in mid-February, Frank walked up to me at the gym and asked without affect, "Would you like to have lunch?"

"Yes, I would like that."

"How about we meet this Wednesday at Amara Café at 12:30?" Frank proposed.

"Perfect."

"See you then," Frank said as he turned and walked away. Whether or not he was interested in me was a mystery.

It had been snowing for days, and by Wednesday the streets were solid ice. The restaurant was a few blocks away from my salon. Frank was waiting for me at a table. As soon as I was seated, he began talking nonstop. He described how he had gone from a blue-collar upbringing to studying architecture at the Cooper Union on scholarship and how he had ended up in Philadelphia after briefly working in Italy after graduation. He stopped long enough for the waitress to take our order. He proceeded to tell me about projects he was working on, that he had gone through a painful divorce ten years earlier, and that he had two daughters in their early twenties. Then

Frank told me that his nephew had been murdered the year before. It was around the time I had first seen him enter the gym looking self-absorbed. He was in fact grieving and struggling to contain his anger.

Frank asked the waitress for the tab. So much for a two-way conversation. The man of few words had not stopped talking. He had asked me one question, "What do you do?" I told him that I was now designing dresses. Without acknowledging it, he began telling me about the upcoming gala marking the opening of the Frank Lloyd Wright exhibit at the MOMA in New York. I presumed that he wasn't interested in a dressmaker. He went on, "My friend's wife is the editorial director there, and she gave me two tickets." I was in disbelief. Was he asking me to the much-touted black-tie affair? Frank paid the bill while I waited for the invitation. Wrong again. He was attending the event with someone else. I had to accept the obvious—he was not into me. Yet, Frank insisted on walking me back to the salon, holding onto my arm, steadying me on the ice. I was befuddled. We reached my door, I thanked him for lunch, and we said goodbye. Socially inept, I concluded. As he walked away, I couldn't help shouting out, "Have a nice time at the gala," wondering if he had caught the sarcasm.

Back at the gym, we continued to communicate with one-syllable greetings. Valentine's Day came and went, and I gave up on Frank. In the throes of launching my business, I had enough to worry about—finalizing the floor plan and paint colors, pricing equipment, sewing drapes, and connecting with vendors from my friend Gloria's invaluable contact list. There were also hats to finish for my millinery class. Word of mouth had brought in more clients, and I had begun to consider hiring an assistant.

I had never been to the gym on a weekend. On a Sunday, three weeks after my lunch date with Frank, I felt an urge to work out. I went to the gym later than usual and found Frank on the treadmill. We acknowledged each other's presence. George and Jane were coming over for dinner at 7:30 that evening. Walking home, I was mentally going over my to-do list when it dawned on me—why not invite Frank and round out the table? George liked him. So what if he wasn't interested in me? I called and left a message. At 7:00 p.m., not having heard back from Frank, I set the table for three. I was checking on my vegetarian lasagna when the phone rang at 7:20. It was Frank. He breathlessly explained that he had just gotten the message after having returned from a hike, and as he started telling me about it, I interrupted. "Are you coming to dinner?"

"Am I still invited?"

"Of course! Jane just called and said they won't be here until 8:00, so whenever you get here," I said while adding another place setting.

"I just need to jump into the shower. I'll be there ASAP." It was the first time I heard him sounding enthused.

As soon as my friends arrived, the doorbell rang, and Frank ran up the flights of stairs. He came in out of breath, smiling. He was decidedly ruggedly handsome. George and Frank seemed genuinely happy to see each other. Frank slowly perused my apartment, commenting, "You have a nice place." We sat down to a bubbling lasagna, and the wine and conversation flowed. Everything about the evening was wonderful. Frank appeared to be completely at ease. It was as if the four of us had been getting together for years. Even though it was a "school night," the three of them did not leave until past midnight. Frank lingered behind and asked if he could reciprocate the dinner the following Saturday night at his place.

There was a definite electricity between us. All week I tried to diffuse my excitement about dinner with Frank and go without expectations. I arrived at the private entrance to his third-floor apartment with a bottle of cognac and rang the doorbell. I could hear him bound down the stairs. He opened the door, beaming. He led me up the stairs under a brilliantly colored Chinese paper dragon kite. His apartment was a world of whimsy. Kites, a carved wooden angel, and various orbs and objects hung from the ceiling. Books were everywhere. The bay window was swagged with strings of lights, and another one ran the entire length of the hallway ceiling. Evocative beats of third-world music pulsed, and a symphony of aromas filled the air.

All of my senses were buzzing. A table overflowed with colossal shrimp, an array of vegetables and dips, and an artisanal whole-wheat baguette Frank had baked himself. Clearly comfortable in his environment, conversation was easy as he poured wine while I piled my plate. As I complimented him on his clever dinner presentation, a timer went off. Frank directed me to the small table set with two place settings and a lush flower arrangement and ordered me to close my eyes. Dinner was about to be served. I closed my eyes amid the sensory overload.

"You can open your eyes now."

There on my plate was a huge, roasted red bell pepper stuffed with herbed chicken and garnished with caramelized celery and carrot spears. Next to it were Belgian endive boats laden with glistening caponata. I could only sigh as he refilled my glass. He made a toast, and we delved into each other's lives on a deeper level. There was no more guessing about the attraction between us. Frank told me how he was "smitten" from the first time he saw me and described the T-shirt I was wearing. He said that he had considered me out of his league and apologized for his hot and cold behavior. He had projected onto me the goddess-on-a-pedestal, and I had projected onto him my fantasy—the self-confident but sensitive artistic macho man. Now we could start getting to know each other for who we really were.

So, Frank's contradictory behavior had been due to feelings of inadequacy. The utter sincerity with which he exposed his weaknesses disarmed me. The timer went off again. He went to the oven and returned with what, unbeknownst to him, was my favorite pie, blueberry. It was the most beautiful pie I had ever seen. On top of the latticed crust were leaves of dough that had been brushed with different mixtures of egg yolk, egg whites, and milk, giving each one a different hue. Only a man with sensitivity and goodness could possibly conjure up this kind of presentation. It was the best blueberry pie I had ever tasted. I could learn to handle his insecurities. How lucky to have had the uncharacteristic urge to work out at the gym on Sunday, find him there, and invite him for dinner as a friendly gesture. Frank put Chopin on and led me under the string of tiny lights to the bedroom where candles flickered.

That was the beginning of my life with Frank. He was kind, compassionate, and exceedingly helpful with putting my salon together. He built the cutting table and partitioned off the dressing room. Frank rolled paint on the walls while my friend Michael painstakingly hand-painted the plaster garlands. While Frank dove into the relationship head first, he perceptibly held back from expressing intimacy. Was he still afraid of me? After a few months of trying to figure it out, I decided to consult a therapist.

David and I clicked immediately. His large head with a thick mane and bushy beard would alternate between bobbing animatedly and hovering perfectly still in rapt attention. We had two sessions. In the first one he asked questions. I told him that, while deep down inside I knew that Frank had strong feelings for me, he was not demonstrative. David wanted to know what the family dynamic was like at home growing up. I told him that, as in many Greek households, everything was amplified. There was a lot of noise, many strict rules, and an abundance of love. We yelled when we talked. When I was little, my father would twirl me while heaving me up in the air, dive down to the floor on my level, and run around the house while carrying me on his shoulders. David asked me what I knew of Frank's childhood. From what Frank had told me, he grew up without rules or boundaries in a family where one was discouraged from asking questions.

At the following session, I anxiously anticipated David's read-out. He lost no time hitting nail after nail on the head. "You were raised in a home full of affect and, therefore, you need to be thrown around the room to feel loved. Frank, however, was raised in a home with little affect. He may love you more than you love him, but he is not showing it in the manner you are familiar with because he doesn't know what that is." My perspective changed completely. Frank's affect had nothing to do with me. It was not fair of me to expect him to express his feelings in a way that was foreign to him. Instead, I resolved to show him the love and affection I had so freely received.

The long-awaited salon opening was upon us, and Frank was making some last-minute finishing touches. Working side by side, we made a great team. Friends came early to help with the food. Flowers were delivered throughout the day. Michael sent a splendid floral mantelpiece. The wedding cake-like interior sparkled under the chandelier. The entire space was filled with friends and acquaintances from different facets of my life. Mrs. Ward, my dear elderly landlady, sat in a chair holding court. My first creation, Elaine's wedding dress, floated like a cloud on a mannequin in front of the window. In the midst of celebrating, I stepped back to take in the moment. It was hard to believe what was happening. Sophia Demas Couture was in business, and I was in love.

CHAPTER 11

War, Peace, and
Real Estate

Two brides made appointments for wedding gown consultations in one week. I had started a marketing fund but decided that word of mouth was going to be my strategy. It certainly was working. Instead, I would use the money to hire an assistant. I placed an ad in the paper. Applicants spanned the spectrum. An elderly, highly skilled Polish lady only wanted to work two days a week and charged extra to work with black fabric due to failing eyesight. A young woman who had just gotten out of jail with no prior sewing experience decided that she was going to be a dress designer. A talented Korean woman spoke undecipherable English. I was beginning to lose hope when Heidi appeared. Wholesome and confident, armed with sketches and an impressive resume, she asserted her design and pattern-making skills. We agreed on a salary and a six-month trial. I offered to provide lunch.

Gloria's contact list of vendors was invaluable. She took me to the garment district in New York and personally introduced me to fabric and sewing notions merchants she had used for years, who offered me discounts. One vendor found out that I had briefly dated Steve Prefontaine in college. The record-setting Olympic runner who had died at the age of twenty-four was his idol. He showed me a frayed paperback of Prefontaine quotes and reverently asked if he could touch my arm. After that, he sold me fabric at practically cost.

Renting out evening gowns at One Night Stand had turned on a light bulb—what about maternity evening clothes for rent? If we could produce beautiful, low-cost, one-of-a-kind cocktail dresses and gowns, pregnant women could show up at an event feeling elegant and sexy in a dress they didn't have to buy or wear again. Heidi offered to make the patterns and sew the dresses for $100 each.

The dresses were a hit. We were featured on the front page of *The Phila-delphia Inquirer*'s Lifestyle section with Heidi modeling them. The article was picked up by *Reuters*, and the phone was ringing off the hook. A story about our pregnant brides made the cover of the paper's weekend magazine. The father and manager of Whitney Houston, the singer, contacted us about custom designing maternity gowns for her. Unfortunately, she miscarried. The free publicity was priceless.

Frank was my one-man cheerleading squad. He balanced my city ex-istence by introducing me to the outdoors. He took me on picnics and hikes where he would point out tree species. Once, he climbed halfway up a tree, plucked an abandoned bird's nest, and presented it to me. We went camping in North Truro on Cape Cod where he had spent many of his summers. I was not exactly the outdoorsy type. When I told my friends, they all reacted the same. "You? Camping?"

As nature was being revealed to me, so was another side of Frank. He began exhibiting what I came to refer to as emotional eruptions. The first time it happened, we were on our way to a restaurant when he suddenly went silent, and I noticed a scowl. Until then, we were having what I thought was a nice conversation. When I asked him if everything was okay, he continued walking in silence. The flare-up happened at the restaurant. Without telling me what it was I had said, he accused me of belittling him. I was blindsided. When I tried to explain that nothing could be further from the truth, he blasted me for negating his feelings. The more I contested, the more irate he became. His behavior was totally contradictory to his mild-mannered nature. I lost my appetite and asked him to take me home. The next day he called and apologized profusely. This happened again, and then again. What Frank perceived as an attack could be something as innocuous as my putting on music, which he took as me tuning him out. When I protested, he would become enraged at my "tone." This was followed by the silent treatment. Nothing about this was logical. I suggested he see a therapist. He refused. Been there, done that after his divorce.

Frank's behavior reminded me of my father's rages that came out of the blue. The punishment never fit the crime. Consequently, I developed a strong reaction toward injustices of any kind. As a child, I could not call the shots, but as an adult, I could. After one such episode, without giving Frank an ultimatum, I told him that I was not going to tolerate being unfairly accused of perceived wrongs. In a letter placed through my mail-slot the next day, Frank declared that he was deeply in love with me and that our relationship was the most important thing to him. He acknowledged his erratic behavior and stated that he wanted to change—not just for me, but for his sake as well—and that he had already made an appointment with David, my therapist. He asked for my support and to please phone him. With a measure of cautious optimism, I told him that I, too, valued our relationship, that taking responsibility for his actions had impressed me, but that I also needed some time to warm up to him again.

The blowups were sporadic but potent. I joined him at his sessions with David, who acted as our mediator, referee, and interpreter. I was also diligently studying *A Course in Miracles*. It was uncanny how the teachings were undeniably relevant to whatever issue was at hand. After one of Frank's volcanic episodes, I also exploded, slamming the door behind me as I left for work. Frank called, but I did not pick up. He left a message that he wanted to talk and was coming over at nine that evening. I had plans to meet my friend Meg for happy hour but would be home by then. I was done, but I wanted to hear what he had to say.

The topic that dominated my get-together with Meg was Frank's conduct. I told her that it had come out in therapy that growing up, his father related more with his older brother, who was big and resembled the father, and Frank, who was small, felt dismissed and insignificant. Consequently, as an adult, any perception of feeling less-than triggered him. I was bewildered at how a sane, compassionate, helpful human being could allow something irrational to risk our relationship. Meg flatly pronounced that I had given him more than enough chances and wished me luck. Something told me to read from the *Course* before Frank showed up. I plopped on the couch with the book just as I heard Frank clomping up the stairs. There was no time to read. I was paralyzed with dread. In a panic, I looked up, raised my hand, and from my core said, "Jesus, help me!"

Still wearing his bicycle helmet, Frank walked in scowling. He was a scary sight. I wanted to scream at him to go away, but instead, I was astonished to hear the words that came out of my mouth. "You were in a lot of pain this afternoon, weren't you?" They were spoken in a calm and steady voice. Those were not my words; my mind did not form them. It was as if I heard someone else speaking. In fact, I hadn't thought about his pain once! As I sat there on the sofa, stunned, staring at him, Frank's face became soft. "Yes, I was," he said as he came over and crumpled down next to me, and we embraced. After regaining his composure, he acknowledged the pain his behavior had inflicted on me and expressed genuine sorrow. The rancor had utterly disappeared. What had just happened here? Moments earlier the atmosphere had been charged with fear and anger. I had asked for help from the depths of my being, and the words I spoke, foreign to me, had disarmed Frank. Love had conquered fear. Each of us had had a shift of perception. Both of us had experienced a miracle.

Therapy was helping. After more than a year since the incident when my words involuntarily came out and acknowledged Frank's pain and detonated his anger, Frank wanted to take our relationship to another level. He still reacted to perceived attacks, but he was learning to stop himself and apologize in a timely manner. Though he still kept his apartment, he had all but moved in with me. Every now and then we would talk about formally moving in together, which would leave me squirming. We continued to see David and iron out misunderstandings, but it was the *Course* that had become my direct line to a cosmic life coach.

My landlady's niece called from Washington, D.C. to express concern about her aunt. Mrs. Ward had had lunch plans the day before with her nephew, who was visiting from New Mexico, but she had not answered the doorbell. I went down to the second floor and knocked loudly on her door. No response. I called the police. Two officers arrived but were reluctant to knock the door down, citing liability. "There's a dead lady in there!" I screamed. After assurances from Mrs. Ward's niece that she would take responsibility for any damages, they kicked the door open. Sweet Mrs. Ward had died in her sleep.

Sadness gave way to fear as the ramifications of Mrs. Ward's death sank in. How much longer could I stay in my apartment paying ridiculously low rent? Nothing had been done to the building since the '50s, and the new owner surely would make substantial renovations and increase the rent significantly. I loved my neighborhood, but one-bedroom apartments around the Rittenhouse and Fitler Square areas were unaffordable. I would have to start looking for an apartment in not-so-nice areas beyond Center City.

I had always dreamed of owning my own home and for fun would peruse the real estate section of the newspaper, monitoring housing prices. At the time, brownstones on Delancey Place went between $450,000 and

$650,000, way, way out of my league. Mrs. Ward's niece and nephew were the only heirs to her estate. Her apartment was cleared out and the building put up for sale by the executors, Mrs. Ward's lawyer, and accountant. Julie, the third-floor tenant, had salvaged Mrs. Ward's wide-brimmed straw hat from the trash, and we hung it on a nail next to her door as a tribute. To acknowledge Julie and me for our kindness toward Mrs. Ward, the estate gave Julie a plant and a carton of unopened orange juice, while I received what was even more useless—her remaining Friday matinee Philadelphia Orchestra subscription for one and a box of envelopes inscribed with the house address in script. I worked on Fridays and was about to move! I placed the box on the bottom shelf of my pantry.

It was during my mother's visit that the building was put up for sale for $265,000. Although it was considered an investment property, the shockingly low price was determined by a formula that reflected the low rents we were paying. Still, the price was beyond my reach. I was certain it would sell in a matter of days. "We should consider buying it," my mother threw out.

"All of my money is going into my business. I can't afford it."

"You have your stocks. I'll match you for the down payment," she offered, "and you can raise the rents."

"I would love to, Mama, but the timing is not right."

Mr. Rial, Mrs. Ward's accountant and an elderly gentleman, was also the listing agent for the property. I anxiously waited for the onslaught of offers, expecting it to sell overnight. A constant stream of realtors would parade prospective buyers through the building without follow through. I was boggled by the lack of interest. This wasn't a covert offering—there was a huge sign jetting over the sidewalk, and the price was half of what other buildings were selling for in the area. The building next door had been converted into condos, and a one-bedroom first-floor unit had just sold for $225,000! What was I missing here?

The building had been on the market for more than three months, and no one had made an offer. When an agent brought his clients and their architect through for a third showing, a siren went off in my head. Frank and I sat down, estimated the cost of expenses and needed repairs, including a new roof, and ran the numbers with different interest rates. Each of the four floors consisted of a one-bedroom unit. We figured out that, with the increased rental income, my purchase budget was $225,000 max, the same as the purchase price of just the condo next door. But, what bank would lend money to someone who had yet to break even on a new business, even with a cosigner?

One morning, I woke up with the decision—I was going to submit an offer. What did I have to lose? The worst they could do was to say no. I decided to call Mr. Rial when I got to the salon. My heart pounded as I descended the stairs. When I reached the second floor I was on the brink of a panic attack and touched Mrs. Ward's straw hat for good luck. In that instant, I heard the words, "Don't worry, Sophia, don't worry." There was no one there, but I heard them as if someone had spoken. I leaned on the railing in disbelief. My apprehension had vanished. I felt emboldened. I marched to the salon on a mission, the comforting words I had just "heard" replaying in my head.

Mr. Rial and I had become friendly. He knew of my interest in the property as well as my financial situation, so when he answered the phone, I got right to the point. "I am prepared to make an offer."

"I'm glad to hear it."

"You are aware that the roof is shot and all of the apartments need serious updating," I continued with my newfound mettle, "and I'm not going to apologize for my low offer because it is what I can realistically afford."

"No need to apologize," Mr. Rial chuckled. "It's better than anything we've gotten so far, which is nothing."

"I'm offering $190,000 with a new roof." I felt as if I had grown hair on my chest.

"Fine, I'll present it to the heirs for consideration, and I'll get back to you."

Clearly, the lack of offers had the estate unnerved. After countering back and forth, my final offer of $220,000 was accepted, and I was asked to obtain two estimates for a new roof. Amazingly, immediately thereafter, a bidding war ignited topping $300,000. The estate honored our gentleman's agreement without a signed contract! It was as if the Red Sea had parted long enough for me to cross over to the other side to safety just in the nick of time before it drowned the competition. Mr. Rial referred me to a mortgage broker who helped me procure a no-doc loan with my mother as cosigner, despite my inadequate income. I hired an acquaintance, a lawyer and real estate agent, to go over the contract for a nominal flat fee. Settlement was scheduled for the end of March, but he didn't think it would go through, saying that it was the most unbelievable real estate deal he had ever encountered. I had to smile. I had been directed not to worry.

To celebrate Valentine's Day and two years of togetherness, Frank and I went to a luxurious inn on Gramercy Park in Manhattan. Frank's eruptions had derailed romantic getaways in the past, but the cognitive techniques he had learned in therapy were helping contain the flickering flames of his perceived slights before they turned into an all-consuming blaze. Therapy had benefited me as well. It helped me to better understand that his behavior resulting from childhood issues had nothing to do with me, and to not allow it to deeply wound me. I chose instead to focus on what I regarded to be his true nature—his high moral fiber and loving kindness. Both of us needed this escape.

We arrived at the inn Friday evening after a stressful drive. Frank appeared to be unusually agitated with the other drivers and annoyed with any attempt I made to calm him. By the time we arrived at our two-room

suite, he seemed to have settled down. Frank had made dinner reservations at a nearby highly touted restaurant that offered American Nouveau
cuisine. It was right after the wine was uncorked that I noticed Frank's
frown. We toasted to Valentine's Day and to love. Midway through our
meal, Frank's sullenness left no doubt about the downward direction the
evening was heading. When I asked if anything was wrong, he shot back,
"No, is anything wrong with you?" Conversation ceased.

After we returned to the inn, Frank took out the cognac—a positive
sign. To stave off any further spiraling into the abyss, I stayed silent and went
into the bathroom to change. When I walked into the bedroom with two
glasses filled with water, his face suddenly turned red with anger. Yelling,
he accused me of dismissing his offering of fine cognac by filling the glasses
with water instead. He might as well have slugged me in the stomach. I
tried to explain to him that I had spotted two, stemmed, finer glasses in the
sitting room. He accused me of being insensitive to his feelings. The more
I attempted to plead and reason with him, the worse it got. His cognitive
toolbox had gone out the window. It was as crazy as if he were insisting
that there was an elephant in the room and then raging at me for saying
I didn't see it. Any expectation for intimacy in a romantic setting with the
man I loved was dashed. I fell asleep in a fetal position.

When I awoke in the morning, I played dead. Going over the events of
the night before, I drew a line between what I was and wasn't willing to put
up with. After both of us got up and dressed, I broke the silence. I needed
him to acknowledge his irrational behavior. "No, you owe *me* an apology,"
he bellowed as he lit into me about his perceived rejection. The same old
pattern was playing out before me. I fell into the trap of defending myself
against the wounding injustice of being falsely accused. That is when Frank
took it one step too far—he ridiculed me. "You're pathetic," he said as he
glowered at me. An alarm went off. I knew one thing for certain; "pathetic"
was not a word that anyone would use to describe me. "It's over," I said

flatly. Frank's head jerked back as if someone had punched him in the face. "What?" he said.

"It's over. Just take me home."

The sound of silence was deafening during the two-hour drive back to Philadelphia. What had crystallized for me was a deep, inner-knowing that my value as a person was inalienable and that I did not wish to be with anyone who said otherwise. As soon as the car safely stopped at my front door, I could not have jumped out and grabbed my bag fast enough.

All of my friends liked Frank and voiced their puzzlement at his paradoxical behavior. They had been cheering the progress he had been making in containing his anger and strengthening our relationship. Now they were even more bewildered and supported my decision to end it.

What I had come to rely on most for spiritual sustenance were the teachings of the *Course*. I read that if my brother is broken, it is because he is in fear, and only the curative powers of love and forgiveness will heal him, but I was not moved. As my "brother," I could forgive Frank, love him from afar, and pray for him, but I didn't have to be with him and subject myself to emotional abuse. I tried to divert my attention to other pressing matters—getting roofing estimates and gathering financial information in preparation for the settlement of the property. Also Heidi, my indispensable assistant, gave her notice. She and her three sons were joining her husband, who had accepted a job promotion in Wisconsin. It was not going to be easy to replace her.

A month after our breakup on Valentine's Day, Frank called to ask if he could hand-deliver a letter after work. In a pained voice he told me that it was important. I was flustered. I had enough reasons to avoid being reeled back in to a relationship with a man harnessing deep-seated issues. I was not going to live my life tiptoeing through a minefield, anticipating the next explosion. Wasn't I getting ahead of myself? All Frank asked for was to present me with a letter, and I was curious. I agreed.

While waiting for Frank to arrive, I read from the *Course*. The doorbell jarred me. I met him out on the sidewalk. He had roses for me. With his gaze squarely on mine, he placed the envelope in my hands, and as he cupped them with his, he told me how deeply sorry he was for what had transpired and grateful that I had agreed to accept his letter. And with that, he turned around and walked away. I went back in, placed the roses in a vase, poured a glass of wine, and sat at the big, round table to read the five handwritten pages.

In my hands was the soul of a man laid bare. In it was a reverential declaration of love, a genuine reflection of his shortcomings, an empathic acknowledgment of my emotional injury, an ardent plea for forgiveness, and an impassioned avowal of hope. Frank articulated his broken heart and his desire to change with introspection and eloquence. Just as I was thinking *I've heard this all before,* he stunningly announced that not only would he continue his therapy sessions with David but that he had joined Menergy, a therapy group of male ragers from all walks of life who were willing to take responsibility for their anger issues. This required a conscious commitment to change. Perhaps Frank was ready to leave behind the talk and now walk. I sensed something shift inside me. I felt admiration. My icy heart melted.

I called Frank to congratulate him on being proactive and to offer my support. He suggested that we talk face to face over dinner. We met at a favorite Thai restaurant. Frank told me that he had stumbled upon a newspaper article about Menergy months ago, prompting a discussion of his pattern of procrastinating and his taking action only when finding himself at rock bottom. He asked me if I would give him another chance. Unlike me, Frank was a private person, and I knew that joining a men's group where he would openly expose his flaws would be orbits outside of his comfort zone. It communicated to me how much our relationship meant to him. We were compatible on the highest levels—emotional, intellectual, and existential. Best of all, we laughed a lot together. I told him that I was going to adopt a wait-and-see attitude. First, I would also resume therapy with David alone to explore why the injustices I perceived were so debilitating. I asked him to pay for my sessions. Frank agreed, expressing relief and gratitude. We agreed to talk on the phone and that the next time we would see each other would be two weeks later at the settlement table.

In the meantime, I turned my focus on my business. Fortunately, it didn't take long to find another terrific assistant. Maxine, with her years of experience making costumes for the Opera Company of Philadelphia, brought an added layer of refinement to the production aspect of the operation.

More than a few large women, not pregnant, were happy to rent the maternity gowns. One of my regular couture customers, a stunning woman who was a size twenty-eight, told me that the last gown I had designed for her made her feel sexier than anything she had worn since she was a size 8. She became my muse. Designing dresses for perfect bodies had lost its allure. I set out on reconnaissance missions to survey the plus-size retail market and found that sexy evening clothes for large women were too few. My gowns were going to change all that.

My goal was to have a collection of eighteen pieces in upscale stores for the late fall market. This gave us a very small window of time for production. I furiously sketched ideas and ordered fabric samples while Maxine made the patterns. The palette of solid colors—pomegranate, gold, sand, taupe, dusky blue, and of course black—coordinated with two multi-colored, hand-dyed, fluttery, chiffon scarf-coats that coordinated beautifully. The time constraint forced us to scale back on our couture customers. Producing the line was an exciting investment for tomorrow, but it was not bringing home the bacon today.

The property closing was just three days away. Despite having been warned that the deal was too good to be true, I felt confident. I called Mr. Rial to point out that nothing had been done about a new roof. Acknowledging our agreement, he offered to average the two estimates and give me a check for $10,000 at the closing. Knowing Frank was going to be at the settlement table with his keen attention to details was reassuring. We had had meaningful phone conversations. He had taken his commitment to Menergy seriously and shared with me newfound realizations about the sources of his anger. His perseverance to change made me hold him in even higher regard. I looked forward to our celebratory dinner and spending the evening together.

When the estate emptied the basement, Mrs. Ward's shoeboxes had been overlooked. I threw everything out except for a pair of sleek, black Ferragamo pumps that were too narrow and a size too big for me. In silent tribute to Mrs. Ward, I went to the closing wearing her shoes. There were nine people present. After signing countless forms, Mr. Rial handed me the check for the roof. My attorney, who until then did not believe the deal would go through, covered his head and put his forehead on the table. Afterward, Mr. Rial gave me a memento of Mrs. Ward—a small scrapbook she had kept with the invitation to my salon's opening along with newspaper clippings of articles written about me and the clothes. She had been there, too.

Mrs. Ward's shoes made my feet hurt, but I was deliriously happy. The Universe had fulfilled my long-held dream of owning real estate, let alone in such a prestigious area. Frank had made dinner reservations at Fri Sat Sun in the neighborhood, a mainstay from Philadelphia's "Restaurant Renaissance" days in the early '70s. We toasted, clicked glasses, and marveled at how smoothly the settlement had gone. Frank told me that as a housewarming gift, he was having the house address affixed in gold leaf on the glass transom above the front door.

The conversation turned to our relationship. Frank made it clear that he would do whatever it took for my trust to be restored. In part, it already had. I saw his commitment not only in his eloquent words, but in the actions he had taken outside of his comfort zone. It was a teaching I had read in the *Course* that had brought about a real change of perception in me—the "special" relationship is the realm of the ego, where separation, attack, fear, and guilt are fostered, and only forgiveness can transform it into a "holy" relationship, where love overcomes all. I felt that our relationship had made that shift. I invited Frank to have a cognac at my apartment, in the building that I now owned.

Frank put on a CD of *Deep Breakfast* by Ray Lynch and poured the cognac. We cozied up on the sofa to classical guitars in the soft light. I thought of the words, "Don't worry, Sophia, don't worry," I had heard after touching Mrs. Ward's hat and remembered the box of envelopes I was given after she died. I went to the pantry and brought the box back to the sofa. "Look, Frank," I said as I opened it and pointed to the address engraved in script. "It's as if Mrs. Ward is saying, 'See, I told you so.'" He leaned over and kissed me.

Frank asked me what I thought of us living together. My expression must have conveyed the wave of fear that hit me because he quickly retracted the idea, saying, "It's too soon, I know." Wasn't it fear that had sabotaged my relationships in the past? Did I really want to continue to propagate fear in my life? I closed my eyes and shot out a plea to the Universe. "Help!" The message I received back was, "I am with you." I opened my eyes, and without a hint of apprehension I said, "I want to work toward that." I meant it, and it felt good. Frank's shock was audible. I knew that Frank's lease was up at the end of July, and Julie had given her notice. The third floor apartment would be available in two months at the end of June. "Frank, why don't you move into the third floor?" It seemed like the perfect first step to a long-term commitment, which I had avoided for so long. Frank did not have to be sold—he was elated. I was euphoric. I had slain two dragons in one day—I had acquired a substantial property and had overcome the gnawing undercurrent of fear of commitment that had plagued me. I felt like an adult. We fell asleep in each other's arms, exhausted and happy.

The next two months became an intensive landlord boot camp. Frank dove right in with me, solving problems and fixing things. The first lease I drew up was for the first-floor apartment. The kitchen hadn't been touched since the '50s, and I told the new tenants my plans to remodel it. Luckily, the couple found it to be "charming" and "kitschy" and asked if it could be left as is. After nine years of doing my laundry in a dingy laundromat around the corner, my first serious purchase was a state-of-the-art, energy-efficient, coin-operated washer and dryer for the basement, greatly improving the quality of my life.

Frank was going to take the first two weeks in July to move in bit by bit. We decided that it would be terrific to have a housewarming party in a completely empty apartment. What better way to celebrate the next level of our relationship than with 4th of July fireworks!

About eighty friends accepted the invitation. Frank made two tables out of old doors and sawhorses, one for food and one for drinks, and we borrowed as many folding chairs as we could. Guests could also congregate in my apartment or sit and eat on the stairs. Frank was in charge of the music, and Ann and Gloria came early to help set up.

Early on the morning of the party, my reading from the *Course* was exceptionally powerful. The gist of it was that we make our own heaven or hell here on Earth. Although reincarnation is not rejected in the *Course*, it does suggest that preoccupation with past or future lives is not helpful while living in the present. While the Buddhist view is that it sometimes takes many lifetimes of suffering to rise above ignorance and achieve a higher level of consciousness, the *Course* teaches that unless we face our fears and work through them in this lifetime, we will keep finding ourselves in similar situations until we do. I did not want to keep reincarnating to work on the same distorted issues and experience the same outcomes. Nor did I want to continue to repeat the pattern of ending relationships because of fear of commitment in this lifetime. I decided to trip up the dynamic. The only way I could break through any remaining vestiges of fear was to make a full and unconditional commitment to Frank.

I have no recollection of who brought up the idea, let alone if there was an actual proposal, but that day Frank and I decided to get married. He would move in with me and rent out the third floor. The housewarming was turning into an engagement party. After forty-five years of staving off marriage, I was going to enter into holy matrimony, and it would soon be broadcasted to our friends. There would be no going back after that. I felt strangely tranquil. My inner knowingness confirmed that this was exactly what I needed to do. I couldn't wait to tell my mother.

There was a hesitant silence at the other end of the phone. It was not the reaction I expected. My getting married had been my mother's main wish since I could remember. Marriage and cooing babies were her definition of happiness. "Are you sure about this?" she finally asked. "You know, men don't change." She had expressed concern about Frank's anger issues. I extolled Frank's many virtues and the actions he had taken to change. It wasn't until I told her that, after my prayer for help, I received the message, "I am with you," that she let out a yelp. She too had asked for divine guidance about whether to marry my father and had received it. "Oh, Sophia, you could not have made me happier," she said excitedly and heaped blessings on our union.

The party was in full swing when, according to plan, Frank turned off Motown blasting from the stereo and clanged on a pot lid, yelling, "Announcement! Announcement!" Word passed along to our friends circulating on both floors. After everyone had gathered on the third floor, glasses with champagne were distributed, and Frank announced that he would be moving in with me and we would be getting married in October. There was whooping and clapping, and a wellspring of good wishes were shouted out. Just then, as if on cue, the fireworks over the Philadelphia Museum of Art began lighting up the sky. Our happiness could not have been better expressed.

As I watched the display of brilliantly colored lights bursting in air, I mused. My business was growing. Against all odds, I now owned a valuable property. I recalled my panic before making the low offer and the encouraging words I had heard out of the blue instantly extinguishing my anxiety. My fear of commitment and years of avoiding marriage had given way to a will bigger than mine. The readings from the *Course* and the assurance I received after asking for help miraculously had changed my perspective. I felt victorious, as if having scaled up Mt. Everest. The power of love had trampled fear and had healed my heart in the process. Love won.

CHAPTER 12

Cosmic Wedding

*M*y brother, on my right side, and my mother, on my left, are walking me down the aisle to where Frank is standing with Steve, his best man. Frank is wearing a tuxedo and a big grin. The church is full of smiling wedding guests who are all standing as we slowly make our way. All eyes are on me. From the top of my head down, I am inside a full, floor-length skirt made of rows of ruffled lace with a slit in the front. My headdress is an exquisite papier-mâché torso of a doll wearing a tiara and veil. Her bent arms are holding a bouquet of flowers that is resting on my forehead. I designed the gown and made the doll myself, and I am thrilled with the dramatic effect. I am thinking, She's getting married, not me. *I feel like a wedding doll float in a parade, and I am annoyed that my brother keeps smirking to stifle his embarrassment. My mother is smiling blissfully. She and my brother give me away and take their seats in the front pew. Frank removes the doll torso with the attached skirt and lets it fall on the floor in a frothy heap, as I emerge wearing a long, simple, white silk sheath. I am free. I feel like a butterfly who has just shed her cocoon of fear.*

David could hardly sit still as I told him my dream. He was in total glee, alternating between grinning from ear to ear and forming an "O" with his mouth like a child rapt with wonder at its first glimpse of the pile of presents under a Christmas tree. He was visibly having a field day with this one. "You finally shed your cage!" he shouted out as soon as I had finished.

"Wow, that never occurred to me," I said, seeing David's point. My fear of entrapment was exactly what had caged me! In my past relationships, I had sought liberation by ending them. The dream beautifully illustrated how the power of love can render the clutches of fear impotent.

Gaining understanding of the dream's meaning was not the only reason I had come to see David. I found the layers of symbolism of the wedding doll get-up so utterly fantastic that I wanted to make it and actually wear it at the wedding. My friends knew how my fears had sabotaged past relationships, and this would allegorically express the "shedding" of my old, mistaken way of thinking and reveal the new, emancipated me. I thought that everyone would be enthralled with the idea, but instead the reactions I had gotten ran the gamut, from Michael falling off a barstool laughing hysterically to Sandi's expressed indignation that I would be mocking the institution of marriage.

"So, what was Frank's reaction?" David asked.

"He thought the dream was fabulous, but when I told him I wanted to wear the doll on my head, he just stared at me. He looked pained and then started stammering something about the wedding being a "special" and a "serious" occasion and that the "costume" might trivialize it. How much more special and serious can you get than emerging from what was caging me, metamorphosed, while the fears that no longer served me were left discarded on the floor?"

"How did you two leave it?"

"He said, 'I hope you will reconsider.'"

"That's fair. It's his wedding, too," David pointed out. He talked about how rites of passage evoke deep-seated, unconscious emotions. "Is it possible that you used the doll as a decoy, hiding under it so that you didn't have to feel that it was you walking down the aisle? You did say, 'She's getting married, not me.'"

He was right again. "Yes, maybe the doll is a kind of crutch to help me walk down the aisle, but this is such an opportunity to use this rich visual symbolism as an art form! David, what is your opinion about me wearing the wedding doll dress?"

"It's a marvelous vehicle to help you process overcoming fear of commitment and in understanding whether your fear was based on something real or artificial."

"The doll isn't the real bride, is that it?"

"Exactly. I have a feeling the elegant dress will triumph in the end. What was your mother's reaction?"

"I haven't told her yet."

"That's your homework."

After dinner, I called my mother and related my dream while she laughed uncontrollably. When I told her that I wanted to make the wedding doll outfit and wear it, there was a momentary silence. "Are you crazy? What are we turning this into, a circus?" Clearly, she was not getting the metaphor.

I understood that this was not just my wedding, or even our wedding— it was also my mother's dream. I resolved that I was not walking down the aisle with an unhappy mother and an embarrassed brother, only to meet up with a pained groom. The wedding doll idea was abandoned. Perhaps this was the perfect time to negotiate our long-standing debate over whether or not I wore a veil. "Mama, I just want you to know that the only way I'll wear a veil is if it's on the doll's head," I declared, to which she shot back, "So don't wear one." End of discussion.

The guest list would consist of about 110 family members and close friends. We set the date for October 4, precisely three months after the 4th of July party. Certainly this was more than enough time to plan a nice event.

Frank and I shared the same tastes, and our ideas melded smoothly. My job was selecting food, drink, and flowers, while Frank focused on the music for the church and reception. The venue did not have to be grand to evoke old world elegance, a look that surely could be generated with the help of our creative friends. One thing was a given—in deference to my mother, the ceremony was going to be held at a Greek Orthodox church, St. George's Cathedral in Philadelphia. My friend Voula's husband, Fr. George, would be one of the two officiating priests. What I wouldn't give to have my father present, though I knew his essence would be there with us.

It quickly became apparent that the amount of time and money we budgeted to pull off the kind of wedding we wanted was somewhat naïve. The church was available, but many of the charming, old Philadelphia reception venues had been reserved for months, as were caterers, photographers, and bands. I couldn't believe how expensive everything was. Undeterred, we began thinking outside the box. The right lighting, fabric, and flowers would make even an empty warehouse look beautiful. Who needed a photographer, anyway? By placing instant cameras on the tables, the guests could take candid shots.

The College of Physicians called to say that a function scheduled for October 4 had been canceled and that the ballroom in the historic Beaux Arts building was available. The building also housed the Mutter Museum, which offered one of the country's finest collections of medical history. An extra fee would allow guests to roam the exhibits, which included a tumor display, preserved mutated human fetal specimens, and the body of the Soap Lady, whose fat had turned her corpse into soap. Though beyond our budget, Frank and I, desperate at this point, were seriously considering it. My friend, Barbara, a sought-after event planner, urged me to procure it.

"I'll help you put this together," she offered. "It'll be my wedding present. My friend Ed will oversee the food. He works with a fabulous chef who will do it for a reasonable price." At the time, I had no idea how significant Barbara's help would be.

Just after Barbara's generous offer and before sending off a check to the College of Physicians, an auspicious coincidence gave new meaning to synchronicity. I dialed my friend, Ann, at her artist studio, and a man answered. When I asked to whom I was speaking, the man asked me surprised, "Sophia? It's Jerry. You called me! I just got out of the shower and am late for a meeting. Can I call you back this afternoon?" Befuddled, but recognizing that the voice belonged to a social acquaintance, I pressed him. "Jerry, I called the wrong number and got you. This is crazy! You have to call me back." He promised.

Jerry called later that afternoon. As a real estate developer and fixture on the Philadelphia social scene, he had purchased the Barclay Hotel in foreclosure for a phenomenally low price. Right on Rittenhouse Square, the Barclay had at one time been one of America's most prestigious hotels where practically every visiting celebrity stayed. We both marveled at how extraordinary it was that we were on the phone as a result of a misdial. Chitchatting, I told him that Frank and I were getting married and that the ballroom at the College of Physicians had fortuitously become available. "Forget it," he said dismissively. "You can have the ballroom at the Barclay. It'll be my wedding present as long as I can come with my girlfriend and you have the chandeliers cleaned."

"What?" I said after finding my voice. "Of course you can come, and those chandeliers will sparkle if I have to swing from them myself with a bottle of Windex!"

Jerry went on to throw in a two-night stay in the yet-to-be-updated presidential suite where President John Kennedy and Jackie had stayed. "Wow, thank you, Jerry," was all I could muster. "Wait. Jerry, what is your telephone number?" The number he gave me was the same as Ann's except for the last digit. We made plans to see the ballroom the following day.

"Fantastic," Frank said under his breath when I called to tell him the news. Barbara expressed delight and incredulity at the coincidence. Jerry met the three of us in the stately lobby and led us through an elegant foyer off to one side, which he offered us for the cocktail hour preceding the reception. He flung open a pair of gigantic French doors and turned on the lights. Three, enormous chandeliers lit a magnificent, cream-colored paneled room. With fluted columns, heavy swagged drapes, and crystal sconces, it stood before us with the imposing presence of a faded grand dame, bejeweled and bedecked in the finery of another era, ready for the ball. At the opposite side of the room was a stage with a grand piano. Transfixed, we just stared. It was way beyond what Frank and I had fantasized as a perfect setting for our wedding celebration.

An additional set of incredible coincidences brought about another wedding highlight. The winter before, I had received a voicemail message from a woman who identified herself as Lisamarie to inform me that she had found my Oregon driver's license in Rittenhouse Square. She had tracked me down at my Philadelphia address and wanted to know the best way to return the card, adding that she lived very close by. I hated carrying a handbag while maneuvering in snow and ice and often stuffed money, keys, and credit cards in my coat pockets. Sure enough, my driver's license was missing. I returned the call and left a message to thank her and ask her to drop it off in my mail slot. Later, I found an envelope on the vestibule floor with my license, along with a lovely note about how she and her boyfriend love Oregon so much that they visit every year.

Two weeks after accidentally dialing Jerry, I answered the phone, and a woman asked for me.

"Speaking."

"Hi, this is Lisamarie? I'm the one who found your driver's license some months ago?" She spoke in questions. "I know this will sound really strange, but I just found your ATM card?" I don't lose cards. She had my full attention.

"No way!" I replied, amazed as I furiously tried to wrap my head around the odds of the same person finding two of my lost items. "Where?"

"At the ATM at 18th and Spruce?" she went on haltingly. "When the screen said, 'Do you want another transaction?' I hit no, and the card that came out had your name on it. I was in shock!"

"Not as shocked as I am! Lisamarie, we have to meet," I blurted out. "Can you come over to my salon?" She said she would come the next afternoon.

I answered the doorbell to find a lovely, young woman with sky blue eyes and pixy cut blonde hair. "Come in! This is so unbelievable," I exclaimed. I brought out tea and cookies while she gushed about eastern Oregon, the drier part of the state. I gave her a beautifully packaged soap handmade in Oregon. Clutching it to her chest, she thanked me. She said that she was a violinist who had studied at the venerable Curtis School of Music. We talked about coincidences and fate as if we had known each other for years. I told her about the upcoming wedding, that I wanted Rodrigo's *Concierto de Aranjuez* to be the music for the walk down the aisle, and asked her if she had ever played it. Of course she had. Then, Lisamarie's eyes lit up. "I would love to play it at your wedding, if you'd like."

If I'd like? Although the piece was composed for the classical guitar, I had never thought of going with anything other than an organ played by the regular church organist. "There is nothing I would like more!"

"And I'll see if my friend Allen, who plays the classical guitar at Le Bec Fin, will be available to accompany me."

"Really?" Le Bec Fin was the only restaurant in the city with a five-star rating, and Allen was an acclaimed musician and composer.

"My playing will be my wedding present, but you can give Allen, say, $150."

"Thank you, Lisamarie." What else do you say to someone who finds your driver's license, months later finds your ATM card, and then offers to play your favorite music at your wedding on the violin with a virtuoso classical guitarist?

"Fantastic, fantastic!" is how Frank reacted to Lisamarie's offer. A man of a few words, whenever he said "fantastic" twice, it meant that he was really thrilled. "These things only happen to you." He echoed what my friends always said when I related to them my "miracle" stories. I never bought their theory, but I also could not discount the fact that having two absurdly incredible chains of events, which had brought about a beautiful wedding venue and a violinist within a critically narrow window of time, was pretty remarkable.

With the wedding day less than two months away, snap decisions had to be made. I consciously decided to "let go, let God." Having consulted with a good number of brides and their mothers, I had heard too many horror stories resulting from wedding micromanagement. Expectations were not always met, leaving all parties unhappy. I decided to give everyone creative license. There would be no food tastings. I trusted Barbara and her team and simply told her what I wanted: Greek-style roast leg of lamb studded with slivered garlic, lemony roasted potatoes, Mediterranean baked fish with tomatoes and olives, and salad. We would purchase the wine ourselves. We reconsidered the decision to only have instant cameras. Harvey, a long-time acquaintance of Frank's and a documentary photographer, was available to shoot the wedding. I gave three of my friends a color scheme of varied shades of creamy pastels and let them have a go with the flowers. Helen, a botanist, would create the arrangements for the church, Gloria, the wedding party bouquets, and Michael, the table centerpieces.

I sketched the dresses in one sitting. A quick trip to New York yielded a

periwinkle blue dupioni silk for my niece's dress, my only attendant, a heavy
three-ply rose silk for my mother's, and a stunning, white silk brocade for
mine. I would be wearing a long, fitted, two-piece dress with three-quar-
ter-length sleeves and marabou feathers around the neck. Far from the
papier-mâché wedding doll headdress of my dream, I wasn't going to put
anything on my head.

Frank's research into bands was coming up with dead ends. I called
Kenny, an old acquaintance and a superbly versatile musician, who performed at prestigious venues but was completely out of our budgetary
range. I told him that I was getting married and asked if he knew of any
budding bands that wanted to break into the wedding scene. He told me
about his side band that played at private events, the Ken Ulansey Ensem-
ble, and asked for the date. Surprisingly, the band was available; although
Kenny would be performing at a concert that night, he would join us at the
reception afterward. I was up front with him about our budget for a trio,
and he assured me that he could work something out. When Frank and I
met with Kenny, he offered us a seven-piece band, including a vocalist, for
the entire evening for just $200 over our budget. They would even play
Greek music for the traditional circle dancing. We were agog. Kenny asked
what song we wanted for our first dance as husband and wife. Acknowledging the sappiness, I told him, "This Magic Moment," the oldie.

While at the chiropractor's office, I was chatting with the receptionist
only to discover that she had been a singer with the Count Basie Orchestra
and was now part of a gospel choir. I love gospel. We agreed that she would
come to the wedding with her cousin. As soon as the ceremony was over,
both of them would break into a jazzy rendition of Handel's "Hallelujah"
chorus from the choir balcony, expressing my mother's joy and relief.

For the reception dinner, Barbara was having a large, oval banquet
table created out of three, round tables in the center of the ballroom so
that we could sit together with our families and have our friends at round

tables surrounding us. Jerry called to say that we didn't have to clean the chandeliers—the opera company had used the ballroom and had cleaned them. I picked up Frank's wedding band at Voula's father's quaint jewelry shop. It cost exactly one hundred dollars, which I paid with a one-hundred-dollar bill my father had inexplicably handed me the last time I saw him before he died.

Wedding presents began arriving, but the best gift of all was family and friends coming together and their participation in our marriage celebration. Local friends offered to host those coming in from out of state. Claire, Frank's sister and a cake and candy maker, was creating three cakes with whipped cream frosting in a Chantilly lace pattern. My friend Ann surreptitiously bought me the Stuart Weitzman silk pumps I had put on hold. Our friend Jack announced that he would host a brunch for us and the thirty-five out-of-town guests the morning after the wedding at his rowing club on Boathouse Row, featuring planked salmon on the grill.

The weather forecast for the fourth of October was sunny and seventy-five degrees. My family was staying in the third floor apartment, and Frank was spending the night with his friends from college—his best man Steve and his wife Tina. I woke up alone, and the first thing I did was read from *A Course in Miracles*, the book I credited with helping me overcome my fear of commitment and bringing me to this day. Tears rolled down my cheeks as I read about what was, as always, uncannily apropos—how joy and love are propagated by the holy relationship and a litany of blessings. I felt embraced by the Universe.

I wanted to savor the state of grace I felt, so I took an early morning walk around Rittenhouse Square and passed the Barclay. It was as if I were having an out-of-body experience. Everything familiar seemed different, more energized. Everyone was up when I got back. After breakfast, my mother, sister-in-law, niece, and I went off for manicures, hair styling, and just being together.

The ceremony was at four in the afternoon, and it was time for everyone to get dressed in wedding finery. My heart burst at seeing my mother looking ecstatic in the elegantly draped rose silk sheath. My niece, with her long, blonde hair, was beautiful in the long periwinkle blue dress and bolero. As I donned my gown with the marabou feathers around my neck and long, white leather gloves, I wondered what I would be thinking had I not been guided away from my vision of hiding inside a lace cage with a doll on top of my head.

The limousine arrived earlier than the 3:30 scheduled time, and we decided to take advantage of it. Since the church was only ten minutes away, we directed the chauffer to drive around the Art Museum, along the Schuylkill River on Kelly Drive, across the Falls Bridge, and back downtown on West River Drive. My brother had brought along a bottle of cognac and passed around shots while telling jokes. Nerves were too taut for the alcohol to have an effect other than a calming one. The driver pulled up to the church, and we looked on as guests arrived.

At precisely 4 p.m., we emerged and entered the church, where Barbara was waiting with the boutonnieres and Gloria's lush bouquets. Helen's glorious floral creations cascaded on each side of a table on which were framed photographs of Frank's father and mine. Frank in his tux, handsome as ever, stood in front of the iconostasis next to his best man, Steve, beaming with joy. His mother, Mother Mary as I called her, insisted on ditching her wheelchair and haltingly walked down the aisle on the arm of her grandson holding a lit candle, which she placed in the holder next to the photograph of her husband. Before my mother took my nephew's arm, she turned to me with shining eyes and embraced me, holding me tight. Barbara handed her a lit candle, and my nephew proudly escorted her down the aisle to the table where she placed it next to the photograph of my father. My niece, radiant, followed them and took her place opposite the best man.

On cue, the Adagio of the *Concierto de Aranjuez* began emanating from the stringed instruments, and my brother and I began the trek that would end my life as a single woman. Glancing at the smiling and teary faces of friends and family, without a trace of apprehension, I felt as if I had achieved the impossible. As I walked to the finish line toward the man with whom I would exchange vows of unconditional love and commitment, I was filled with an inexpressible love. Frank and I took the candles our mothers had placed in the candleholders and jointly lit the tall candle between them, two flames making one. Seeing the photograph of my father, I knew there had been no coincidences on this journey. My father had been pulling strings and, bigger than life, he was indeed present.

One cannot go through the Orthodox Sacrament of Holy Matrimony and not feel extremely married. The ritual is long and filled with symbolism. The chanting, incense, lit candles, and wine shared by the bride and groom from one cup arouse all senses. There are no "I do's." Why would anyone, logic holds, subject themselves to this if they weren't ready to "do" it? It is believed that the actual moment of our union was when Voula, our *koumbara*, or spiritual sponsor, placed the crowns, or *stefana*, joined by a ribbon, on our heads after exchanging them three times. The priest then led us around the table three times in a ceremonial walk, which symbolizes starting the new journey together. He then placed the gold bands on our fingers, also exchanged three times. Fr. George and Fr. Jim heaped blessings upon us, declaring us married. Not waiting for instructions from the priest, Frank grabbed me and kissed me while a cappella hallelujahs boomed from the balcony. As we turned to face our witnesses, a thunderous applause broke out. My glowing mother was the first to embrace and kiss us before our exit march.

Outside, there was a continuous fest of hugging and well-wishing as we greeted friends and family pouring out of the church. The guests left for the reception while we stayed behind to sign the necessary documents. Frank and I then got into the waiting limousine, alone for the first time that day. We could only look at each other giddily. We did it!

We arrived at the Barclay and waited until Barbara told us that all the guests were seated, so we could enter. When the doors to the ballroom were opened, I looked onto a twinkling fantasy. The crystal chandeliers shimmered, two-foot tall tapers on the tables illuminated faces, and votive candles flickered around Michael's centerpieces, orbs of creamy roses and greenery. Everyone spontaneously stood and applauded. As Frank and I walked down several steps, through the cheering crowd, and onto the dance floor, the band burst into, "This Magic Moment," for our first married dance. The schmaltziness of the song set the mood for a fun evening. We invited everyone to join us on the dance floor and were quickly surrounded by their warmth. The partying had just begun.

The faces of our family members sparkled around the oval "feast" table. Frank and I led them to the aromas wafting from the buffet. Table after table, the rest of the guests followed. The food was visually enticing and could not have been better prepared. Toasts were made evoking happy tears. Guests packed the dance floor as rock music interspersed with disco, pop, jazzy tunes, and by our request, predominantly Motown and other oldies.

In her amazing soprano voice, Voula walked onstage and sang *Oraia Pou Einai I Nifi Mas*, "How Beautiful is Our Bride" in Greek, and the band didn't miss a beat. This prompted the shift to traditional Greek dancing. Voula and I took turns leading circle dances as Frank and more guests found the courage to join in. My mother hadn't danced since my father had died but had promised to dance at my wedding. As I was heading the line of dancers, she approached and took over the lead, skipping to and fro and twirling excitedly.

Frank's friend Marek decided the affair needed to be infused with some Jewishness. Suddenly, Frank and I were sitting in chairs, hoisted up in the air as the band cranked out "Hava Nagila." Marek lost his balance, and I toppled onto the floor as he fell on top of me, leaving both of us in hysterics. The band went on break, and my old friends who were part of the The Juggernaut String Band, Peter on his banjo and Janet her fiddle, got onstage, plucking and twanging bluegrass tunes. Other friends who had brought instruments joined in. The dance floor had turned into a foot-stomping hootenanny.

Just after Frank and I had ceremoniously cut Claire's cake, Kenny appeared with his saxophone and played with his band until well after midnight, ending one of the most fun parties I have ever been to. Savoring every minute of it, arm in arm, Frank and I went upstairs to spend our wedding night in the presidential suite.

The next day was equally warm, sunny, and perfect for family and out-of-town friends to gather for brunch at Jack's rowing club. Ever the quintessential host, Jack effortlessly grilled salmon fillets on wood planks he had fished out of the river, which he served with Bloody Mary's, mimosas, and beer.

The main topic of conversation was the wedding, from the ceremony to the reception—how meaningful the ritual was, how every aspect of the celebration had come together perfectly, and how everyone left it feeling warm and fuzzy. I listened, steeped in gratitude for the collective efforts of our friends who helped make our affair memorable. Leaving each one to their own creativity yielded spectacular flowers, food, and music. Although Frank and I had put effort into it, it felt as if the perfect wedding had come together on its own in a remarkably short amount of time, for relatively little money, no less.

Many of those present had not heard about the coincidences that had manifested Jerry and the ballroom, or how Lisamarie and Allen ended up playing the music at the church. As the stories were retold, the general re-action to them was incredulity. I took a moment to absorb the congruencies that had occurred myself. Though improbable, it was plausible that one could misdial a number and reach another person whom they happened to know. Equally far-fetched, it was not impossible that someone could find two cards, months apart at different locations, belonging to the same total stranger. What most amazed everyone was how both of these coincidences yielded such fortuitous gifts. I marveled at the outcomes myself.

The celestial frying pan came crashing on my head as a light bulb turned on, shedding light on my role in the manifestations. The coincidences had gotten my attention, but the secret ingredient was action. I took action. When I got Jerry on the phone instead of Ann, I could have expressed my astonishment, chalked it up to coincidence, and told him that it wasn't necessary for him to call me back. After Lisamarie called the second time to tell me that she had found my ATM card, I could have mirrored her shock about the odd chances, thanked her profusely, and asked her to drop it in my mail slot, as before.

It was my inner voice, an unconscious cognition, that recognized what the coincidences were communicating. I had listened. Without a clue of what was in store, I took direction and became proactive. I begged Jerry to call me back. I invited Lisamarie to bring me the card in person so that we could meet and I could show her my appreciation. My impulsive reaction to each of these cosmic messages, communicated via synchronicities, had allowed events to unfold and ultimately manifest the miracles. I returned to being present with my family and friends, feeling saturated with wonderment.

That evening, together with my family and Frank's two daughters, we ordered pizzas and beer up to our suite and opened presents. We said our goodbyes to our family and spent our second night at the Barclay. In the whirlwind of it all, we had hardly thought about the honeymoon. We only had one day to pack and get ready for the 5:30 a.m. direct flight to Mexico City.

After a quick breakfast, Frank and I walked the few blocks home. We climbed the three flights of stairs to our apartment for the first time as husband and wife. Frank dropped the bags, picked me up, and carried me over the threshold.

CHAPTER 13

Typhoon Honeymoon

Every October Michelle would traipse off to Rancho Cerro Largo, a rustic resort between Huatulco and Puerto Escondido in the south of Mexico. She stayed in one of the adobe huts clustered atop an isolated cliff with a breathtaking view of the turquoise ocean. Upon her return each May, she would relate the adventures her alternative lifestyle provided. The mini-compound's creator was also a Cordon Bleu-trained chef, and she would describe his mouthwatering culinary concoctions. It sounded so dreamy and romantic. What better place for a perfect honeymoon! Frank was immediately on board.

The dizzying pace of preparing for the wedding in such a short period of time made me rely on Michelle for help planning the trip, and she answered the call. She made the initial contact, introduced us to Mario, and presented us with a hand-drawn and colored map of the coast marked with secret paths and coves she had discovered. The plan was to fly into Mexico City, where we would catch a local plane to Huatulco, then take a taxi to the secluded compound where we would spend most of our twelve-day honeymoon unwinding. The map also included Puerto Escondido, where her friend Barbara owned and operated the Hotel Santa Fe, a lush resort that served meals made with organic herbs and vegetables grown on the premises.

I felt excited waking up and leaving for the airport in the middle of the night. Our bags were packed with summer clothes, bathing suits, two bottles of red wine, and one of brut bubbly left over from the wedding. Next to Frank in the backseat of the cab, I sensed the warm comfort of being watched over. We arrived at the airport with time to spare before our non-stop flight to Mexico City. When we reached the counter to check our bags with tickets and driver's licenses in hand, we were asked for our passports. I told the agent that my passport had expired and that I had learned from more than one source that I didn't need a passport to enter Mexico, only a state-issued ID.

"That's correct, ma'am, you don't need a passport to enter Mexico, but you'll need one if you want to come back to the States," said the agent, trying to deliver the bad news as neutrally as possible. Frank and I could only look at each other with shock and dismay. Why hadn't any of the travel articles mentioned that part?

"It's our honeymoon," I said, as if that were going to make a difference.

There was empathy in the agent's face. "You can come back into the country if you have a birth certificate along with a driver's license," he offered as a solution. "Do you have time to go home and get them?"

With a half-hour before boarding, Frank finally spoke, "No, we don't."

"I'm sorry," he said, and as we turned to walk away, he added, "You can get on any plane to Mexico City that has available seats."

I had no idea where my birth certificate was. "Why are you doing this to me, God?" I asked as we got into a cab. The disappointment was in direct contrast to the wedding euphoria we were still feeling. Dejected, we lugged our bags up to the fourth floor. I flung myself on the sofa despondently. Frank offered positivity without success. Suddenly, he had a thought—why not get on the next available plane? We could have dinner and spend the night in Mexico City.

I perked up. "That's a fabulous idea, but what about a place to stay?"

"I'll take care of the airlines and hotel. "You start looking for your birth certificate," he ordered. Thankfully, it was in the documents folder where it belonged.

"We'll be on the 9 a.m. flight," Frank said as he got off the phone and unpacked *The Lonely Planet* guide to Mexico. Things were coming around; Frank turned lemons into lemonade. We decided on the Hotel Bamar on the Plaza Alameda, one of the few buildings in the area that had survived the devastating earthquake of 1985. We called for a taxi and, back at the airport, checked our bags and boarded the plane without incident, our good moods restored.

Stories of a dangerous Mexico City abounded. However, we found it to be a beautiful, cosmopolitan metropolis sliced with wide boulevards bordering large plazas peppered with palm trees. The hotel lobby with its dark paneling, marble floors, chandeliers, Roman-looking sculptures on pedestals, and a huge globe of the world in the center, looked like a scaled-down version of a Las Vegas casino. Our room faced the plaza, where a raucous political rally was being held. We strolled to a restaurant highly recommended by the concierge that was located in the colorful Zona Rosa, a hub of Mexican nightlife. Frank's brilliant idea of coming here for the evening instead of moping in Philly had saved the day.

On the way to the airport the next day, our driver informed us that a strong storm had hit the southern coast. That could be exciting. We were dropped off at the domestic flights terminal and quickly reached our gate only to find that our flight to Huatulco had been canceled. Another missed flight? I felt my heart in my throat. *God, where are you?* I thought. Frank asked the agent why.

"There is a hurricane," he replied.

"A hurricane? I don't care!" I was now screaming, "It's our honeymoon, and we have to go to a place between Huatulco and Puerto Escondido!"

"*Sí, Señora.* Go there," he said, pointing diagonally across the hallway, "There is a plane leaving for Puerto Escondido in twenty minutes."

Frank and I turned and ran, pulling our suitcases. There were only two seats available. How lucky! We hugged. The ping pong of emotions in the last twenty-four hours had left me limp in the seat of a very small plane. The pilot announced that all other flights to southern Mexico were indefinitely canceled. Overnight, a tropical storm had morphed into Hurricane Pauline, and we were flying right smack into it. I didn't know whether to laugh or cry.

Visibility decreased as we neared our destination. Patches of green flashed through dark gray, and the torrential rain belted the windows as if continuous buckets of water were hitting them. Turbulence got worse as we prepared to land in what felt like a toy plane. I tried to find comfort by the pilot's apparent confidence while he calmly gave us status reports. Frank and I held hands. We touched down in a ferocious wind that shook the plane as we taxied on the tarmac. It was not raining on the ground, but when we emerged onto the stairway that had been wheeled up to the door, we were met with slapping gusts. Fighting the wind as we walked toward the tiny terminal, my eyes were glued to the palm trees whose tops all pointed horizontally in one direction. We jumped into a waiting taxi and felt some assurance as the driver nodded after I showed him the address of Michelle's friend's resort. He told us that the airport was being shut down and that after letting us off he was going home.

We arrived at a beautifully landscaped setting where a rambling Spanish Colonial villa and courtyards were interconnected by stepped walkways trimmed in colorful tiles. Barbara came to greet us at the office. In her late forties, she looked New-Agey with long, blonde hair, flowing pants, and hand-crafted jewelry. Since many rooms were available due to cancelations, she led us to a corner one with great views of the ocean. She opened the door into a spacious, white room with large windows shuttered for the storm, tiled floor, and painted wood furniture. I asked her what to expect from the hurricane. "Nothing happens here," she said with a dismissive wave. "The cove is protected, but here are candles and matches just in case."

All of a sudden, I felt very hungry. In the blasting air, we followed Barbara past two swimming pools to a huge, open pavilion with tables and chairs and an enormous, round thatched roof. I was heartened to see people having lunch. The plates of food looked fresh and colorful. Mexican guitar music from speakers competed with the pounding gusts. "Everything we serve here is organic," Barbara assured us.

There was something thrilling about a hurricane. The weather was hot and humid. *But we're here*, I thought. There was one other couple still seated when our food arrived. My salad was a feast for the eyes—perfectly ripened avocado and tomato chunks, grilled shrimp, and grated cheese topped the mound of the freshest lettuce. The albondigas soup was the best I had ever tasted. Three giant tacos were placed in front of Frank. As we ate with gusto, I noticed the help scurrying. The couple hurriedly got up and left. I saw something in my soup that didn't belong. It looked like dried hay. My trusty inner siren started blaring. "Frank, look, there's roof thatch in my soup," I said as I stared down.

"It's time to go," Frank said matter-of-factly.

Frank signaled the waitress, who was now running back and forth from the kitchen. I got the picture. The staff was getting ready to close up and go home, which left dinner up in the air. The waitress came over, and I asked her for a menu to order something else.

"I'm sorry, the kitchen is closing," she stammered apologetically. "The cook is making us something to eat, and then we're going home. It's going to get worse."

"We'll take two of whatever you're having and two liters of water, please."

The wind gusts had intensified, and it had started to rain. The waitress returned with two potato omelets wrapped in aluminum foil and the water, double bagged. We tipped her well. From the bussing station I took plates, napkins, silverware, wine glasses, salt and pepper, and hot sauce and placed them in one of the plastic bags with the omelets. I put the other one on my head. Frank and I bolted down the walkway, clutching the bag with both arms. Rain was whipping our backs, and the plastic bag over my head was utterly useless.

By the time we got to our villa, we were waterlogged. Frank turned on the light switch. No power. The floor had been flooded. One of the shutters had come unlatched, and we had an indoor waterfall. I secured the shutters and lit candles. Frank grabbed a broom and bucket from the utility pantry outside. The absurdity suddenly hit me. This was not a movie. It was our honeymoon, and we were in the middle of a typhoon. Giggling, I grabbed the camera, jumped on the bed, and started taking pictures of Frank sweeping water out. While I found it funny, it apparently turned Frank on. He dove on the bed and tackled me.

After discovering that we had no running water, the amusement waned. I recalled that the huts at Rancho Cerro Largo, where we were supposed to be, had no running water, either. But we had each other, and we were going to make the best of it. I did not want to think about how people were faring who were not in a sheltered cove. That night we had one of the most romantic dinners ever. With rain and wind raging outside, we lit all the candles. Frank uncorked the champagne and poured it into the stemmed glasses. We made toasts to our life together and promised each other that we would never lose our sense of humor. We vowed to make the best of everything—that no matter what, we would make it through thick and thin as a team. The omelets were delicious, and the tortillas feather-light. Sated, exhausted, we blew out the candles and fell asleep.

The first thing I became aware of upon waking was the absence of sound. I got up and flung the shutters open. Bright light poured in. All was calm. The storm had moved on, leaving significant debris on the beach. Frank and I used the rest of the bottled water to freshen up before going on a reconnaissance mission. On the way to the café, we saw the swimming pool full of mud and branches. Big chunks of the pavilion's roof were missing.

TV, phone, and radio lines were down, and guests huddled around transistor radios. Barbara had been up early putting crews to work and making sure that there was a breakfast made out of what was available— fruit, eggs, and tortillas with sugar and cinnamon. We got coffee and joined the group. We learned that roads were closed and communities were cut off from each another. The hurricane had moved northward toward Acapulco, leaving unknown numbers of people in the area dead or missing.

Road access to the idyllic isolated getaway that we had reserved would be closed for at least two days. Frank and I walked to the center of town in silence. Streets, sidewalks, and storefronts were covered with mud. The main street was completely washed away, leaving large craters. People furiously cleaned while others walked around dazed. The road to the airport was open, so we were not held hostage here. Why not ride out the whole mess while exploring Mexico inland? On the spur of the moment, we bought two roundtrip plane tickets to Oaxaca, the capital of the state with the same name, and flew out the same day.

As our plane made its ascent, the scope of Hurricane Pauline's destruction became even more evident. The lush green we had seen through the gray clouds flying in was now a camouflage pattern of desolate browns. Once we crossed over the mountains, Oaxaca emerged from under the clouds, oblivious to the havoc that had wracked the coast just 160 miles away. We arrived with information about the city from what we had gleaned from the guidebook, and without expectations. We were richly rewarded.

Spending the next four days in a city steeped in history and rich in culture, we became immersed in Mexican culture. Although we passed on the chapulines (fried grasshoppers), we could not get enough of the renowned Oaxacan cuisine. Dish after aromatic dish of fresh vegetables, meats, and fish prepared with a variety of spices, peppers, and mole topped off with shots of smoky mescal left us swooning. We spent one day at the site of the ancient pre-Columbian Zapotec city of Monte Alban with its multiple terraces and mud-baked ruins. On the way back, we stopped at an unassuming, sparklingly clean diner to have *pescado a la Veracruzana*, a deliciously baked fish with tomatoes and flavors I still savor.

The eyes also feasted. We visited museums and the flower market, where a kaleidoscope of colors spread before us like an Oaxacan embroidered shawl. The Zocalo, the city's central plaza, was surrounded by ornate colonial buildings and cafés from which spontaneous musical performances erupted.

Strolling through the plaza, we were stopped in our tracks by the lyrical voice of a sultry young woman, a Frida Kahlo look-alike, accompanied by a guitarist. Captivated, we listened to her sing Mexican folk songs, operatic arias, and American blues. She stopped to introduce herself in an American accent as Lila Downs and the guitarist as her husband. She told us her mother was a Mexican Mictec Indian singer, her father an American university professor, and that she had grown up in Oaxaca and Minnesota. That explained her vast repertoire.

The Zocalo was lined with stands of artists and craftspeople selling their work. We went from one to the other admiring the quality of workmanship and then encountered a jeweler whose artistry particularly stood out. Frank bought me a pair of exquisitely wrought silver earrings with blue glass and red coral for my birthday, which Frida Kahlo would have surely fought me for.

Oaxaca had left us rested and recharged. It was the first time in the last few months of riding a roller coaster, from fast-tracking a wedding to flying into a typhoon, that we didn't have to plan, think, or solve anything.

Back in Puerto Escondido, we saw progress. The walkways had been hosed, and the swimming pools shimmered. Guests sat in the pavilion under the thatched roof with gaping holes, unfazed. Much of the debris on the beach had been removed, and surfers had resumed riding turquoise waves onto the stretch of white sand. Best of all, the toilets flushed.

We ran into Barbara at the café and got the good news and the bad news. The good news was that the coastal road had been cleared and the local bus was running; we could leave in the morning to visit the enclave where we had originally planned to stay. As details of the hurricane trickled in, we got the bad news. According to reports, 173 people had died and about 200 more were thought to be missing, mostly in shanty areas near Acapulco. The number of fatalities would later increase dramatically. On our first walk on a Mexican beach, I felt a deep solidarity with Frank. I sent out a thank you to the Universe for our protective cove. But it was when the sun began to set and the blues, golds, mauves, and oranges of the sky dazzled, reflecting on the water like glitter, that I experienced an uncontainable wave of gratitude. All at once, I felt that we, the sounds of the ocean, and the light and energy from the sun were all one. There was no separation between us and the grandeur unfolding before us, or from each other. There, I met God, a benevolent creator who was as much a part of me as I was of Him. Frank saw my tears and, without words, embraced me for a very long time. The next day was my birthday. It doesn't get much better than that.

There were several people waiting at the bus stop the next morning, all locals. The midmorning sun was hot, and everyone looked glum, staring into nowhere. I wondered how the hurricane had affected them and how they were coping.

Until then, whenever I heard about a tropical hurricane on the news, I never gave it further thought than what it was called and how many deaths it had caused. The people I was standing next to put faces on the statistics. The bus was late, and the heat was intensifying. It finally appeared bedecked like a Christmas tree, with colorfully painted borders and village scenes. I showed the driver our destination on the map, and riders switched seats so that Frank and I could sit together.

At the top of the bus's windshield, under a purple satin valance with gold fringe were decals of Mickey Mouse, horse heads, and the face of Jesus with a crown of thorns on His head. On the middle of the dashboard was a figurine of the Virgin Mary with a vase of plastic roses on either side. The further away from town we went, the less the roads had been cleared. Most of the trees still standing had lost their foliage—a winter scene in the hot sun. The driver dropped us off at an intersection where idle taxis hovered. One took us to a desolate spot at the edge of San Agustinillo and pointed toward the cliff. We got out and stood in what seemed like the middle of nowhere. There was no *bienvenido* sign as the dot showed on the map. The only indication of humans was an old, muddy pick-up truck parked at the side of the road. The stark desolation looked nothing like Michelle's photographs. Instead of tropical flowers in every conceivable color and lush foliage, all we saw were wet mud and bare branches. We put the useless map away and followed a recently-made path.

Trudging through the mud and loose twigs, we came upon two beehive-shaped mud brick structures and several people sitting around a large cooler speaking English and drinking beer. They stopped talking and looked at us quizzically. I introduced us and explained how the hurricane had kept us from spending our honeymoon there. A man jumped out of a hammock and introduced himself. It was Mario, the owner, manager, and chef. He invited us to join them while someone brought out two, white, plastic chairs and offered us beers. Mario introduced us to a couple from the States, a German man, and a Canadian couple who were the caretakers.

"*Hola*," I said, feeling an undercurrent of discomfort. "Where are the other huts?"

"Down there," Mario responded, pointing to the bottom of the cliff as he got back into the hammock.

"What do you mean by that?" I asked. Qualifying assumptions is always wise.

"There was a mudslide. This is the only one that survived, and we have all been sleeping in it." He gestured at the other one. "That one, the roof caved in. The rest, *adios, amigos*."

Frank and I picked up our beers at the same time and started guzzling. The reality of what we had been spared was beginning to sink in.

"Where were you when it happened? Was anyone injured? What did you do?" I asked, as I conjured up what could have been.

Mario put it in a nutshell. Although the huts were regularly exposed to hurricanes, except for the two standing, they could not withstand the ferocity of this one. He expressed his good fortune that one had escaped major damage, provided shelter, and that everyone had survived in that hut for five nights living off their stored food and water. Obviously smarter than we were, the rest of the guests had canceled their reservations rather than insisting on flying into a tropical hurricane. This was the first day that their supplies had been replenished.

I expressed my incredulity but felt that our palpable relief of being spared was not shared. "Before we go," I said, drawing our visit to a close, "can we see the rest of the place?" Mario voiced concern about the conditions and asked the Canadian man to accompany us. We slowly made our way to the edge of the cliff to find a coastline vista more breathtaking than any of Michelle's photos or descriptions. We took pictures to show Michelle, thanked Mario, waved goodbye to all, and left.

Actually seeing the two remaining huts and knowing that the other seven were gone had suddenly made the reality of the destruction hit home. Speechless, I was processing what we had witnessed. Had we not missed our plane, we might have been killed in the mudslide. Or, what if we had been badly injured with no one to rescue us? Not only would we have been trapped here with the others, we would have shared the one surviving hut with them, sleeping on top of one another. Frank spoke for both of us, "Wow, we came that close." Nothing more was said as we walked down to wait for the next bus. I thanked God over and over for the narrow miss and for the protected cove.

We arrived at the palapa for dinner that evening to find a beautiful centerpiece of tropical flowers, compliments of Barbara. After the last of the Baja wine was poured, we ordered flan for dessert. Frank made a birthday toast to being alive. Both of us were now ready to talk about how lucky we were. What we had initially perceived as obstacles had in reality saved us from peril. Amid the now tranquil setting, my mind and heart were allowed to expand and feel the oneness. What was not supposed to happen on a honeymoon had made us feel blessed. The waitress approached with two flans, one with a lit candle. A trio of musicians appeared out of nowhere and began playing and singing "Happy Birthday." I blew out the candle, but what more could I wish for?

We were flying out of Puerto Escondido early the next morning to return home. Our plane from Mexico City was not to depart until that afternoon, and we had hired a driver to pick us up and take us on a four-hour sightseeing tour before delivering us to the airport. The two places I most wanted to see were dedicated to women, one secular, whom I idolized, the other one, holy, to whom I prayed—the house in which Frida Kahlo, the long-suffering artist and wife of Diego Rivera, had been born and had died, and the Basilica of Our Lady of Guadalupe, honoring the Virgin Mary.

Frida Kahlo could not have been more secular or more self-obsessed. She had good reason to be. For thirty years she painted self-portraits with objects symbolizing her debilitating physical and emotional agony as a result of an early accident, and living with a philandering husband whom she loved. Throughout it all, she looked fantastic with her long, braided hair, brilliantly colored Mexican folkwear, and dramatic jewelry. It was her grit that I found most inspirational. I admired her for grabbing what she could out of life, tempestuous as it was, and making it original. Nobody else was going to tell her how to live it. I wished I had known her. Being in "The Blue House," now a museum that contained her belongings and her energy, I felt as if I had.

When we emerged from the taxi to visit the Basilica of Our Lady of Guadalupe, we were confronted by thousands of pilgrims making their way to the modern rotunda—some in wheelchairs, others walking on their knees brimming with tears and hope. My motivation was curiosity. Despite my unassailable connection with the Virgin Mary and faith in the power of miracles, I was skeptical of the story of how the image of "Our Lady" had physically manifested onto fabric, now displayed in the Basilica. In the 1530s, after the Spanish conquest of the Aztecs, Juan Diego, a poor, indigenous man, was said to have seen apparitions of the Virgin Mary. The bishop would not believe him. The Virgin instructed Juan Diego to pick roses in the snow and take them to the bishop. When Juan Diego unfurled his cloak exposing the roses, the bishop, knowing that roses don't grow in the winter, saw the image of the Virgin Mary on the inside of the cloak and believed. To commemorate the event, a church was built on the hill nearby more than 150 years later. Many scientists, scholars, and clergy have examined the image on the fabric. Its physical properties have continued to astound all sides. Whether it had divinely materialized or had been painted by a native Aztec artist as doubters charged, the Virgin Mary's appearances coincided with the conversions to Christianity of more than eight million Aztecs.

Inside the Basilica, the life-sized portrait of the Virgin of Guadalupe hung high above the crowd. She watches over everything with the gaze of a loving mother. I immediately became skeptical. How could this clean, bright image on intact fabric be more than four hundred years old? Perhaps it was a representation of the "real one" kept somewhere else. I sidled up to an English-speaking guide who had been leading a group of tourists and posed the question to him. He assured me that this was indeed the original and added that its age was never disputed, only its maker. If that was the case, whether by human hands or miraculously imprinted, its incorruptibility could only be explained by divine intervention. I went back to scrutinize it one last time. Absorbed, trying to accept its authenticity, I heard words resonate in my ear from a soft, steady voice, "Sophia, open your heart. It is a privilege to walk on Earth. You will find your purpose."

I reeled at the interruption. I believe the Virgin Mary communicated to me that what I knew deep, deep inside me was true. How the image was imprinted on the fabric was not important. What mattered was the awe it invoked. Overwhelmed with the power of faith around me, I sensed one humanity in its suffering, hoping, and loving. As I looked upon the reverent, upturned faces under her gaze, it hit me—this was the exact church in which the Virgin Mary appeared to Fr. Domenic in a vivid dream, silently directing him to turn his attention away from himself and focus it on the needy. My purpose was abundantly clear—to be truly helpful to others. I vowed to never doubt again.

Once again, something had shifted in me. I left Mexico feeling different. As we walked back to the waiting car, I thought about how many times during this trip I had thanked God for the gifts freely presented to us, for all that is here to fill the senses, and for our very lives. Insisting on imposing my will and knowingly boarding a flight heading into a hurricane had put us in danger. We were also given a glimpse of the suffering and possible death that could have befallen us had we not been miraculously spared because of a missed flight. I promised myself that I would be more conscious of obstacles and pay attention whenever I felt as though I were swimming against the current, seeing them as possible messages that could actually save my life. Feeling profoundly grateful, I held on to Frank's arm. Yes, it *is* a privilege to walk on Earth.

CHAPTER 14

From Rags to Richness

Back at the ranch, there was no time to lose getting back in the saddle. The focus on wedding preparations and a honeymoon hiatus without communication with work had resulted in matters of consequence. Necessary renovations to our apartment—additional closets and a real kitchen—had been placed on the back burner. My sister-in-law's report about my mother's increasing forgetfulness had been met with denial by the rest of us. With the Asian financial crisis and a jittery economy, black-tie events were sparse. Alterations and repurposing were keeping the salon afloat—people were hanging on to what they had. A cash crunch could force us to liquidate the maternity rentals. Maxine and I needed to review the status of the plus-size line and the direction of the salon. She would oversee production while I found part-time design work. I would explore every avenue before getting a business loan. Everything rested on the line's success.

Frank and I resumed our sessions with David. The honeymoon had come and gone without major eruptions between us. Instances of subterranean rumblings, however, could not be denied. Now and then, without warning, Frank continued to perceive my suggestions as being told what to do and then would lash out and withdraw in a moody haze. He viewed any attempt to discuss the incident as me trying to control him. David suggested we take tango lessons with the idea that it would introduce a healthy balance between assertiveness and surrender. After his initial eye rolling, Frank agreed to weekly Argentinian tango classes. Once we got past tripping on each other's feet, the challenges of this sensual art form—learning the steps, how to communicate with our eyes, how to anticipate each other's moves, and how to allow our bodies to give and take direction—seduced both of us into embracing it on a more serious level.

I was thrilled to find that Maxine was almost finished with the patterns. Monica, my Wharton MBA coach, had graduated, and I missed her organizational savvy. Because we lacked business acumen, Maxine and I operated from the gut. It felt that it was time to order fabric. It felt that we needed to hire more help. It felt that we needed more money, more exposure, more advice. There was no doubt about one thing—I knew that I wanted Saks Fifth Avenue's Salon Z to carry the dresses. It was the only department store that carried designer clothes beyond size 16, but only up to 24. My line was offering luxurious, dressy clothes to women up to size 32. An advocacy organization called NAAFA, the National Association for Fat Awareness, was having their national convention in Philadelphia and would be featuring a fashion show. It would be the perfect vehicle to debut the clothes and get feedback from the population we were targeting. With less than four months to complete the line, it had become our goal and highest priority.

One by one, as each sample garment got its finishing touches and was hung on the rack, the fall collection came to life. Everyone who saw it swooned. There was exuberance in the air knowing that we were on the right track. As beautifully as it came together, my fashion investment was seriously draining finances. I put the word out that I was seeking work in the design field. Just as I was preparing to sell off the maternity gowns, I received a call from Michael, my friend who had initially introduced me to Amy and One Night Stand. He excitedly told me that a nationally acclaimed local interior designer who specialized in kitchens and baths was opening a showroom offering custom-made, high-end Italian walk-in closets and cabinetry. She was looking for someone to custom design them.

"Closets! Me, designing people's closets?" I asked contemptuously.

"You wouldn't be organizing their clothes, dummy," he chirped. "This is a top-of-the-line Italian system that offers sleek entertainment units, shelving, kitchens—the possibilities are endless . . ."

"First of all," I cut him off, "it sounds like a full-time job, and second, I was done with kitchens a long time ago. Now I'm going to design closets?"

"The showroom will be next to her three other ones, so maybe her employees can fill in. She," as Michael and I would refer to the grand dame designer from then on, "wouldn't touch anything unless it was the best of the best, and I'm sure you would get a commission on top of your salary," he said, weakening my wall of resistance.

A salary with commission did sound attractive in a time of financial need, but still, "I don't do closets, Michael," I said, surprising even myself at the trill in my voice. "I design things to put inside closets."

"It won't kill you to meet her," Michael offered in a last-ditch effort. "You would at the very least find her interesting."

"Okay, fine," I said, giving in. It was not easy to counter Michael's effusive enthusiasm.

"Grrrreat!" He let out a victorious shout and offered to introduce us personally. Spontaneously, he invited me to a feng shui lecture at 8 a.m. the next morning at his design firm.

Why not? Feng shui, the ancient Chinese practice to optimize chi— the energy of space—for health, well-being, and good fortune, had intrigued me ever since a few years earlier a friend had informed me that the placement of my bed was "bad chi." It was during one of my break-ups with Frank. I moved the bed, Frank and I got back together, and we were married in less than a year. Along with yoga and astrology, I would look into anything that has been implemented by entire cultures for thousands of years.

Cradling a cup of coffee that I was hoping would keep me alert, I was not prepared to receive vitally pertinent information first thing in the morning. When I heard the woman giving the feng shui presentation describe the worst-case scenario for the prosperity of a business—a street that is perpendicular to its door—I sprang to attention. The chi energy picks up speed as it snowballs down the street and, "like a spear, it will kill your business as an arrow piercing the heart." I pictured sleepy Manning Street coming at my door like a dagger. The "cure" she suggested, placing a fountain in front of the building, wasn't going to work. "And if that isn't feasible," she went on, "banners or kites in the wind can reshuffle and slow down the chi, and mirrors are excellent in deflecting it."

The first thing I did after I got to the salon was place a hand mirror in the bay window facing ominous Manning Street until I could come up with a more permanent solution. Frank came by after work to survey the situation. We went straight down to the basement where he found a small, round, frameless mirror that implausibly happened to fit perfectly in the little, round window above the building's Gothic entrance. While Frank was on the ladder installing it, I ran into Tom in the vestibule. A children's book illustrator who worked from home on the third floor, he was asking why Frank was on the ladder when Dave, a physicist who lived on the second floor, came in. I explained as best I could how the bad chi from Manning Street was piercing our door, how it was ruining our finances, and how the deflecting properties of mirrors were going to save us. I was met with blank looks.

The next evening, I met Frank outside the salon to walk over to our favorite Thai restaurant. After crossing the street, Frank turned me around to face the building. Besides the round mirror over the door and the hand mirror in my bay window, there was a hand mirror hung upside down in

Tom's third floor window. When I saw the second floor bay, I stepped back in astonishment. In it was a huge triptych mirrored bathroom cabinet. Where could Dave have found it overnight? Our resident quantum physicist was taking no chances dealing with bad chi.

I called the preeminent kitchen maven as Michael had insisted. She had been waiting for my call. Michael had obviously told her about me. She loved that I had worked in architecture. She loved that I was a dress designer. She loved that I spoke Italian. I tried to be up front about my situation and that I was only available to work three days a week, but she would have none of it. It was as if she had already decided that I was her girl. Any concerns I brought up were met with snappy retorts. "We can work around that," and, "We'll iron out those details." Her voice was captivating and exuded utmost confidence that things would go her way. We made a date for the three of us to meet in her tile showroom.

For our meeting, I chose an austere Anne Klein, steel gray, wool dress with a long, flared skirt that made me feel like a prison camp commandant. I needed the armor. Michael and I met in the lobby of the Design Center, which housed showrooms catering to interior designers and their clients. Exiting the elevator, one could not ignore the extent of the kitchen queen's empire. I followed Michael into the tile showroom across the hall. The variety of colors, textures, shapes, and sizes of tiles induced sensory overload.

Everyone we encountered greeted Michael enthusiastically. Amid the banter of introductions, an imperious woman paraded in dressed all in black. Her demeanor left no one to wonder who owned the place. Everything about her—head, eyes, cheeks, mouth—was large, and her round, tortoise-shell glasses were framed by a short, blonde bob with bangs cut straight across her brow. She had perfect posture and strode toward us purposefully, practically singing Michael's name, "Helloooo, Michael."

They air kissed. She then turned to me, cocked her head back, and trilled, "You must be Sophia; I'm so glad to finally meet you." Giving me a sweeping look from head to toe, she added, "I like your dress."

With the gestures of an orchestra conductor, she directed us into the adjoining kitchen showroom. She pointed out the hand-wrought French stove and such as if they were jewels in her treasury. She had a right to exult over her realm—the quality and taste level that she offered was unparalleled. We followed her back across the hall to another showroom, her latest triumph. Closet, cabinet, and wall units featuring sleek wood and glass doors exemplified the system's capabilities. The floor was shiny blonde maple. Furniture was also for sale. We sat at a state-of-the-art engineered square table, but not before she demonstrated its flawless conversion into a dining table for eight, made possible with ingeniously designed, invisible German hardware.

In the midst of discussions, Michael brought up feng shui and the mirrors my neighbors and I placed on the front of the building to deflect the bad chi and improve finances. Momentarily, she appeared to be tepidly amused before re-launching into the system's potential success, not so subtly signaling that our meeting was not about fun and games. She became rhapsodical about how she was the only retailer in the state given exclusive rights to sell the product. She informed me about my training schedule as if I were already in her employ.

I found an opportunity to interrupt. "It sounds like this is a full-time position."

"It is," she declared, peering at me over those glasses as if shocked that I would think otherwise. Michael shifted in his chair.

"I thought I was clear when I told you that my business would limit me to working no more than three days a week," I said, feeling as if I had had the phone conversation with someone else.

"No," she said as she rose regally, "I need someone here five days a week the first of the year!" She seemed genuinely surprised that the meeting was coming to a close without getting what she wanted.

"I'm sorry, but this isn't going to work for me," I said as Michael and I stood up, "but thank you for the offer. It was a real pleasure meeting you." I meant it.

Her eyebrow shot to the ceiling, and as she stared down at me with a wide frozen smile, she said, "Well, maybe that mirror will fall down and break, your business will fail, and then you can come work for me!"

I could not have walked out of there faster. "Can you believe she said that, Michael? That woman just put a hex on me! Is she for real?"

"It's just who she is," he said matter-of-factly as we were getting into the elevator.

"Well then, I don't want to work for someone who is who she is."

As our apartment was being renovated and we camped in the living room, the search for part-time work was shelved. In the midst of dealing with contractors, we visited my mother for a long Christmas weekend. At eighty-eight, she was still the best go-to source for advice, but now reports of burned food on the stove, incontinence, and memory loss were ramping up. We found her to have more difficulty walking and standing for more than a short period of time. She repeated herself over and over. When I brought it to her attention, she would laugh it off saying, "I would buy extra brains if someone would sell them to me."

This was the first Christmas my mother showed no desire to trim a tree, something she had looked forward to doing each year "for my grand-children." My brother put one up anyway, and children from his church came over with ornaments they had made to decorate it and sing carols. Most disturbing was the accumulation of dirt at the back of the kitchen counters and in the corners of the floors. My suggestion that we get her help with housecleaning was met with a strong backlash. Her whole iden-tity was based on being a gracious housewife, keeping a meticulously clean home, and preparing delectable Greek food and pastries. The thought of someone else doing her job was an existential threat to her and to her independence. My heart bled. When I took her to have her eyes checked, it was determined that she needed to have cataract surgery. That explained everything, I thought—it was all due to poor vision.

One of the first tasks of the New Year was to submit the application to NAAFA to show our clothes. A woman called to announce that the line was enthusiastically received, referring to it as stunning and dreamy. Not only would our clothes be modeled at the fashion show, they would be saved for last as the show's climax. We were also given a booth at the "boutique," where vendors sold their wares. Since ours was a sample line, we would take measurements for special orders. Just before hanging up, the woman added, "Oh, and don't bother bringing anything under size twenty-eight; the average is thirty-six." Our largest size was thirty-two. We had no option but to bring what we had and hope for the best.

The weekend of the convention arrived. Frank and I loaded the garment bags into the car and drove to the hotel. We met Maxine and Michael in the hotel lobby. It was filled with very large women and the men who loved them. None of my garments would fit around one of these women's thighs. While just about everybody stopped at our booth to admire the clothes, a few women who were able to fit into them agreed to model them at the fashion show. The other deterrent was the price point; it was higher by far than that of the other vendors. We made one appointment for a couture consultation but did not get a single order.

After waiting in a long line for the fashion show, the doors opened, and we took our seats. It began with a booming beat. One by one, magnificent, queen-sized women bounced and swayed with abandon down the runway under the bright lights. There was no shortage of self-esteem as they modeled lingerie—teddies, thongs, and panties made from yards of lace—while the audience hooted and howled. It was wonderful to see women accept themselves for who they were, displaying their bodies with pride. The lights softened and our models appeared in shimmering silks and chiffon scarf-coats, sashaying to "Let Me Entertain You." There was a hush and then a burst of applause and a standing ovation. It gave me the courage I needed to make the call to Saks.

I got the buyer for Salon Z on the phone on the first try. He seemed genuinely curious. He asked to see the clothes at the end of March, a few weeks away. It could not have gone better.

With just a few more pieces to augment the collection, two couture wedding gown deadlines, and a backed-up rack of alterations, I thought everything was on track and going smoothly. I was wrong. Maxine asked to have a talk over morning coffee. She announced that her husband Mark had accepted a job in Portland, Oregon and that he was leaving in a week. She would remain to pack up their belongings, work until the end of March, and join him the beginning of April. I was losing a second gifted assistant thanks to yet another husband's out-of-state job promotion.

The same week I received two consequential phone calls. The first one left me worried. My sister-in-law informed me that my mother had left a pan of oil on the stove, which caused a fire. Luckily, my nephew was there and was able to contain it. She suggested that we unplug the stove and stop Mother from cooking altogether. The second call was from the preeminent kitchen maven. She was direct and to the point. "After interviewing thirty people, I decided I would rather have you for three days a week than somebody else for five. Are you available to go to New York for training in two weeks?" I accepted without hesitation.

My attention was pulled in different directions all at once—my new job at the showroom that required training, finding another assistant, worrying about Mother, and getting ready for Saks. I knew that if I could keep the boat on course, I would eventually get to the other side. I was working three days in my gleaming new showroom and three at the salon. After interviewing prospective assistants to replace indispensable Maxine, I hired Betty Jane, a young mother of two with a professional demeanor and substantial experience in patternmaking. With a new assistant and additional income with which to fend off debt, I could see a speck of light at the end of the tunnel.

The dresses were pored over for snags and missing hooks, steamed, and packed. Frank took off from work to come with me and help with the dress bags. We loaded up the car and headed for Manhattan and Saks Fifth Avenue's executive offices. As we made our way through the city, the pulsating streams of yellow taxis, honking cars, and streets swarming with people revved up my excitement. At the same time, I felt oddly serene knowing that the clothes were perfectly finished inside and out. It was overwhelming to think that an order from Saks would mean that, for the first time, women over the size of 24 would be able to walk into a department store and try on ready-to-wear designer clothes.

I tried to put the brakes on fantasizing as we were led into an office. The buyer stood up, greeted us, and, pointing to an empty rack, said, "Let's see what you've got." Frank and I methodically unzipped bags and hung the dresses up as the buyer squinted and peered at each one from afar as if looking at a whole painting and then darting close in to scrutinize inside seams and trim details. "Nice," he would intermittently mutter. After he finished, he let out a long, drawn out, "Fab-u-lous." I was so caught up watching his reaction that I only caught the tail end of his remark, ". . . after deciding on sizes, styles, and colors. We would be ordering around two hundred pieces. Are you prepared for that?"

"Of course," I lied.

I left thumbnail sketches, fabric samples, and an order form I had hastily put together. Frank was beaming. We thanked the buyer, got into the elevator, and waited until we were out of the building to whoop it up. Frank and I celebrated over one very expensive Reuben sandwich while rehashing details of what the buyer had said and done. It was not until we were in the car on the way home that the replaying began: "Two hundred pieces, are you prepared for that?" I felt an ever-so-slight prickle in my gut. My dream was coming true, and I was ecstatic, for God's sake! My head, however, felt like a runaway train of fear, calculating the price of fabric and manufacturing costs, not getting paid for sixty days after delivery, and various other pickles. I tried to tell myself that one had to spend money to make money and that risk is part of the game. The resistance, however, was formidable, and I couldn't put my finger on it. Frank asked if anything was wrong. I told him no and vowed to be jubilant about my triumph.

The first person I called was my mother and got her usual "whatever God wants" reply. The second call was to Maxine, now in Oregon. Her enthusiasm should have buoyed me, but instead, the tugs in the pit of my stomach escalated. I confided my fears to her. She told me that I would have no trouble getting a bank loan with a commitment from Saks and that I couldn't do better than having Saks selling my clothes—I would make my money back in no time. It didn't matter what she said—fear had reared its ugly head and was holding me in its clutches.

Determined to relax, I was soaking in the tub when I sat up with a jolt. Something I had heard surfaced from my subconscious—Saks had engaged in dubious business practices. There were rumors that Saks had improperly withheld "markdown money" from vendors, claiming they were forced to markdown merchandise that wasn't selling, and canceling orders by falsely claiming late shipment or workmanship that didn't match the sample. A designer I knew went out of business as a result of such practices and because she didn't have the funds to litigate. Well, neither did I.

Was dressing women to make them feel confident worth the risks? Was there some other way to help them increase their self-esteem? I spent a week talking to my friends, colleagues, and even the mailman. Within six days, three people close to me, including Frank, said that I should be a therapist. Frank said, "You listen to people talking about their problems anyway. Why not get paid for it?"

Something about Frank's urging turned on a light bulb. I had secretly contemplated what it would be like to be a therapist. Listening was one of my strongest assets, and nothing fascinated me more than human behavior. I could visualize sitting with people all day listening to them, delve into their motivations, help them overcome their fears, and empower them.

Whipping up a new dress that, once donned, made a woman feel good about herself certainly took less time than months of therapy. But, wasn't that a superficial fix? Was I prepared to walk away from Saks Fifth Avenue because of hearsay? I felt powerless to make a decision on my own. Confused, my last thought before going to sleep that night was "God, help me!"

When I woke up the next morning, the path I needed to follow was clear as day. The notion of becoming a therapist was exhilarating. I was ready to bring my ten-year fashion career to a close. It was the very beginning of April. I could wrap up my business with a blowout clearance sale and look at schools that offered a master's degree in counseling. My mind spun as it made plans.

Later that very day, Nathalie, a lithe, natural beauty, came in to make an appointment for a wedding dress consultation, and she was delighted to hear that I was free to do it now. I brought out the tea and cookies. In her lilting French accent, she told me that she already had a formal gown for the Belgian ceremony in her hometown and wanted a simple, silk sheath for the celebration on the Italian Riviera where her fiancé was from. We talked about everything from her wedding plans to uncertainties about her future. In passing, Nathalie mentioned that her mother had died three years ago and that planning the wedding had brought up grief. Incredibly, this would be my seventh wedding gown, and all seven of my brides had lost their mothers. We talked in depth about her mother. As Betty Jane took her measurements, I thought back to that afternoon five years earlier when

Elaine came in to One Night Stand in search of a wedding dress and asked if I would make it for her, catapulting my couture business. Before leaving, Nathalie told me that she felt better than she had felt in a long time and hugged me. It was the confirmation I needed about my decision. Nathalie was my last bride and couture client.

My friends, though disappointed that I wasn't going to become a famous dress designer after all, were all supportive of my newest endeavor. I immediately redirected my energy into researching counseling programs offered at universities nearby. I whittled the list down to a three-year, part-time program at Temple University designed for people with day jobs. I was accepted for the coming fall. It didn't matter that I would be the same age as the mothers of most of my schoolmates or that I hadn't written a paper in twenty years. I was eager to study what had interested me most of my life—human behavior—and signed up for an introductory summer course. I told my boss that I needed to leave early two days for classes, and she proposed I work four days instead of three. Perfect.

We had wound down the alterations work. Before I had a chance to notify Betty Jane about closing the business, she announced that she was quitting as soon as Nathalie's gown was finished. It felt as if the chain of events was happening on its own, and I was watching from the sidelines, marveling at the timing. Asking God for help worked for me. Praying for what is best had brought about fortuitous changes, solutions, and answers that were exactly what I needed.

My mother's situation was growing dire. The house was getting dirtier, and Mother would shoo away the cleaning ladies my sister-in-law sent to the house. She could no longer go down to the basement to wash clothes. Her difficulty walking made her rely on my brother to bring her food, which was left to rot in the refrigerator. After the stove was shut off, my sister-in-law had Meals on Wheels bring her prepared meals daily. I shuddered. Our denial of our mother's deterioration, which Mother had cheerily tried to cover up, had brought us to this. I flew to Portland to assess the situation for myself.

I was not prepared for what I saw. I walked into a house smelling of urine and a bathroom smeared with feces. I found Mother lying on the bed, happy to see me but too weak to get up. Five or six Styrofoam containers of hardly-touched food were stacked up on the counter emitting a foul smell. That meant she hadn't eaten for days. I found my thirteen-year-old nephew on the couch watching TV. "What's this uneaten food doing here?" I asked, stupefied. "She won't eat," he responded. I revved up into high gear. I hired a team of three professionals to clean and disinfect the house. Clothes were washed and the bed changed. I bought a wheelchair and made appointments to see her doctors.

I confronted my sister-in-law. How could she have allowed my mother to end up in such a condition? "I have been trying to tell you," she said resignedly, "but everyone's been in denial. I just couldn't do it anymore by myself. I guess you had to come and see for yourself." She was right. I needed a bucket of ice water poured over my head to accept the truth.

What was most harrowing was interviewing potential caregivers. Some were downright frightening. One actually screamed at me. I put calls out to everyone I knew. Two days before I was to return to Philadelphia, a friend of my mother's called to refer Zimam, an Ethiopian woman who attended my mother's church. Mother took to her immediately. We hired her as a caregiver and to cook and clean three days a week. By the end of my stay, Mother had perked up and gotten stronger. I had finally faced the music. I returned home feeling lighter, ready to start my counseling program.

First, I had to close my business. The maternity gown rentals that had made so many party-going pregnant women happy were sold at a clearance sale. I placed ads in the paper and sold the industrial sewing machine, drapes, dishes, even the floral mantelpiece that Michael had given me for my opening, now a beautiful, dried arrangement. It was not until I sold the cutting table that Frank had painstakingly built for me that my heart left the rag business for good.

In architecture school it was all about design. I hated taking exams and came up with creative alternatives to write papers. Now, I was to embrace these things I had avoided in the past. I had a new purpose. A combination of well-timed events, signs, and information, along with a trusty inner voice and a divine answer to a plea for help, were opening up a whole new way of helping people that made more sense to me—doing good on a different level.

CHAPTER 15

Life, Death, and
More Real Estate

I told myself that I would be content with passing grades. My summer class on different counseling modalities, however, sucked me into academia headfirst, and by the fall, nothing but an A would do. Those first papers took me forever to write, while my twenty-something schoolmates would spit them out in a couple of hours. At first, Frank would proofread them and hand them back to me covered in a sea of red ink corrections. I got better and was thrilled the first time I came to a page without one little red squiggle.

At age forty-eight, I was one of the oldest students in the department. I found it refreshing to pal around with my young schoolmates. They sought me out to join their study groups, partly because of the life experience component, but mostly because I said things in class they were feeling but afraid to express. I was having fun while discovering that my listening abilities and desire to help others feel good about themselves were making me stand out as a student.

I couldn't wait for spring semester to begin my internship and apply techniques I had learned to real clients. I was assigned to a mental health agency in Cherry Hill, New Jersey, less than half an hour away. Luckily, my supervisor was a gifted therapist who approved of my creative approach to counseling. Close to me in age, she became both a mentor and a peer. I looked forward to Monday morning staff meetings where therapists shared difficulties and successes they had with their clients and were given constructive criticism. Soon, the cases assigned to me were progressively more challenging. I took my role seriously and viewed the client-therapist relationship to be a holy one. It was an honor to have clients trust me enough to share their innermost feelings. Before each session I would say the prayer from *A Course in Miracles*.

I thought that I had nothing to offer children and teens. After agreeing to see a reportedly despondent teenager, I witnessed her confidence blossom in a short period of time. Word got around about my effectiveness, and I was on my way to becoming teen counseling queen. I did not take one moment I spent with my clients or what I learned from each of them for granted. By the end of the semester I had the highest rate of returning clients among the interns, higher even than of some of the staff therapists.

Not once did I second-guess my decision to leave the fashion world behind. I was much happier. And thank God for my job designing cabinets—it was the ideal counterpoint to school. It provided a creative outlet and a quiet place to do my homework. I also practiced my newly -acquired skills on my customers. Musing over moving out of our cramped quarters, Frank and I rode our bikes around looking for dilapidated buildings to remodel and empty lots on which we fantasized designing our dream home. Our tango dancing continued to improve. When we finally had gotten the rhythm down, I rewarded myself with a pair of handmade tango shoes.

It wasn't all rosy. Tango or no tango, Frank continued to have periodic flare-ups, though less frequently and not as intense. The problem was not just Frank—the build-up of my frustration level with his surprise eruptions would lead to my own meltdowns. This resulted in periods of silent impasse with both of us ending up on the herringbone tweed armchairs in David's office. I particularly resented that I had to use "time out" and "intentional dialogue" among other tools I used with my clients with my own husband. From another perspective, it was an opportunity to put myself in the clients' shoes and experience their discomfort. There were times when I didn't want to continue living with an active time bomb. In these moments, two lists would flash in my head—a long one with Frank's assets juxtaposed to one with his single detriment. The pros won every time. I vowed not to take his anger resulting from insecurities personally.

Zimam, who came in to help my mother three times a week, announced that she had to give notice. She was very straightforward with her assessment that my mother needed daily care. It was the end of my first year of school, and as soon as finals were over, I flew to Portland to reevaluate the situation with my brother and determine the next step. I visited assisted-care facilities and talked with social workers. When I brought up the subject about moving to my mother, she balked at the idea of leaving her home.

There had to be a way Mother could stay in her house. Up to now, social security and her stock dividends were covering expenses, but hiring a full-time caregiver from an agency would be prohibitive. I went through the list of women I had interviewed months earlier. I met with Sharon, who was older with some health issues of her own, but her advocacy for the elderly had impressed me. She was available and referred Camila from Guatamala as a backup. We met and worked out the logistics. They would take turns. My mother's reaction was lukewarm, but I got her to agree on a trial period. Camila, the cook of the duo, asked her what her favorite dish was. Only after tasting Camila's deliciously prepared lamb and Sharon offering to take her to church did she warm up to them. Under the circumstances, it was the best quality of life we could give her.

I sailed through my second year of school. Mother's situation, however, was constantly on my mind. She had been diagnosed with dementia and now needed twenty-four-hour care. Camila had moved into an upstairs bedroom. The caregivers did their best, but there were slip-ups. Not only were Sharon's health issues limiting her physical ability, but she was also easily distracted. Once she forgot to secure Mother in her wheelchair, and she slid off onto the pavement. Whenever Camila had not done what we had asked, she would blame the misunderstanding on her poor English. Although Mother never directly complained, her slips of the tongue made it clear that she could barely tolerate "strangers" in her home.

The following summer I spent a month in Portland taking care of Mother, giving Sharon and Camila a break. Mother was so happy. Her change of attitude did not escape the caregivers' notice. Sharon took me aside and implored me to move to Portland and care for her. "That's out of the question!" I said, shocked by her impropriety. "I have a husband and a job, and I'm in school on the other side of the country. There is no way I could make it work."

The economic downturn had my brother worried about Mother's finances and the cost of her care. My concern was her quality of life. We had focused on her being able to stay in her own home but were not addressing her discontent. It was obvious that she was happiest with her family around her, especially her grandchildren. She had devoted her whole life to our well-being. It was now our turn to look after hers. My brother and sister-in-law proposed caring for Mother in their home for half the cost of paying the caregivers. My niece agreed to take the morning shift as her college job. I was beyond grateful. Now, confined to a wheelchair and bedbound, Mother required that everything be done for her. What they were taking on was not going to be easy. My sister-in-law recoiled at having outside help in her home, increasing the risk of burnout. When they were ready, I flew back out to help move Mother in. I went from room to room in the house in which I grew up, said thank you, and let go. It had done its job and now was just a string of memories. I left my mother in her new home with family, smiling.

Graduation was nearing, and I got right to work studying for finals, writing the last papers, and saying goodbye to my clients. I was proud of my achievement and looking forward to receiving my diploma and celebrating with Frank, who had so staunchly supported me. I had no idea where my degree would take me. Wearing my robe and mortarboard with tassel, parading into the athletic arena with my young friends, I felt like a walking, beaming strobe light.

That August, I went to Portland to stay with Mother for two weeks in my brother's home. Her room was downstairs next to my brother's office. I found her propped up in her hospital bed, a shadow of the person I had left there at Christmas. She was weak but at peace with her living arrangement. It was the first time that my mother didn't throw her arms around me and kiss me upon seeing me. Her food and water were barely touched. Because the kitchen and dining room were on the main floor, her meals were brought down to her, thereby limiting her interaction with the rest of the family.

I had my meals with Mother and egged her on when she pushed her food away. Not having attended the church she so loved, I asked her priest to come and give her Holy Communion. After just one week she became livelier; her humor had returned along with her appetite. With her short-term memory gone, she repeated stories of her girlhood in Greece, her life there during World War II, and her coming to America. She retold old jokes, and we laughed as if I had heard them for the first time. My sister-in-law had expressed her aversion to changing Mother's diapers. I could certainly understand why and was indebted to her for having done it anyway.

Halfway through my stay, I sensed a distancing from my sister-in-law. The tension in the house mounted rapidly and could be cut with a knife. Her demeanor was that of a taut elastic band ready to snap. Any suggestion

I made was perceived as criticism and met with indignation. My niece told me that she couldn't stand her "job." I reminded myself that they were doing their best. They had been taking care of Mother for sixteen months, something I had not done.

My brother took me aside. Having other people in the house created stress, so he politely suggested I not come and stay for extended periods of time. I told him I would not be elbowed out from spending time with our mother and alerted him to the possibility that, without outside help, his wife and daughter could experience burnout, which would be detrimental to everyone involved.

The evening before returning home, I had dinner upstairs with my brother and his family. I looked at the faces around the table. Caring for Mother had taken a toll on all of them. She never complained or showed any discontent as she had with the ladies taking care of her in her home. Being with family was what mattered most. How could I ask them to give her more personal attention without detonating a bomb? After everything she had done for us, she deserved the best quality of life in the time she had left. So did everyone else. Without any hesitation, without weighing the pros and cons, out it came:

"What if I moved back here and took care of Mother?" There was stunned silence.

"We can move her back to her house, and I can take care of her there," I continued, waiting for a reaction.

My niece's face lit up, her eyes darting between her mother, father, and me. With both of her parents motionless, she let out in one breath, "That sounds great!"

"Well, we could do that," my brother spoke up. He warned, "There's not a lot of money, stocks are down, and we don't know how long she has left . . ."

My sister-in-law cut him off. "When do you think you could come?"

"I don't know exactly. I have to talk to Frank, but I'd like to try for Thanksgiving," I said, feeling unexpected peace.

I called Frank, and he gave me his full support. I went downstairs to tell Mother, "Mama, I'm coming back with Frank for Thanksgiving. You and I will move back to our house." With shining eyes, she threw her arms around me and kissed me.

There was no point in looking for a job as a therapist if I was going to move to Portland in three months. I would continue working in the showroom until then. As I was exploring creative ways to utilize my counseling skills, I received a call from my friend Ann with an idea and a request. She was volunteering at the Working Wardrobe, a non-profit organization that collected business clothes donated by professional women and made them available to women who participated in welfare-to-work programs for their job interviews at no cost. Believing that more than clothes were needed to secure and keep a job, Ann was putting together an all-day workshop of one-hour presentations on resume writing, makeup application, and how to dress and conduct oneself in an interview. Citing my fashion background, she asked if I would give a talk on appropriate attire. "What a great idea! But Ann, you're always so well put together; you give the talk on how to dress. What if I talk about healthy self-esteem?" Ann enthusiastically agreed.

My interest in the role self-esteem played in a person's well-being had been spurred when, as an undergraduate, I had done an independent study on territoriality and personal space, working with incarcerated women in Portland. Using a questionnaire that I had created, my objective had been to measure how much of their territoriality diminished over time as their defenses decreased. To establish a bond with the women, I had made weekly visits to the prison and applied makeup on them. Within two months, the warden had reported that their behavior had improved. Was it the makeup or the personal attention they were receiving that was key?

Whatever it was, they felt better. According to their answers on the questionnaire, the women's self-esteem had improved.

The workshop I did with Ann was sponsored by the Philadelphia Electric Company, which was conveniently located across from where I worked. A hundred and forty women filled a large conference hall. I began my presentation by explaining how self-esteem is established in early childhood. If a child is given encouragement, they develop healthy self-esteem. Conversely, if the child is repeatedly being told he or she is worthless, the brain gets wired with the negative message and is carried over into adulthood. "This is how negative self-esteem is propagated generationally. If you were beaten as a kid, you most likely will beat your kids." I paused. You could hear a pin drop. I ended with a guided meditation, allowing the women to visualize themselves as successes. It was followed with exuberant applause.

Several women came up to me afterward to share their stories. A tall, noble-looking woman stood to the side until the others had their turn. She approached me teary-eyed and said, "I hit my child, and I didn't know why. Now I know and I will never do it again." I congratulated her, telling her that it takes some people years of therapy to gain that awareness. That evening I found a folded piece of paper from Ann in my mail slot. The women were asked to fill out an evaluation form about the presentations. She had compiled a list of the favorable comments on mine. My talk had hit home. I knew that this was the direction I needed to go—helping at-risk women get rid of their negative wiring and enhance their self-esteem.

Frank and I bought his daughter's old Honda and planned on taking eleven days to drive cross-country to Oregon. The possibility that Frank might have one of his eruptions on the open road with me trapped in the car had crossed my mind. We went to see David, and he suggested that we have two phone therapy sessions along the way as a safety valve. I gave my notice at work and wrapped up my projects. We packed the car with snow chains, food provisions, a space blanket in case the car broke down in snow, and my winter clothes. There was no way of knowing how long I would be away.

First stop was Falling Water, Frank Lloyd Wright's architectural masterpiece in Mill Run, Pennsylvania. We headed northwest. I had always wanted to go back to Dearborn, Michigan and see the house where I spent my early childhood before moving to Greece. Once a white blue-collar suburb, Dearborn was now an Islamic enclave with store signs in Arabic. We walked by the small, brick, elementary school that I once had thought to be enormous. At the Ford Museum, I was surprised to find a prototype of Buckminster Fuller's Dymaxion House.

We drove through Chicago up to Neenah, Wisconsin to stay with my ex-assistant Heidi and her husband in their big, old farmhouse. Then west through the moonscape-like Badlands of South Dakota, where we saw Mt. Rushmore, which was smaller than I had expected. Crazy Horse Monument, the Native American chief carved on the side of a mountain, was much bigger than I had imagined. Zigzagging south through Wyoming, we arrived in Boulder, Colorado, where we stayed with old friends of my parents. We continued west through Salt Lake City into Idaho. Twice we parked on the side of the road to have our therapy sessions with David. When we reached Pendleton, Oregon, we turned west. Driving alongside the Columbia River, we finally arrived at our destination. After eleven days without incident, our relationship remained happily intact. Frank stayed for a few days and then flew back to Philadelphia, leaving me with the Honda.

Frank and I made a pact not to be apart more than a month and a half at a stretch, alternating visits to opposite coasts. The family friend who took care of Mother when my brother and his family went on vacation would take care of her while I was away. Before I brought Mother back to her home, I oversaw construction of a ramp leading to the front door. The family room turned into a sunny bedroom with the hospital bed next to the large window looking out onto the fruit trees and beyond, where her garden used to flourish. There was space in the room for a loveseat for visitors. When my brother brought Mother home, she was dazed and confused. She had deteriorated into frailty.

I was determined to make ends meet on the barebones monthly allowance we received from my brother along with a small stipend from an agency advocating care at home. Mother was assessed and found eligible for hospice, which turned out to be a team of visiting human angels. Doris, another lifesaver, took over caregiving for twelve hours one day a week. Partly funded by insurance and partly by hospice, she came every Tuesday, giving me much-needed time for myself. Nothing gave me more fortitude, however, than the support of my friends, and Frank, who was there for me on the other end of the phone, day or night.

We soon had a routine. At first I had Mother's friends come over for coffee every Tuesday morning, but as she increasingly withdrew, their visits stopped. She loved having me read her the Bible in Greek. On Sundays when she was having a good day, I would dress her in her classically tailored clothes and a wide-brimmed hat and wheel her to church several blocks away. The highlight of her week, however, was every Thursday evening when my nephew, Yianni, came over for dinner. This is when she was at her best. As her grandson put her to bed she would say, *"Kalinihta, palikari!"*—good night, you strapping young man!

The idea of creating a program to enhance self-esteem in incarcerated women had begun percolating. Mother's naps and Doris' Tuesday visits gave me the opportunity to do some research and development. Positive feedback I had received from the women at the welfare-to-work conference confirmed the importance of healthy self-esteem. In a box of old school projects, I stumbled upon an article entitled, "Self-Esteem Through Femininity: Feminine Development Program for Women in Correctional Institutions," a program sponsored by the W. Clement and Jessica V. Stone Foundation. It had been given to me by the warden at the women's prison where I had done the makeovers. After only two months, he had observed significant improvement in the women's behavior. I concluded that it was because they felt better about themselves. A 1971 article in *Sepia Magazine*, with an even more dated title, "Prison Charm School," claimed that at one reformatory that had implemented the program, only 6 women out of 117 returned to the facility after being released. This was a 5 percent recidivism rate compared to 50 percent for those who did not participate in the program. I knew I was onto something!

Expanding on my presentation at the conference, I created a twelve-workshop program to address body, mind, and spirit, entitling it *Living a Fearless Life* (LFL). To develop rapport, we would begin with appropriate makeup application and hairstyle makeovers. Before and after photos would prove that change is possible. Sessions on diet and yoga introduced a healthy lifestyle. After developing trust by addressing the superficial outside, the ensuing workshops guided the women to look inward and determine what worked for them and what didn't. The program came full circle, giving them exposure to a grander outside—the benefits of integrating with community and giving back. The graduation ceremony acknowledged the women's achievement of completing something, which some of them had never experienced.

My mother was withdrawing more and more. One afternoon, as she had drifted off with her eyes closed, a raised eyebrow indicated that she was in thought. I asked her what was on her mind. She maintained her silence. "Mama," I implored softly, "if you tell me what you are thinking, you'll feel better." She opened her eyes, looked directly into mine, and said, "I am waiting for God to invite me to His house," then closed them again. I got it. Mother let me know that she had her bags packed and was ready to go. I prayed that her words were heard. She had had a lifelong devotion to the Virgin Mary. What could be more perfect than if she made her transition on the fifteenth of August, when the Virgin Mary had made hers—the *Dormition of the Theotokos.*

Mother was increasingly becoming more spirit than human. She ate less and slept more. As we were talking one evening, she stopped mid-sentence. Her eyes darted behind me to the open door into the living room. "Who are those men wearing sandals?" she asked incredulously.

"What men?" I asked.

"The ones in the living room," she replied, gesturing toward the door.

"I'll go look," I said as I peered into the living room to appease her. The last thing I needed were sandaled men in the house at ten at night.

"There are no men in the house, Mama. The doors are locked."

"I don't care what you say; I saw at least two walk past the door." I believed her. She was being visited. A few weeks later, Mother and I were having afternoon coffee on the patio. She looked utterly ethereal. I noticed she had fixated her gaze beyond the opposite edge of the table. Smiling, without averting her eyes, she asked, "Whose children are those?"

"I don't know. What do they look like?" I asked matter-of-factly.

"They're just beautiful. They look like little angels." Mother was seeing what I was sensing—angels all around us. I knew beyond any doubt that we were both being taken care of. August 15th came and went, and Mother was still here. Her wish to leave earth for "God's house" was granted on the 8th of September with my brother and me holding her hand, just like when we were little. She left on the Virgin Mary's birthday.

It took another month to clean out the house. After family members took what they wanted, I sold everything at a yard sale. The last ten months had been my opportunity to help my mother leave this world and repay her for bringing me into it. It had also helped me with the grieving process. I had already said goodbye to each room before Mother had moved out of her home to live with my brother and his family thinking she would never be back. Now it was just a house. Where there is love, there is God. He had protected us and given my mother a miraculous send-off. Before leaving it for the last time, I simply said thank you. I returned to Philadelphia with a profound sense of fulfillment. Fortunately, my job at the showroom was still there.

After contacting Pennsylvania's Secretary of Public Welfare, we met at a cafe. A handsome woman without pretense, she put me in touch with the Commissioner of the Philadelphia Prison System. He seemed intrigued with my program and invited me to meet with him and the Director of Programs. After making my presentation, I offered to pilot it at no cost. The commissioner was enthusiastic about everything but the makeup, voicing his reservation, "We try to get it off of them, and you're putting it on them?" I told him, "No makeup, no program," and explained the importance of building trust and rapport. He relented.

Assumptions I had made about prison employees sharing the commissioner's enthusiasm were quickly extinguished. Some correctional officers played power trips, not only with the women, but with me as well. They questioned supplies I brought in even though they had been approved and made me wait unnecessarily. The women, however, made all the hurdles worthwhile. At first my motives and I were met with suspicion. Realizing that they were not being judged, the women began to look forward to my visits. It was gratifying to see them get the message—that I was neither different nor better than them. By taking responsibility for their actions and making the right choices, they, too, could make their dreams come true.

The administrative hoops I had to jump through were getting more restrictive. Midway into the program, as I was seriously considering quitting, one of the participants approached me to say that she was being released and handed me an envelope. In it was a card that she had purchased at the commissary, in which she had written a poem—a stunning expression of gratitude. How could I quit after that? Something was definitely getting across.

The program wrapped up with a graduation ceremony. The commissioner and other officials who had a role in implementing the program sat in the front row of seats while guest speakers who had participated in the workshops made up the rest of the audience. As each woman came up to the front when her name was called to proudly receive her certificate of completion, I fastened a string of faux pearls around her neck. It symbolized a community comprised of individuals. Frank was there to bestow a red rose to each graduate. Everyone was beaming.

The commissioner was eager to add the program to the curriculum. He brought me in front of the board to have it approved for funding. Dressed conservatively, I walked into a room of thirty-some men and two women. The commissioner gave the program a stellar introduction. As soon as I began my power point presentation, I could see the eyeballs starting to roll. Yawning, dismissive, the men slumped into their chairs. The feedback was direct—my program was not scientifically measured. Since when did the positive effect of healthy self-esteem on one's well-being need proof? The rejection letter came as no surprise.

I knew unequivocally that LFL would help at-risk women find self-worth, but figuring out how to fund it had been discouraging. Uncannily, each time an obstacle blocked progress, something would happen to push it forward. Just when I thought I had come to the end of the road, my friend Barbara invited me to a Sunday afternoon tea. In attendance was Marjorie, a former US congresswoman. As soon as I walked in, Barbara introduced me. "Marjorie, this is Sophia, the friend I told you about who is working with women in the prison . . ."

"Not anymore," I cut her off. "I'm done!"

Barbara responded, "What?"

"Why?" Marjorie chimed in.

"Because I need money, and no one is giving it to me, and I can't do the fundraising thing."

Digging into her bag, Marjorie produced her card. Handing it to me, she said, "Send me a one-page description, and I'll put you in touch with the right person."

Quitting appeared not to be an option. Marjorie set the gears in motion. One introduction led to another, and eventually to Karen, who worked for a state representative. We became fast friends. With her help, I received a $10,000 grant from the Department of Community and Economic Development. My friend Jane, who was on the board of an organization that provided an alternative setting to incarceration for female offenders, introduced me to its executive director. Soon, I was facilitating the program with a group of women who could not have been a better fit.

Everything was falling into place. Frank and I decided that we needed more space than a one-bedroom apartment. Every now and then we would resume talking about designing and building our dream home. With my mother's estate about to settle, it couldn't be a better time. The cost of vacant lots in Center City was prohibitive, and we turned our sights to West Philly.

While scanning the paper for real estate property values, one ad popped out at me: "Two charming Victorian twins for sale." The last thing we needed was another Victorian building. Before skipping to the next ad, I recognized the name of the listing agent, a customer from the showroom. She would know of lots for sale and what newly constructed townhouses went for in the area. I called her.

Nancy was effusive about the twins. Although they needed updating, they were exceptionally beautiful and on one of the best streets in Powelton Village, a pocket of Victorian architecture. They had been on the market for several months, and the owner, who was downsizing to a condo, had priced the properties to sell.

"If you are considering this area at all," she urged, "you really should look at them." Why not? The neighborhood had a nineteenth-century charm, and it would be nice to catch up with Nancy. When I told Frank I had made the appointment, he just stared at me. "You must be kidding," he stuttered. "Come on, Frank. We're not buying. We're just looking. Let's make it a date—we'll take a look and then go out to dinner."

We met Nancy on heavily-treed Hamilton Street in front of the Second French Empire-style Victorian twins. Replete with mansard roof, columns, and curved brackets tastefully painted in contrasting accents, they were beautiful, indeed. We walked through the iron gate and up the steps onto the wrap-around porch. Nancy rang the doorbell. Bob, a robust, older African American gentleman answered the door, welcoming us in his baritone voice. As he led us through the vestibule into the parlor, it was as if we were entering another era. An organ and a baby grand piano were squeezed in. Placed between two floor-to-ceiling Jefferson windows was a magnificent, equally tall mirror. Paintings covered the walls, and artifacts from extensive travels were bathed in a soft glow. My mother would have loved it.

Built in 1868, the house had been divided into three apartments, one of which Bob had turned into a B&B. He lived on the first floor. We followed him through a low passageway under the stairway created to connect the parlor with the rest of the apartment. In the center of the kitchen was a large, round, oak table, which could be replaced with an island. Bob's living room would make a lovely dining room, but the '60s bathroom would have to go. I could perfectly envision Bob's bedroom as my office. The large bay window overlooking the garden could have been part of a provincial French chalet. After showing us the other twin, Bob led us back into his parlor. He brought out pink champagne and glasses. A retired music teacher at a tony prep school, he sat down at the piano and started playing Chopin etudes. I was a goner.

I wanted this house, and I could tell that Frank had done a 180. Bob invited me over the following week to pick over decades of accumulated stuff before he put them out in the annual Hamilton Street sidewalk sale. Frank and I couldn't wait until Monday to tell Nancy. "Call him yourself," she said, sounding pleased.

"Bob, we'd like to make an offer," I blurted out when he answered the phone.

"Oh dear, I sold it," he said under his breath.

"Sold it? When?" He must have been making a joke.

"That Asian woman who had been pestering me for months called Saturday and offered to buy both twins. "I don't like her very much," he added, as if it mattered.

I was heartbroken. Just when I had fallen crazy in love, I got dumped. Frank was befuddled. I took Bob up on his invitation anyway. Something steered me that day to the most expensive French bakery in the city. As if I were on cruise control, I selected a large, glazed pear tart. I asked for extra multicolored ribbons to be tied around the box, and off I went a-courtin'.

Bob answered the door with a big grin. "Come in, come in," he boomed and brought me into the kitchen. I presented him with the box dripping with ribbons. When he saw the tart, his eyes lit up. "Oh, ho, ho!" he bellowed. "How did you know pear was my favorite? I'll make a pot of tea."

Bob and I sat at the big, round table in the kitchen sipping tea while he devoured half the tart himself. He slowly lifted the cup to his lips and asked, "How much would you have offered if the house were still for sale?"

Mirroring him, I took a prolonged sip, set the cup on my saucer, and replied, "$350,000." After Bob took another sip in slow motion, he said, "I would have accepted." He was fishing. He wanted to know if our offer was viable in the event the opportunity presented itself. It gave me a glimmer of hope.

The conversation turned to our departed mothers and their importance in our lives. I could swear I felt the presence of mine in the room. Bob led me to the folding tables set up in the parlor, piled with vases, African figurines, and mismatched china. A handsome pair of ceramic roosters sitting in the corner of floor caught my eye. Bob sold them to me for twenty-five dollars. He escorted me out to the front gate and, closing it behind me, said, "I'm going to pray for you."

In that instant I knew. I called Frank. "It's ours!" I said as soon as he answered.

"What is?"

"Bob's house. Frank, we're getting it!"

"Did the deal fall through?"

"No, not yet. I'll explain later, but I'm telling you right now, the house is ours!"

Three weeks later, Bob called to ask if we were still interested. He had been waiting for the inspection. When the buyer demanded extensive repairs, Bob nullified the agreement. He wanted us to have it even though he was losing the sale of the adjoining twin. His and my prayers were heard. As sure as I was that my father's divine intercession helped me acquire the building on Delancey Street, I knew my mother had a hand in manifesting this one.

The euphoria waned as soon as we took possession. Empty in the unforgiving daylight, the flaws were glaring. We hadn't noticed the network of extension cords in the soft romantic lighting while sipping champagne, inferring the wiring was not up to code. We prioritized. Living on third floor while workmen banged away below was not fun, but it was all worth it. One step after another, one day at a time, our dream home was materializing.

I sketched up my fantasy garden, and Frank made it happen. He created a brick patio surrounded by ferns, shrubs, and flowers. We found the ideal fountain at a garden store's sidewalk sale. The fireplace mantel had been removed when forced-air heat was introduced at the turn of the 1900s. I acquired a period-specific gray marble mantel at auction for a song that looked like it had returned to its home just like Bob's ceramic roosters did. The rugs that I inherited from my mother fit perfectly. We invited Bob over for dinner, and we became family.

In the spring, daffodils, irises, and lilies of the valley sprang up in the front yard. The neighbors' tall trees and climbing ivy surrounding the garden in the back provided rare privacy and the feeling of being in a terrarium. One by one they appeared—hydrangeas, irises, and peonies. Sitting there with my morning coffee, watching the water gurgle from the top of the fountain and spill over glistening as it hugged the tall column and fall into the basin, I thought about how many times things did not go my way, yet it could not have turned out better.

How many times had I wanted to quit my program for at-risk women only to have the obstacle replaced by an auspicious event, pushing me to go on and allow me to reap the rewards of being truly helpful? I had scoffed at the idea when my mother's caregiver had suggested I leave my job, home, and husband to take care of my bedridden mother. Thank God my perception changed. That decision yielded me a miracle—one of the richest experiences of my life.

Nothing was going to daunt my will to design and build our house together. Yet, by allowing a spattering of coincidences to realign my focus in a completely different direction, I was brought to this moment of profound gratitude for our perfectly suited home. All of it was a confirmation that an omniscient force of love had better answers than mine, that obstacles were blessings, and that struggles were not to be seen as enemies, but as teachers.

CHAPTER 16

The Split and a Shift

For our ninth wedding anniversary, Frank and I planned a romantic getaway to Venice. Then on to Lucerne to visit my friend Erika, with whom I had recently reconnected, more than twenty-five years after we were students in Florence. Our first stop was Greece to introduce Frank to the "homeland" where I had spent an unforgettable part of my childhood.

The last time I had visited Greece was with my mother almost twenty years before. I was looking forward to seeing my relatives on my mother's side in Argos and my father's in Manesi, a small, rural village between the ruins of the legendary ancient cities of Mycenae and Medea. My cousin Aikaterini had invited us to stay in her home in Argos where she had been raised with her three sisters and now lived with her husband, Kanellos.

The train from Athens only went as far as Corinth, which was halfway to Argos. Aikaterini and Kanellos were waiting to pick us up. That evening, they took us to a play by Euripides at the same 20,000-seat ancient amphitheater where it was first performed at the end of the fourth century BCE. The reunion with my cousin was heartwarming, as if no time had lapsed. An instant bromance developed between Frank and Kanellos. They would laugh incessantly together without understanding a word of each other's language. The five days in Argos and Manesi were spent gathering in various cousins' homes, sitting down to endless home-cooked feasts. The goodbyes came too soon.

We toured the rest of Peloponnesus by rented car, visiting the highlights of ancient city-states from Greece's golden age. Once in Patras, we had just enough time to purchase some wine, for which the region is famous, and local delicacies for a picnic dinner on the ferry. After boarding and finding our cabin for the overnight trip to Brindisi, the southern port city in Italy, we located a table and two chairs on deck. As the ferry's anchor was raised, I laid out bread, feta cheese, salami, and sliced tomatoes while Frank uncorked a bottle of wine. I was mesmerized by the twinkling lights dancing on the surface of dark blue waves just before sunset. For millennia, poets, novelists, and historians have attempted to crystallize Greece's beauty into words, but only experiencing it can do it justice. We toasted to the grandeur and to all that awaited us. The scalloped coast fell further away, and I had not a care in the world. Nothing could go wrong.

Our Fiat was ready for us at the rental agency. Our itinerary was loosely outlined to accommodate spontaneous stops and side trips. The Italian I once had spoken fluently was coming back to me, and I couldn't wait to share with Frank the special places I had experienced in Florence as a student. My friend Bianca from Oregon, who was a handbag designer based in Florence, had invited us to stay with her and her young daughter, Olimpia, at her flat near Tivoli Gardens. Everything was as splendid as I remembered it.

As we traveled up the Amalfi Coast to hike the *Cinque Terre*, the five towns, we arrived in Monterosso al Mare. We had decided to start at the most arduous end of the journey early the next morning. Although people take two or more days to walk at their leisure, we chose to hike all five towns in one day. Huffing and puffing, climbing craggy rocks following three Germans, I wondered what we had gotten ourselves into. The stunning vistas of the shoreline and each picturesque town as it came into view made the challenge worthwhile. The Germans suddenly gave up and turned around. Germans surrendering? Who would have thought? It was the shot in the arm we needed, and we picked up the pace. It got easier as we went on. After hiking for eight hours, stopping for lunch along the way, we reached Riomaggiore, the town at the other end, where, victorious, we caught the train back.

Venice was exactly as it appears in photographs. It oozed a Romeo-and-Juliet-like romantic quality. We arrived at our hotel, which had recently been renovated to its original glory, filled with antiques, hand-painted porcelain, gilt clocks, and richly framed paintings. There was nowhere else I would rather be celebrating our anniversary. The staff greeted us as if they had been anticipating the arrival of important guests. Our room was unexpectedly large. With its exposed beams and Murano chandelier, it exuded old-world charm. On a side table was a silver tray with two crystal flutes, a hand-signed anniversary card from the staff, and an ice bucket with a bottle of Prosecco. We decided to enjoy it after returning to our room from having dinner. The concierge suggested a favorite restaurant that was a good walk away but assured us that the food was worth it.

The map of the unfamiliar network of canals, bridges, and narrow paths connecting small piazzas was confusing, prompting us to stop and ask for directions. Insisting on speaking English, Frank would stop a a passerby, show them the piece of paper with the name and address of the restaurant, and hand them a map. When the reply came in Italian, I interjected. Finally, the name of the restaurant appeared on a canopy over an unpretentious storefront. Upon entering, we were seated at a corner table with perfectly starched white linens. Waiters whizzed by with platters wafting mouthwatering aromas.

Frank seemed preoccupied. I handed him the wine menu, and he brusquely pushed it back toward me, saying, "Just order one." He would not look at me and began scanning the food menu. The waiter came over, and I nervously ordered a nice Montepulciano. There was silence. The waiter returned with the wine, uncorked it, and poured it into the glasses. I ordered the grilled lamb chops. "Osso Buco," Frank ordered in a crusty tone. As he picked up his glass to drink without clicking, I raised mine and, leaning into him, said, "We're in Venice, Frank. Happy anniversary." His reply, "Cheers," was barely audible. There was no denying it—the atmosphere had darkened. "Are you okay?" I finally asked. He didn't even look at me.

Our food arrived, perfectly garnished. Frank's face had turned into stone. I saw it coming. "Frank, what's wrong?" I asked with dread.

"You cut me off," he growled. "I was asking the guy directions, and you jumped in like I wasn't even there."

"Frank, he couldn't speak English," I said, terrified of what this might be foreshadowing. "I thought I was helping. How could you take it like that?" I knew it was the wrong thing to say as soon as it came out.

"Now you're telling me how I should take it?" Frank's face was beet red with rage. Trying to keep his voice down, he snarled about how I had belittled and treated him as if he were invisible. We had crossed the point of no return. I felt the familiar boot in the stomach. His words came at me like a round of machine gunfire. I stopped hearing. Every cell in my body screamed at me to get as far away from this man as I could. I grabbed my bag and ran out.

It was dark, and I didn't have a map. Stumbling, not knowing which way to go, I desperately tried to remember the name of the hotel, but I could only put together a string of meaningless syllables. After roaming for what seemed an eternity, my anxiety mounted. I asked someone the direction of Piazza San Marco. I finally reached it, but every time I thought that I had a sense of the hotel's location, I found myself in yet another unfamiliar setting. I felt as if I were playing a part in horror film. How could this have happened? Another special occasion sabotaged. After more than forty-five minutes of frantic wandering, I found myself in front of the hotel. My knees buckled from relief. The shock and hurt now gave way to anger. Straightaway, I went up to the room. The door was unlocked. I walked in. Frank was sitting on one side of the bed staring into space.

"Do you have any idea what I have been through? For almost an hour I've been walking the streets in a panic going around in circles trying to find the hotel. Anything could have happened to me. Was there not even a smidgeon of concern to come looking for me?"

"I did look for you." His flat voice shut me down. I felt nothing for this man sitting on the bed. Finding the Prosecco unopened gave me some comfort. I got into my nightclothes, uncorked the bottle, and filled one of the flutes. I sat in the chair next to the table contemplating my fate. Was I really going on to Switzerland with this guy? I told myself I could always fly home. I refilled my glass. It didn't matter that the sparkly was room temperature. There was something different about this eruption that touched an unchartered part of my psyche. Trying to put a finger on it, as I reached for the bottle again, I heard a barely audible voice say, "Can I have some, too?" I poured a third of the other flute and set it on table. That was all he got. I drank the entire rest of the bottle, processing in silence.

The reason for my disquietude was crystal clear. For the first time in my life, I felt abandoned. This, by the man who had always ensured my safety. And when I appeared, he took no action to stop the bleeding. By the time I had finished the last drop of Prosecco, Frank was snoring in an upright position. I climbed into bed and went to sleep on the opposite edge of the bed.

I woke up the next morning in disbelief over last night's disaster. Frank was up and dressed. As I got out of bed, he attempted to approach me. Flushed, sullen, and with droopy shoulders, he looked painfully deflated. I lunged past him, grabbing my clothes to dress in the bathroom. I took a long shower to gather my wits and the courage to even look at him. I braced myself as I walked back into the sun-filled room and sat next to the empty

Prosecco bottle. Frank was lying on the bed with his hands covering his face. He got up, came around, and sat on the edge of the bed. He tried to talk, but words would not come out. He was struggling with emotions he was unable to express. After a few minutes of paralytic silence, I spoke. "I feel utterly abandoned by you, physically, and emotionally."

"I can't tell you how sorry I am, Sophia. I came out looking for you as soon as I paid the bill, but you were nowhere in sight. I was walking around not knowing which direction to go for I don't know how long. I didn't know that it would take you that long to find the hotel, and I didn't want you coming and not finding me here. I was scared, too." It was the first time I thought of the luscious, uneaten food left behind and felt a wave of hunger. I had turned stone cold, and even though I knew that his response would be the same as after every outburst, I had to ask, "Then why didn't you show your relief when you saw me? Why didn't you apologize last night? You knew that I was deeply wounded; why didn't you apply a tourniquet? Why did you let me go to sleep like that?"

Frank began by telling me how seeing the horror on my face and knowing it was a direct result of his behavior had rendered him incapacitated. He acknowledged the terror I had experienced. Next came a play-by-play analysis of his thought process, from his emotions being triggered by his mistaken perception of being belittled, to feeling contrition and sorrow. The more remorseful he was, the more eloquent he became. I remained unmoved as he expressed his abhorrence at his behavior and his inability to control it. Frank wrapped up the familiar soliloquy by declaring his intense love for me and vowing that he would do everything in his power to qualify his perception of belittlement before it turned into another train wreck, followed by, "Sophia, please forgive me."

There was no question that everything he said was with deep conviction, but I was still reeling from emotional desertion. How narcissistic of him to cling to his feelings of imaginary persecution, slash me with verbal abuse, and not provide me with an apology in a timely manner. Once again, he expressed genuine repentance, and I felt for his suffering. I had to make a swift decision. Do I flee or stay with the itinerary? I can always flee, but what to do now? Flailing, I desperately asked the help of the Holy Spirit. Immediately, all anxiety left in a swoosh. I was astonished at the feeling of peace that enveloped me. "I forgive you, Frank." His relief was audible. "You know I love you more than anything in the world," he said softly. I felt limp as he embraced me, but the process of healing had commenced. We stepped out into the treasury of riches that Venice had to offer.

Four days after the incident, we took the train to Lucerne to chronicle the changing landscape. As we sped northward, the almost flat, red-tiled roofs of Italy incrementally morphed into steeply-sloped wooden ones designed to ward off the Swiss snow. The contrast between Venice and Lucerne was striking. We left the dense, three-dimensional Baroque and Rococo styles of the Renaissance and narrow canals veining through a Venice drenched with art like an old countess dripping in her jewels, and we arrived in crisply clean Lucerne. Void of throngs of tourists, there was the main square, ringed with buildings adorned with patterned frescoes, the Chapel bridge surrounded by perfectly maintained flowers, and a magnificent lake against the backdrop of snow-capped Swiss Alps.

Erika had long-standing plans to be away on holiday in the South of France, and she and I were both disappointed that we would miss each other. She graciously invited us to stay in her top-floor apartment. With exposed beams under a high, acutely-sloped roof, it had the feel of a cathedral. A long weekend there afforded us a beautiful setting to heal together before resuming our lives back home.

Upon our return, we were buoyed to learn that my mother's estate had finally been settled and the money dispersed. The agency that had funded my Living a Fearless Life program was no longer giving out grants for limited scope projects, and I could use money to continue to facilitate LFL at agencies that served at-risk women until I found another source.

I did not want too much time to pass since I'd seen clients in a clinical setting, so I took a part-time job as a pay-per-session therapist in a mental health facility serving mostly people on welfare. The working conditions were laughable. Treatment was government-subsidized, and clients had nothing to lose if they missed their appointments. Since we only got paid on completed sessions, wages were dismal. The paperwork was enormous. We were not compensated for necessary correspondence, nor were we allowed to take work home because of "confidentiality" issues. The place was a revolving door of highly qualified therapists. But I wanted the experience of helping clients with as many different disorders as I could, and this was the place to get it. I vowed to stick it out for six months, no matter what, and ended up staying one year.

Our anniversary blowout in Venice had a profound effect on me. That hurtful sense of abandonment, foreign to me until that point, had rocked me to my core, but I had recovered. Or so I thought. Almost two years had passed without incident.

I don't recall exactly when Frank's next eruption occurred or what precipitated it, none of which really matters. All I remember is that it was late at night and that the minute I saw it coming, I shut down. There were none of the usual appeals of trying to reason with him. There was no pleading for another perspective, no escalation in my voice, no demands that he acknowledge my hurt and apologize. As soon as he exploded, it simply came out. "It's over. I want out." Frank's reaction is a blur. I remember whizzing about, grabbing necessities, including the *Course*, and running up the stairs to find sanctuary in the third-floor guestroom. I tried reading about the "Holy Relationship," but nothing made sense. In desperation I asked the Holy Spirit for peace and promptly fell asleep.

The predominant feeling I had upon waking was one of relief. I felt no need to construct a mental pros and cons list of Frank's strengths and weaknesses. I was resolute, as if the decision had been made for me. I was not going to live with a time bomb a minute longer. The last straw had broken the camel's back. Love or no love, I felt a desperate need to be separate from him. I knew I would be taken care of. How Frank would fare was not my problem. Even before purchasing the Delancey property, I had told Frank that my commitment issues and fear of entrapment required that I have a piece of real estate in my name only. I was now beyond grateful for it. I went downstairs to face the music.

Frank was in the second floor sitting room, sunk into the sofa. "I can't tell you how sorry I am for putting you through this, Sophia," he said, covering his face with his hands. "I know you're gone. I've lost you."

He looked beat up. "I'm sorry, too," I said flatly. "I'm sorry for the life ahead of you if you don't let go of your imaginary perceptions of being wronged. I don't want to deal with it any longer." I told Frank that I was not ready for a divorce, only to be away from him. I asked him to find another place to stay while we worked out the logistics. He was adamant that if I wanted out, I should be the one to leave. I really didn't care who moved out. All four apartments at Delancey were rented, and the soonest one would become available would be in three months. The guest room would have to serve me until I figured something out.

Reactions from friends and relatives about the split ran the gamut, but all expressed shock. "Oh, poor Frank," was the common refrain, and although his being a good and honorable man was never questioned, my close friends who were privy to Frank's eruptions from the beginning wondered how I had put up with it for so long. While I processed the separation with them, Frank became solitary and moved about mechanically. David, our longtime therapist, had retired. Specifically seeking out a woman's perspective, Frank made an appointment with a new therapist.

A few days after the rupture of our relationship, I met with the bug exterminator at Delancey for the quarterly spraying. Exiting the building, I ran into Joan, whom I had met several years prior through a mutual friend. She lived with her husband, Daniel, a few blocks away. A stunning woman, tall and lithe, with perfectly tousled hair and an inimitable fashion sense, she came off as a model or a ballerina. Her laugh was infectious. Whenever I ran into Joan, she would be walking her dog, Chudley. We would stop to catch up, and one of us would inevitably end the conversation with, "We should get together and have dinner." We never did. It was Joan who suggested it this time.

"Well, let's!" I concurred.

"Great. Come over to my house," she said brightly, and we made a date.

Joan's stately four-story brownstone was on a corner and had a balcony facing the street, a rarity in the neighborhood. While waiting for her to answer the doorbell, I admired her postage stamp-sized English "garden," carefully planned and tended. Joan greeted me with a hearty giggle. She led me through a huge living room that could have come straight out of the pages of *Architectural Digest*. There were pots of orchids throughout and lots of serious art. Joan uncorked the wine I had brought, and we sat down at a very long dining table set with whimsical, coordinated place settings. As she served the grilled chicken salad, she informed me that she only ate organic.

I learned that she had lost Chudley and now had two cats, Fred, who neurotically darted about, and Guthrie, who had digestive issues and chronically threw up. It was hard to imagine that such a pet would be tolerated in an environment of this level of perfection, but it only made Joan even sweeter. After the initial chitchat, she told me that she and Daniel were divorcing; he had left her for another woman. How could he leave such a lovely creature? For whom? We talked for hours. I told her about my breakup with Frank and that I was looking for a temporary studio apartment.

"I'll be here for at least six months. Why not come and stay here?" Joan asked without hesitation. "I have a large extra bedroom on the fourth floor. Some of my things are stored in another room, but basically you can have the whole floor."

"Are you sure?" I asked to make sure that I had indeed won the lottery.

"Yes," Joan giggled. "I'd love to have the company."

"How much would you charge?"

"I go away a lot. When I visit my mother in Connecticut, I'm gone up to two weeks at a time. I would be grateful if you just fed the cats and watered the plants."

"I'm sorry, Joan," I said, suddenly feeling deflated. "I can't do cat puke." I had never had a pet, and I had my limits.

"No worries," she said cheerfully. "Just put a napkin over it, and my housekeeper will clean it up when she comes."

"But I still have to pay something—for the utilities." After Joan proposed a ridiculously low monthly rent, she took me on a house tour. Off the vast master bedroom, there were two walk-in closets across from each other that looked like high-end boutiques filled with designer clothes and accessories. Going from room to room, we reached the fourth floor and entered what would be my bedroom. Lacking the glossiness of the rest of the house with a mix of antiques, it had a simple charm to it. I felt instantly at home. I could move in that very weekend. How lucky!

Frank was having a hard time with the turn of events. On the one hand, he was relieved that I had found a secure and affordable place but was heartbroken at the prospect of being in our house alone. He announced that he was too glum to help me move. I had never planned on asking him. It wasn't as if I didn't love Frank or didn't feel sadness, but not having to walk on eggshells was liberating. Until now, I had not been aware of the intensity of the dread that had been subconsciously dragging me down.

The first thing that my friend Mary told me after I announced I was moving was to take the *Course* with me. "You don't know when you will need it." When things got tough, we took turns reminding each other of the book's abundant spiritual guidance. Mary had gotten back together with her boyfriend of two years and was in a completely different place. She and Stephen were planning to get married on their favorite beach on Maui in mid-December, seven months away. It was Mary's third marriage and the second time I would be her matron of honor. The reality of the separation with Frank hit me when I realized that I would be going to Hawaii alone.

I ferried my things over in separate trips to make the move less traumatic for Frank. I still couldn't believe my good fortune at the incredible timeliness of running into Joan and ending up in such a beautiful place that perfectly served my needs. It was auspicious for her, too. I became somewhat of an in-house confidant, and we would often process the difficulties the divorce was causing her. I got along better with Guthrie, the vomiting cat, than Fred with the personality disorder. When I had the house to myself, friends would come over to find several paper towels scattered about covering whatever had been emitted. The warmer the weather became, the more time I spent sitting out on the balcony. I was the princess in the tower.

Frank and I would check in on the phone about housekeeping, work, tenant issues, or what came up for Frank in therapy. Every other Sunday he would pick me up, and we would go to church together. In early October, Joan threw herself a birthday party, and I invited Frank. As with all of her soirees, it was a grand affair. Everyone came in evening clothes with Joan stealing the spotlight in a fabulous champagne, floor-length gown. Frank came in a Hawaiian shirt. As the night progressed, he became visibly angrier, like a shaken soda bottle ready to blow its top. I felt the familiar fear grip me and walked over to him to find out what was wrong. He barked. I lost it. I took him outside, sent him home, and told him that I wanted no further contact. The next morning, I asked Joan for her divorce attorney's phone number.

About a week after Joan's party, I woke up one morning feeling terrific. I was so glad to be rid of that jerk! It had been five months since moving into Joan's house, and I had not once read from the *Course*. Each chapter was a couple of pages, and my rule was to read to the end, even if the content brought me discomfort. Feeling light as a feather and free as a bird, I was ready to glean some wisdom about my next life phase. There was nothing I could possibly read that I couldn't handle. I got up and brought the book back to bed with me. Cozily nestled in the covers, I randomly opened it. The title at the top of the page read, "The Healed Relationship." No! But, I had to stay true to my vow and continue reading. I mentally contested the first paragraph. The second one was an apt rebuttal to my argument. I was having a debate with a book! The message I received was that God is in all of us, and if your brother comes to you with his hand outstretched to make contact and you say no to your brother, you are saying no to God. The book won. If Frank called me, I had to talk to him.

Incredibly, Frank called the next day to ask if we could meet in person. How could I say no to God? I agreed, but only if we read from the *Course* together. Joan was away, and I invited him to come over the following Tuesday evening. The Sunday before, my friend Alice had visited me. It was unseasonably warm. Knowing that once I made a decision it was immutable, she wanted me to read to her what had changed my mind. It was about two in the afternoon. For the next hour we marveled at how relevant its counsel was. I knew what Alice meant when she said, "I feel the Holy Spirit all around us."

I was not looking forward to seeing Frank. When I heard the doorbell, I said a little prayer, asked for help, and felt an instant sense of relief. Something bigger than me had my back. I opened the door, and Frank handed me a bouquet of flowers. He was quiet and reserved. I led him into the dining room because I wanted a table between us. I was determined to remain civil, but as soon as we sat down, I stood back up and, pointing a finger at him, said, "I just want you to know that the only reason you are sitting in front of me is because of a miracle." There was nothing Frank could say that could possibly redeem himself.

Frank replied in a soft, matter-of-fact voice, "Well, I have a miracle for you, too."

This was not part of Frank's lingo. "All right," I said as I sat back down, "you go first." He had my full attention.

"I was replacing the pump in the fountain on Sunday when the column part slipped and fell on my hand," he said this as he gestured at his right hand where he wore his wedding band in the Greek Orthodox tradition. I stared at the top of his hand in disbelief as he twisted the ring off his finger. The concrete column that spewed out the water was extremely heavy. If what he said was true, his hand should look like raw hamburger. Instead, there was only a bruise with a slight scratch. "This is what took the brunt of the weight." He held up the ring, now a bent oval, adding, "And I'm not going to fix it."

His wedding ring saved him? I was disarmed to the core. I had to ask, "What time on Sunday did it happen?"

"About two in the afternoon," he replied.

"That was exactly the time Alice and I were reading from the *Course*," I said amazed, and I told him about the chapter I had resisted reading.

"You told me that you wanted to read from the *Course* together. Can we read that one?" he asked. Another first. Frank had never asked me to read from the *Course* before.

I pointed to "The Healed Relationship" and began reading. We both marveled at the relevance of the teaching—how it applied to our turmoil, to our respective fears, and how love has the power to overcome everything. The effect it had on us was the same as it was when Alice and I read it together—a presence of holiness. All of my resentments, bitterness, and defenses that I had brought to the table had vanished. Frank appeared utterly serene. With my eyes affixed on the deformed wedding ring on the table, I felt at peace. He asked me to have dinner with him that Saturday evening, and I accepted.

Frank and I began to see each other again. The separation had been necessary for both of us. Being together now felt different, as if we had entered another level. After about three weeks of meeting and talking on the phone, he asked me to move back home. I agreed. Our relationship had always been built on love, but this new foundation was devoid of the toxicity of underlying fear. Joan had found an apartment and was moving the following month. The timing, again, was incredible. There was a sense that a will beyond ours was pulling the strings. I trusted Frank enough to ask him to accompany me to Maui for Mary's wedding. Hawaii in the middle of December would be the perfect setting for a warm, sunny, fresh, new start.

Everything fell into a new normal at home. Frank had done a lot of soul-searching in therapy. This time he had realized that my leaving had dredged up what he had experienced when his first wife had left him, and he had redirected that anger at me. There were nanoseconds when the familiar, irksome fear would rise up in me of potentially another trip ruined. I staunchly made up my mind that, whenever anxiety crept in, I would turn to faith that our tropical Maui getaway was going to catapult us to a place of harmony and trust.

The cab we had ordered to take us to the airport arrived promptly at 5:30 a.m. As soon as Frank and I got in, I realized that I had forgotten to bring reading material for the fourteen-hour trip. I jumped out, ran into the house, and bolted up the stairs to the bookcases in the sitting room. On one of the shelves, there were seven books I had started reading but had not finished. I arbitrarily picked one and bounded back down, out, and into the waiting cab. I was immediately disappointed. Why didn't I pick a novel? The book was titled *Endless Energy* by Dr. Debra Greene, a kinesiologist. Her approach to healing body/mind/spirit on an energetic level had piqued my interest, but it was not a book to take to the beach.

On the plane, after reading the newspaper and doing all of the puzzles, I picked up and began perusing my book. I became progressively more fascinated with the content, especially with the one-on-one "energy clearing" sessions the author had developed. She claimed that the clearings healed deep-seated trauma by quickly getting to the core of one's energy imbalances, facilitating lasting improvement. What most intrigued me was that, despite that Greene was a scientist who studied what is seen and measured, she was writing about things that were ephemeral. When I would come across something particularly compelling, such as, "prayer works," I'd go to the back of the book to find the source. Flipping back and forth, I came across a page with the author's address and phone number. She lived in Maui on Kihei Road. Our condo was on Kihei Road! I was dumbfounded. We could have been going in any direction, and here we were making a beeline to her front door!

During our layover in San Francisco, I called Dr. Greene, and she answered. I told her about the wild synchronicity and inquired about the individual energy clearing sessions. She told me they were two hours each. I gave her times of our availability, and yes, she could accommodate both of us. It certainly wouldn't hurt to have energy overhauls. I told Dr. Greene that I would get back to her.

After I had explained to Frank my understanding of an energy clearing, I pointed to the address in the book. "Frank, the author lives in Maui. Look, Kihei Road, can you believe it?"

It was Frank's turn to be bowled over. He let out a drawn-out, "Wow."

"I called her when we were in San Francisco to see if both of us could have a session with her, and she can do it." I tried not to hold my breath. "If you say yes, it'll be your Christmas present."

"It looks like it was meant to be," he replied. I was not expecting Frank, a dyed-in-the-wool skeptic, to go for it. This was not the same man I had married.

The wedding ceremony on the beach was to begin at 4:44 p.m., a number Mary believed to indicate angelic presence. When she appeared on her son's arm in a long, cream, silk sheath, she looked like a mesmerizing lit candle. The backdrop beyond the palm trees was a shimmering aquamarine ocean stretching to the horizon. The minister's words delivered to the couple were right out of *A Course in Miracles*. They could not have been more meaningful or relevant to Frank and me—striving for a holy relationship based on the Holy Spirit rather than a special relationship driven by the ego. He said that if the relationship becomes broken, it takes just one person to reach out with love, void of ego, and the Holy Spirit will heal the relationship. That is exactly what had happened to us. I had given up. It was Frank who had come forward to reach out to me, and the Holy Spirit did its work. It took his wedding band miraculously saving his hand to render my ego powerless and humble me. The ring now was a tangible souvenir to remind Frank of the power of God on a daily basis.

The wedding festivities spanned three days, including a day of snorkeling on the island of Lanai, ziplining over lush terrain, and visiting Maui's tropical gardens. Our energy clearings had been scheduled to take place in Dr. Greene's home. We arrived to find a vintage A-frame amidst exotic flowers and fruit-laden trees. Tall, with waist-long hair plaited into a braid, she greeted us with enthusiasm, and I could see Frank's skepticism was put at ease. She asked us to call her Debra.

This was uncharted territory for both Frank and me. I went first. Debra led me into her office and lost no time getting started. After first obtaining general information, she began asking questions and muscle testing without waiting for me to answer. It was my outstretched arm that provided the answers, depending on whether my muscles resisted with strength or collapsed in weakness. Since trauma is impressed in muscles on a cellular level,

Debra was able to pinpoint a traumatic experience I had when I was six years old and had swept under the rug for years. For two, solid hours she bounced back and forth between my responses and consulting an extremely thick binder. The process was fascinating, and her analysis was spot on. At the end she gave me homework. I was to meditate on particular geometric forms while reciting a specific mantra. I wondered about Frank's reaction.

Debra led me out to the waiting area and gestured Frank to follow her. I decided to take the car and drive around in case he attempted to flee. When I returned two hours later, Frank had yet to come out. This was a good sign. I waited in the airy, open space expecting him to emerge rolling his eyes. After more than a half hour, Debra and Frank appeared and embraced. Frank was blinking wildly as if having being holed up in the dark and had just been exposed to a bright light. "How was it for you?" I asked him as we headed toward the car.

"There's something to this," Frank answered as he continued blinking.

"So, what happened?"

"I don't know." Finally looking at me, he mumbled, "I need some time to think about it." He was obviously processing something big.

It wasn't until after we had returned home that Frank was ready to talk. He hadn't realized how much resentment he had internalized growing up with a large, beefy father who related more to his equally hulking football player older son than to Frank, a slight child who drew pictures of buildings. For a man of little affect, Frank was emoting from the gut. He spoke about how he had felt like an outsider, how his brother getting a send-off party before entering the United States Naval Academy while Frank did not get one before going off to the Cooper Union had deeply affected him, and how much guilt he carried for the deaths of both his brother and his father. "This is where feeling 'less than' comes from. I can't explain it," he said, shaking his head, "but I feel like I can let it all go."

I was buoyed to hear Frank express his newfound awareness. I knew all of this. We had discussed it many times. Something had happened during that energy clearing for him to express true understanding of the muck he had been carrying all of his life and allow him to release it. I had not a speck of doubt that Frank had experienced healing. A great weight lifted off of me. An inner knowing assured me that I never had to tiptoe through a minefield again. "I am so happy for you," I said, embracing him. Our energy fields meshed as if we were one, and one with the entire Universe, floating in perfect peace. Any fear I was carrying from the past had evaporated. Never before had I felt this level of unconditional trust and forgiveness with Frank. I finally understood what a holy relationship truly meant.

"I feel peaceful," Frank said as we let go of each other. He had felt the same thing.

"Did she give you homework?" he asked.

"Yes."

"What do you have to do?"

I told him about the mantra I had to recite while imagining geometric forms, once a day for eight days.

"I guess I have more catching up to do than you," he said smirking. "I have to do mine twice a day for twenty-eight days."

What had transpired in a little over six months was truly miraculous. It started with running into Joan and getting together for dinner, something we had put off for years. It happened at the exact time I needed to leave Frank, with no place to go. Inexplicably, my friendship with Joan subsequently vaporized and she moved away. Regardless, I would be forever indebted to her for what she had provided me at a time of need. It brought Rob to mind, the man I had met when I was nineteen. While in the midst of struggling with existential angst, he appeared, interpreted my confounding dream, and in a matter of a few months, helped me resolve my issues. Then he was gone, leaving me with an entirely new perspective. In each case, like an angel, a fellow human traveler showed up at just the right moment, helped me, and then vanished. Sometimes, that's just how the Universe works.

Regardless of how strong and stubborn my will was to divorce Frank, God wasn't having any of it. I had lived with emotional abuse and had multiple valid reasons to leave him, and once again, *A Course in Miracles* had presented itself, this time in a chapter titled "The Healed Relationship," with which I had a mental dialogue. Frank's hand was saved by, of all things, his wedding band, and this is exactly what I needed to hear to soften my heart and open my mind. It also provided him with what he needed, a constant reminder that miracles can happen to him, too.

A synergetic chain of events helped me put my ego aside and align myself with God's will so that both Frank and I could be healed. I was on a plane reading *Endless Energy*, a book that I had grabbed in a rush, only to discover that its author just happened to live at our destination, and who was available to help lift the muck that traumas had embedded in our bodies.

No longer did miracles resulting from "coincidence" leave me awe-struck. I had it figured out—I now knew my part. I had taken action. For me, these coincidences were not chance occurrences but directly communicated to me by an omnipresent, omnipotent, omniscient force, Universal Consciousness, God, with whom I had developed a personal relationship, and whom I trusted with all of my heart. Without a trace of doubt in my mind, I knew that, as long as I act on the coincidences, I would continue to experience the miraculous—the apt career, the right job, the ideal house, the healed relationship—without any worries as to what to say or what to do. I knew that I would be taken care of for as long as I lived on Earth, my heaven. And there is nothing more to say, over and over again, but thank you, God. My unadulterated faith says it's so.

CHAPTER 17

The Big One

I t had been over a year since Frank and I had gotten back together.
The shift in our dynamics had healed our relationship at the core. The
perceived attacks ceased. His fight or flight reflex was transplanted with an
ability to not take things personally. If he did, he caught himself. He apologized in a timely manner. The *Course*'s influence, the crunched wedding
band memento, and the energy clearing by Dr. Debra Greene, all had
contributed to Frank finding his self-confidence. When I had first met him
at the gym, I had wishfully projected onto him the characteristics I sought
in a man—confidence and quiet strength. Now he was that man. Letting
go of my fear and letting down my guard had elevated his self-assurance.
I had drawn boundaries; he did the work. A few miracles helped us along.
Finally, I had my dream guy. We were entering 2011, and what a way to
start my sixth decade on the planet!

In the past, a period of self-reflection preceded each approaching birthday, while decade markers required deeper introspection. Surprisingly, the
big "six-oh" did not instill in me any desire to go off somewhere alone and
reflect. Without the dread of a potential eruption, I was looking forward

to celebrating with Frank, and I didn't care where. I hadn't given it any thought.

Frank surprised me on Valentine's Day with an attempt at recreating the first dinner he had made for me, which had worked in reeling me in. He poured a well-aged French Bordeaux and made a toast, comparing it to our evolved relationship, which had also improved with time and effort. We clicked glasses, and Frank asked what I wanted to do for my sixtieth birthday in October.

The query provoked a bizarre reaction. Suddenly, I visualized myself on my deathbed lamenting not having seen the pyramids of Giza, the Hagia Sophia in Istanbul, the Taj Mahal in Agra, and not having walked the Via Dolorosa where Jesus is believed to have carried the cross on the way to his crucifixion at Golgotha. "Frank, there are things I want to see in the world before I die." I told him of my vision. "October would be a perfect time— we'd be avoiding the throngs of tourists and summer heat."

"Let's do it," he said as he raised his glass, and we clicked again.

Several years earlier, I had had a reading by Dianne Lawson, an astrologer for whom I had great regard. Everything she said rang true until she told me that my approaching Saturn return would present me with an opportunity to write a successful book. I had zero inclination to hole myself up somewhere with no particular topic to write about. "That's not in the cards, Dianne," I had said with certainty.

Dianne dug in her heels. She described the powerful attributes of this cyclical phase then paused to consult the chart. "I see you writing a book and having tremendous success."

"But I don't want to write a book," I contested.

"You will be successful doing whatever you want," she retorted.

"Then, why can't I do something else? I would love to have my own TV talk show and interview interesting non-famous people."

"Why not?" was Dianne's quick comeback.

"Really? I can just walk into a TV studio and say, 'Hi, my name is Sophia Demas, and I want my own talk show?'"

"What were you doing when you were twenty-eight years old?" she asked pointedly.

"That was one of the best periods of my life," I said, recalling the fortuitous events that precipitated my move from Portland to Philadelphia. "It was right after I graduated from architecture school and went to work for Buckminster Fuller."

"You told me that he was your hero for years before you met him, right?" asked Dianne. "If someone had told you that you would meet him and work with him, would you have believed them?"

"Absolutely not."

"But you did, didn't you?" she asked, building her case. "That's what I'm talking about—the winds are in your favor."

"Thank you, Dianne. I'll keep it in mind," I said, thinking how off-base she was with the book idea. She couldn't be right about everything. She did, however, have a point. How everything had come together, culminating with me working with Bucky was undeniably incredible.

A few months after Dianne had interpreted my chart, my friend Virginia asked me if I would accompany her to a consultation with Vickie Gay, an internationally-renowned medium and "lightworker" from the West Coast. She was headlining the annual Body Mind Spirit Expo the following month in New Jersey. Virginia wanted answers about her mother's untimely and mysterious death, and she wasn't going to leave any stone unturned. I said yes—I had always been fascinated with mediums.

Just days before the expo, I suddenly felt a strong urge to have my own session with Vickie Gay. It didn't make sense because I had nothing I wanted to ask. I couldn't shake the desire, so I looked her up. She had been hired by the FBI to find missing people and bodies. Intrigued, I called her and explained that I did not want to disturb my dead friends and relatives, but I wanted to have a session out of curiosity. She was personable and direct. Vickie told me that spirits do not necessarily show up just because one asks. She had been completely booked for some time, but just that morning, the person whose timeslot followed Virginia's had miraculously called to cancel. She said, "It looks as if you've been invited." I made the appointment without a second thought.

Vickie had thick, blonde hair that cascaded down below her waist. The way the process worked, she explained, was that it was going to be a three-way—Vickie, me, and Spirit, who would act as Vickie's intermediary between her and the other spirits. She asked me to first visualize a ring of light around me as she called for my protection, which made me nervous. As I silently questioned what I had gotten myself into, she gestured with her hands. "Walls, walls—you are putting up walls." She then launched into a prayer beseeching only the purest spirits to join our session. I relaxed a bit. Vickie said that Spirit had come through right away. She marveled at the number of other spirits that had shown up.

"There is a spirit next to me nudging me, but the message is for you. There is also a spirit kneeling next to you smiling, eagerly urging you to do something." Vickie paused, then went back and forth between looking at me and glancing just past my left ear as she related what she was seeing and what Spirit was telling her in clipped sentences. "Yes. You have your glasses on. You are at your computer. You are writing. It's not spell check. It's more like you are editing. You are intently trying to express what you mean. You are writing a book. You are writing *your* book." I told her what I had told the astrologer, that it was just not going to happen. "Spirit says," she continued without missing a beat, "when she's ready, there are many spirits here to help her, and many hands on Earth." Not only earthlings were insisting that I write a book; now spirits were doing so as well!

Virginia's experience with Vickie was more spot on and credible. Vickie had provided her with answers. How could she have given her such apt advice without knowing the circumstances? When Virginia asked me how my session went, I told her that I felt as if I had taken a hundred-dollar bill and flushed it down the toilet. I had to admit, however, that it was quite peculiar that both Vickie and Dianne, coming from completely different milieus, had told me the same thing.

A few weeks after Valentine's Day, when Frank and I had decided on the bucket list trip, I was on the phone with a childhood friend with whom I had lost contact for more than thirty years. We were catching up on our lives, and I told her about my separation from Frank and the serendipitous events that had brought us back together. After I had described how Frank's wedding ring had saved his hand from being crushed, Rita laughingly said what people had been telling me most of my life and which I had shrugged off: "These things only happen to you!" This time, the comment resonated with a ring of truth. I felt a cosmic boot kick my stomach. Although the wedding ring miracle was a key part of the story, it had happened to Frank, not me. Inexplicable, fortuitous occurrences do happen to people. They happened to me, however, over and over again. It was befuddling.

My inner voice was screaming for clarity. I called upon the Holy Spirit for help. Swiftly, I recalled that monumental dream I had had at the age of nineteen that I thought was predicting my death. It had sent me into the arms of a young man whom I had just met, whose wisdom helped me alter my perception of the world and who disappeared as suddenly as he had surfaced. It was not just the string of coincidences and timing that were in-credible. The miraculous part was the result—I was changed for the better. That experience had made me begin paying attention.

That was it—awareness! One *aha!* followed another in quick succession. From a young age, I had begun to understand that synchronicities, which provided me with exactly what I needed, were more than coincidences. What I had not figured out then was how action, intention, and emotion factored in to create space for the miracle to occur. Experiences that had presented me with the best possible outcomes flashed through my head like streaming video snippets. Some of the miracles had happened because I had prayed for them, some had occurred as a result of not having my prayers answered, some had materialized right after expressing deep gratitude, and some as a result of becoming aware of a coincidence. When I had taken action to express my intention through prayer or gratitude, it was in conjunction with a strong emotion emanating from the heart. When a coincidence was brought into my awareness, again I took action with intention and emotion. There was another factor that was key, but I couldn't put my finger on it. I thanked the Holy Spirit with all my heart for guiding me to what was best. Immediately, I became aware of my faith. I had been having a personal relationship with God for a long time without even knowing it. I was now given the key—coincidence, action with intention, emotion, and unshakable faith were the components that had worked so well for me, the components that had manifested my miracles!

If my system rewarded me so well, why couldn't it also serve my fellow humans or inspire them to develop their own? The desire to share my spiritual toolbox with others was overwhelming. It was as if something was directing me. In that instant, the notion of writing a book, which I had so vehemently resisted before, now seemed the most natural thing in the world to do.

Deciding to write a book and writing it are two different things. Driven, I dove in. Not having a clue about how to start, I chose to write a prologue. Though I had heard that it is best written after the book is finished, I regarded it as a means to formulate an outline. Soon, I was flailing. It was as if I had plunged into the deep sea knowing only how to tread water. My excitement turned into anxiety. I found myself directionless, preferring to run an errand or scrub the toilet rather than face the computer. Desperate, I went to church and lit two candles, one to the Virgin Mary and one to my mother, asking for their intercession.

Soon thereafter, I received the first of many divine signs that I was on the right track. I began to question the prologue approach. Ideas bounced around in my head, but they didn't correlate to one another. I was stuck. Walking down Chestnut Street one day, lost in thought as I tried to prioritize what I needed to express, doubt reared its ugly, little head. I'm not an author. Why would someone want to read my book? There are many bona fide authors whose books are rejected, so why would mine get published? As I digressed in a downward spiral, my father's favorite refrain, which he would throw out whenever I brought up something that he deemed frivolous, jumped out at me. "Who do you think you are?" I closed my eyes and ranted silent gibberish in an attempt to erase the intrusive thought. *No, I am going to do this*, I thought resolutely. "God, I know I'm supposed to write this book." And, raising my hand as if swearing on a Bible, looking up at the sky, I added, "But I need a little sign."

Just then I was walking by the Whodunit Bookstore, a Philadelphia institution whose owner had a passion for books. On fair-weather days, a folding table on the sidewalk was piled with an eclectic assortment of used books where one might find anything from how to create a terrarium to a biography on Ringo Starr. Now and then I would stop by to look over the selection, but I had never found a book to buy. To distract myself, I walked over to the table for a cursory glance. Scanning the titles, my eyes landed on *When God Winks at You: How God Speaks Directly to You Through the Power of Miracles* by Squire Rushnell. Really? The title was no coincidence. I paid the three dollars and, walking home, thanked God for the immediate response.

Once home, as soon as I began reading, my expectation of being spellbound quickly dimmed. The true stories, some more compelling than others, were of the feel-good, heart-tugging variety. I was looking for Earth-shattering. One nice, little, short story after another left me flat. That's nice. Nice outcome. Nice, but was it really worth turning this into a whole chapter? *I can write better than this*, I thought. When I came upon the last story, after having read the first half of the first page, I froze. It was as if the Universe, having had enough of my cavalier judging, zapped me with a lightning bolt. It was grippingly cinematic. In this true story, a series of co-incidences resulted in the most beautiful act of forgiveness I had ever heard. I read, sobbed, and savored. Reaching the end, I clutched the book to my chest thinking, *God, it doesn't get better than this!* Once again, God had wasted no time in letting me know that I was wrong. On the next page, the book ended with a short piece entitled, "The Clarity of Quests." With my heart wide open, I began reading instructions that appeared to be addressed to me. When I had experienced self-doubt that day, I had asked for a sign. The words could not have been more germane. They assured me that I would attain my goal and resonated my mother's regular sign-off—"Keep putting one foot in front of the other." I made it my directive and taped a copy of it on my office wall.

My mentor, Fr. Stephen, was coming over for coffee the next day, and I couldn't wait to tell him about my *godwink* experience and discuss my writing issues. Next to President Jimmy Carter (who shares his initials with Jesus Christ), Fr. Stephen was the person most like Jesus I had ever met. Over lunch several years earlier, my friend Voula stopped midsentence and, beaming like a light bulb, blurted, "You and Father Stephen have to meet." Fr. Stephen, she explained, was not only an Albanian Orthodox priest with a small parish in Northeast Philadelphia, he spearheaded shelters for Covenant House, an organization that housed homeless youth. She spoke of him as if he were a magician or a saint as she jotted down his contact information.

Connecting with Fr. Stephen was not easy. I waited weeks to hear back from him. When he finally did call, his voice was exuberant, as if he had just found his long-lost cousin. Upon meeting at a Starbucks, his eyes twin-kled as he greeted me. "Hi, cuz!" That day, Fr. Stephen became more than a friend—he became the mentor and confessor I had yearned for. During our regular bi-monthly *kaffee klatsches*, we would discuss God, faith, love, death, life, quantum physics, and, my favorite topic, human behavior. He was not your ordinary person. He dedicated his life to getting kids away from the "bad guys." Sometimes, when there was a crisis, he would dip into his own pocket to pay for bus fare or a hotel room. Fr. Stephen gave to all the kids what they craved most—love. Frank and I began attending Fr. Stephen's church. The only word I can summon to describe what I felt there during the liturgy is "holy." I became convinced that Fr. Stephen could read minds. He would go up to friends and family members I brought to church and tell them something personal and specific they needed to hear, which made it look as if I had disclosed their intimate secret. I had no doubt that he had a direct line to heaven.

Fr. Stephen had told me about a Turkish girl who had ended up at the shelter in Atlantic City. He was taking her to get her cap and gown for her high school graduation and asked if he could bring her along to our coffee. Of course! I would do anything for Fr. Stephen.

It was warm and sparkly out—a perfect day to sit in the garden. I set the table under the wisteria for coffee and pastries. Fr. Stephen arrived with a stunning young woman. Her name was Hayal. She had luxuriously thick, dark brown hair cascading over her shoulders, doe eyes, and a dazzling smile. Wearing a lovely pinstriped sundress and espadrilles, she could hardly contain her excitement about her cap and gown. I made her put them on and took pictures. Fr. Stephen proudly stated that she had been accepted at Stockton University and that she was waiting to hear back from Chestnut Hill College, her first choice. My curiosity was piqued.

Sitting down with our coffee, I learned that Hayal had progressed from the shelter to the Right of Passage facility, where kids who had found jobs could have their own apartment until they were financially able to live independently. She had just turned nineteen and was working at two stores in the outlet mall.

I began by asking the most obvious question—what had brought her to the United States? Hayal's English needed polishing, but she was extremely articulate. She told me that her biological mother, who had abandoned her when she was three, lived with her husband in New Jersey. Out of the blue, her mother started beseeching Hayal to come to live with them, promising her a dream education. At first, Hayal wanted nothing to do with her. Her unhappy circumstances, however, ultimately forced her to accept her mother's offer. After coming to the States a year and a half prior, she had found her mother to be mentally unstable. Three weeks after Hayal's arrival, her mother changed her mind. She bought Hayal a ticket back to Turkey, took her cell phone and green card, drove her to the airport, and dropped her off, abandoning her yet again. I overcame my speechlessness to ask, "Then what happened?" Fr. Stephen looked at his watch, slapped his hand on the table, and stood up, saying, "I've got an errand to run. I'll see you back here in an hour and fifteen minutes."

Hayal matter-of-factly explained that, while waiting for her plane's departure, she questioned with whom in Turkey she would feel safe enough to live. In a snap decision, she borrowed someone's cell phone and called one of her two half-brothers, whose existence she had learned of only after arriving in the United States. A serial abandoner, her mother had also left her first husband and her three- and four-year-old little boys before marrying Hayal's father. She had recently brought over her now grown sons to live with her, but they had moved into their own apartment. Incredibly, this woman had collected her children to create a fantasy family she was incapable of dealing with. "And then what?" I kept repeating,

While Fr. Stephen was gone, Hayal told her story of systematic abandonment and abuse that was too extreme for one person to have experienced at such a tender age. We were still at it when Fr. Stephen returned. I felt like a cement truck churning with mixed emotions of horror and admiration for her. My mind was stuck on the logistics. If she was accepted to

Chestnut Hill College, the more than hour-long commute to Atlantic City would be a hardship. We had turned our third floor into a guest suite. She could stay with us! Interrupting my daydream, Fr. Stephen announced that it was time to go. I walked them to the gate, and Hayal thanked me profusely. I felt love for her. After I congratulated her and kissed her goodbye, she said, "I really hope to see you again."

Now I just had to break my game plan to Frank. After he came home from work and complained of a stressful day, I poured him a generous vodka on the rocks. "Frank, remember that pamphlet you showed me about taking in a Chinese student?"

"Yeah," he answered, surprised. "What do you think?"

"I have a better idea." I told him about my visit with Fr. Stephen and Hayal.

"Let's consider it," Frank responded without hesitation.

"How about we take her out to dinner for her graduation and then discuss it," I suggested. I was elated. Frank had given me the green light.

We took Hayal out to a Turkish restaurant where she swooned over İskender kebab, a favorite spiced lamb dish. After toasting her graduation, she told us that she had been accepted to Chestnut Hill and that more than half of her tuition and room and board would be covered by grants. It took just one look between Frank and me to seal the deal. After she was convinced of our sincerity, her big, brown eyes sparkled, conveying her delight even before she could speak. We toasted again. I felt unexpected utter joy. We told her of our planned trip in the fall and that she could come to stay at the house whenever she felt like getting away. We would move her in the following weekend. I couldn't wait to tell Fr. Stephen! I wondered if he had planned the whole thing.

Fr. Stephen, jubilant at the fortuitous connection and our decision, gave all the credit to God. I secretly knew that my mother had something to do with it, too. Poised, gracious, and studious, Hayal was the daughter my mother had always wanted. She transitioned into our home seamlessly, as if she had belonged there all along. My friends didn't know what to make of it. Reactions ranged from amazement and joy to warnings that possibly a shrewd conniver was plotting to take advantage of us. I began to refer to her as my daughter. This did not fail to elicit blank looks.

Hayal possessed an innate sophistication and insisted on developing financial independence. She was hired by Coach, the leather goods store, and soon went on to become one of their top salespeople. Hours of talks over coffee yielded more insight into a young life that had suffered because her biological parents hated one another to such an extent that they loathed her for reminding them of each other. How can a person at her age possess such dignity and sense of self despite repeated abuse? How could love like this unfold between strangers? What did I do to deserve this joy? I would ask Fr. Stephen, and he would just chuckle.

After meeting with various professors, Hayal decided to major in molecular biology with a minor in philosophy. She wanted to become a doctor. I worried that her less-than-perfect English would put her at a disadvantage. I worried about her emotional well-being. I worried about her coming home safely. I felt a strong need to protect her and give her a home and the normalcy she craved in contrast to her friends who couldn't wait to fly the coop. Knowing she had lacked healthy male role models, Frank held back from being physically affectionate with her, waiting to first gain her trust. He was at the sink washing a pot one day when Hayal came up from behind him and gave him a warm hug. With that, she had given him permission to express his love, too. Soon, Frank and I were actively parenting.

As soon as Hayal's request for a single dorm room was approved, we went into decorating mode. Frank and I were planning on going on a major trip, not on sending a kid to college. We would have to be more financially aware. To save money, we got creative. We scoured Ikea and Craigslist. Hayal was thrilled with the results, all for under $250. For years, I had watched many of my friends having mixed emotions as they got their kids ready for college—excitement, pride, and the poignancy of a mother bird nudging her young from the nest to teach them how to fly. It was a significant role that I had never expected to experience, yet here I was doing just that. People would say to me, "You are doing such good by taking her in. Hayal is so lucky." To which I would respond, "No, I am the lucky one." With Hayal happily entrenched in college life and me having started writing a book, I couldn't wait to go on our trip.

Frank and I began our trek in Turkey. I had dreamed of visiting Hagia Sophia in Istanbul ever since I was in third grade in Greece when my teacher related a legend about the inception of its design. Emperor Constantine had commissioned the Christian church to be built in 360 CE, and amongst its many reincarnations since, it was converted into a mosque in 1453 by the Ottomans. In 1935, Turkish president Mustafa Kemal Ataturk turned it into a museum. On the day of my sixtieth birthday, my lifelong wish came true as I entered the splendor of this Byzantine architectural masterpiece. Atop a vast column-free expanse floated a majestic dome, through which light poured in and made the mosaics glitter. It evoked the spiritual. This mystical place and I shared the same name, and I felt as if it had been inviting me since childhood. I stood there and wept. Frank silently put his arm around me, allowing me to have my moment alone. For an instant, I imagined it reverted to its original and rightful function as a Christian church, but eons of time and history had rendered the notion virtually impossible.

We took a one-day trip by plane to the ancient city of Ephesus. Its notably preserved ruins brought the glory that was Greece back to life. There was the ancient amphitheater where St. Paul had spread the news of Jesus. St. John, the apostle, had built a church where the first Christians were baptized, but only the floor had survived. He had brought the Virgin Mary there after Christ's crucifixion and had built her a little house on Mt. Koressos near

Ephesus. It became the highlight of our visit. Sister Anne Catherine Emmerich, a German nun who had been confined to her bed for many years, claimed to have had visions of the Virgin Mary, who had described to her the layout of the house and its location. The nun had drawn a diagram of it. After her death in the early nineteenth century, two German priests who were also scholars set out with the nun's diagram and discovered the house. What was most remarkable to me was the reverence it elicited. People of different ethnicities and religions milled about outside, talking and laughing. As they got in line to enter, they became silent, and many were in tears as the line made its way through the house and out the back.

After a four-day stop in Greece to see my relatives, we flew to Mumbai for a one-month tour of India that would take us from coast to coast, across the northern part of the country. Our indoctrination began with a ten-day visit with our dear friends, Pushpa and Scott, who lived in Shillong, Meghalaya, in the Northeast near the Bangladesh border. Not once did we dine in a restaurant. Every meal was a spread of aromatic dishes and local specialties delectably prepared by Pushpa and her cook. Shillong, an intriguing mix of tribal traditions, religions, and remnants of colonial times, offered a variety of cross-cultural events and festivals. The Shillong Chamber Choir, winners of the *2010 India's Got Talent* competition, performed a concert with the Vienna Chamber Orchestra!

The extreme northeast of India is inhabited by tribes that are an exotic mix of Asian, Indian, and Caucasian (thanks to the colonists). Most of the tribespeople speak English and are Christian. The Khasis, natives of Meghalaya, where the highest rainfall in the world is recorded in Cherrapunji, have for generations been a matrilineal society. In the nearby lush, mountainous countryside of Nagaland near the border of Myanmar, the Nagas worked in stepped rice paddies, dressed in colorful traditional garb. It all took our breath away. By allowing us to be immersed in their daily lives, our friends' gracious hospitality gave us the priceless opportunity to experience daily life in India.

Pushpa joined us on the train, acting as our guide for part of the trip. She took us to Khaziranga National Park in Assam, where we took a Jeep amidst wild animals, photographed rare one-horned rhinos, and rode elephants. My highlight was bonding and playing with a baby elephant as he followed me around. In Kolkata we visited Mother Teresa's tomb in the modest building that housed the headquarters of the Missionaries of Charity she had founded. Nothing exemplified her essence more powerfully than her small, simple room with only a bed, table, bench, and her files, where she had slept, worked, and prayed for close to fifty years.

Our next destination was Mirzapur to visit Pushpa's good friend Edward, who had taken over his father's vast carpet manufacturing company. He lived on a compound in a large villa that boasted every state-of-the-art amenity, near the original colonial house he kept as a guesthouse, which was our home base for five nights. In the evenings, he held court, and his sharp wit and booming laugh were as grand as his hospitality. Edward's driver took us on day trips. We visited Sarnath, one of Buddhism's holiest sites, to see the sacred Dhamekha Stupa in Deer Park, where Buddha gave his first sermon after achieving enlightenment. It is here that he proclaimed, "I have found the Middle Way," and where he gathered his first disciples. In nearby Varanasi we went down the Ganges in a rowboat to the Manikarnika Ghat, where cremations are carried out 24/7. Hindus aspire to die in this holy place so that they may attain Moksha, being spared reincarnation and going straight to heaven. I experienced a visceral connection with the mourners in their grief, a universal emotion and part of the human experience.

The time came to part with our priceless asset, Pushpa's company, and go it alone. Frank and I headed to the Monkey Temple in Jaipur, a mountainous locale where abandoned buildings were overrun with monkeys considered sacred, and where we received blessings from Hindi priests. Then on to Jaipur Jantar Mantar, a fantastical astronomical observation site built in the eighteenth century. Of course, a trip to India is not complete without seeing the indescribably beautiful Taj Mahal in Agra. It was love that motivated Emperor Shah Jahan to build it to memorialize his third wife of seventeen years, who died while giving birth to their fourteenth child in 1631.

The magnificent city of Udaipur in Rajasthan, called "Venice of the East," is known for its lakes and palaces. From far away it looks like white lace. We toured the vast City Palace as it was being decorated for a wedding with endless yards of purple and saffron silk and bouquets of birds of paradise, roses, and orchids. I learned that the champagne was flown in from France, as were the chef and his entourage.

That same evening, our driver took us to see an obnoxiously expensive hotel that looked like a palace and had taken sixteen years to complete. There was a huge lobby but no guests to be seen. Two seated concierges in white Nehru jackets and maroon turbans jumped up to welcome us. I asked why it was empty and where could we have drinks. They told us that the entire hotel had been reserved for guests of a grand wedding nearby and that they were getting ready. "We'd like to go to the wedding, too," I joked, pan-faced.

"Are you serious, ma'am?" queried the concierge.

"Of course I am."

We were led to the elevator and directed to the roof terrace. The elevator stopped on every floor, revealing resplendently dressed and bejeweled wedding guests waiting for the elevator to come back down. Of course, they must be going to the wedding at the palace!

There was no one else on the magnificent terrace filled with orchids and candles. Our waiter approached us carrying a silver tray with an envelope. He announced that it was our invitation to attend the wedding and the bride's family wanted to know if we would accept. I was too thrilled to worry about being seriously underdressed and that Frank had on a Hawaiian shirt. "Yes, we accept with pleasure." As we took the elevator down to meet our driver, I fantasized about endless platters of superbly roasted meats, French champagne, and exotic entertainment at the palace.

Hardly able to contain my excitement, I handed our driver the invitation. He began heading in the opposite direction of the city's center and the palace. I asked him if he knew where he was going. "Yes, yes," he kept assuring us. We soon arrived at what looked like the entrance to a national park.

Disappointment gave way to curiosity. We entered a large field. At one end was a stage with a huge, colorful peacock backdrop right out of a Bollywood film. On the stage were the bride and groom and their families having pictures taken. We had arrived just ten minutes before the time specified on the card. Hundreds of chairs had been set up, but there were only about forty people sitting in them. Perhaps events started late here. The bride's father came over and ushered us onstage, and the wedding party posed with us while cameras flashed. I asked the bride's father when the wedding ceremony was going to begin. He brought a man over who could speak English. The man laughed as he shook his head and, pointing to a gap in the trees, kept repeating, "Go eat, go eat!"

Through the trees was an enormous clearing the size of a football field. Scattered throughout were a dozen small, colorful canopies, each with a table and a few chairs. Lining the perimeter were food stations where about eight hundred people stood in lines. As we walked over to the food, Frank searched for the bar. I noticed that everyone was drinking tea. I was looking for roast goat or chicken tikka, but we were only hitting the vegetable stands. In line, we wondered why there was no music. An elegant man in front of us overheard and turned around to break the news. It was a Jain wedding. He explained that the Jains are a Hindu sect that adheres to strict vegetarianism. Music and alcohol were forbidden. Forlornly, I thought of the palace wedding we were missing.

The canopies were all occupied. As we headed back to the empty chairs in front of the stage with our teas and plastic plates loaded with vegetable and bean curries, we noticed a canopy off to the side where the bride and groom sat on a carpet with about two dozen people sitting cross-legged around them. The wedding ceremony was being performed while guests milled about. We finished dinner as fast as we could, went over to the wedding canopy, and sat down on pillows just a few feet from the bride and groom. A priest solemnly led the couple through a series of symbolic rituals. Captivated, we stayed until the end, honored to have witnessed the essence of this celebration—not the pomp, but the circumstance.

We left India from Delhi, intoxicated with sensory overload. In a country where millions live in poverty, where child labor is rampant, and where shanty towns are filled with shelters constructed of found material, people were steeped in spirituality, joy, and gratitude for the smallest thing that came their way. I left feeling deeply humbled.

Egypt was politically shaky and on the State Department's do-not-go-to list. Many took the advice, resulting in a historic drop in tourism, which was shattering the economy. The Egyptians had had it with President Hosni Mubarak, and Tahrir Square was occupied by protesters. Nothing, however, was going to come between me and the pyramids in Giza. When I caught a glimpse of them from the plane, I could feel the power these massive geometric structures had wielded through the ages.

We went directly to Alexandria, the ancient Greek city founded by Alexander the Great, where Pharos, a lighthouse, and one of the wonders of the ancient world once stood. Having eluded modernization, the city took us back in time to when it was a cosmopolitan mecca. Both of us promptly came down with a disturbance of the lower tract. If we had to get sick, it couldn't have happened in a better place. The family-run hotel overlooked the sea. The staff took it as their personal responsibility to tend to us, bringing us lemon soda and crackers on silver trays. Back on our feet, we stumbled upon the home—of the great twentieth-century Greek poet Constantine Cavafy. From the time we walked in until the time we left, we didn't see anyone—visitors or attendants. I could have walked out with one of his original manuscripts.

I have never been inclined to go on a cruise before, but the boat trip down the Nile to see Egyptian art, architecture, and culture spanning five thousand years was genius. It chopped travel time and freed us from hunting down hotels, restaurants, and drivers. While on the ship, we read up on historical and anecdotal information about the marvels we were about to witness. The sheer size, artistry, and preservation of the temples in Aswan, Kom Ombo, Edfu, Karnak, and Luxor were jaw dropping. Walking down the ramps of the Pharaohs' tombs in the Valley of the Kings with hieroglyphics emblazoned on the walls and seeing King Tutankhamen's burial crypt inspired the same childlike awe I had experienced when learning about them in grade school.

Back in Cairo, our driver picked us up to take us to what had been one of the inspirations for the entire trip, the pyramids. There was no letdown here. Built with geometrical exactness, these phenomenal structures fired up the mind. Surely, only aliens from outer space could have plopped them here on Earth. I tried to conjure up what the sheaths of polished Tura limestone reflecting the sun's brilliance from afar looked like before they were plundered. Unbeknownst to me, the interior shaft was open to the public. Our driver told us that only three hundred people were allowed in per day. At peak tourist season, visitors and travel agents begin lining up early in the morning and tickets sell out quickly. Because tourists were sparse, we purchased tickets without a wait. Astonishingly, except for a security guard, we were the only people inside. We walked up and down the shaft of the Great Pyramid of Giza in silence. It was as if the smooth, perfectly precise walls had been chiseled yesterday. We ended a hot day in December by riding camels at the base of the pyramids, and our experience had surpassed any and all expectations.

It was Old Cairo that shifted the rest of our journey into a spiritual one. Parts of a wall studded with forts that surrounded the city with its many Coptic Orthodox churches still remain. Ever since St. Mark first preached the gospel in Alexandria around 50 CE and despite the persecutions, many divergent events made Egypt an incubator for Christianity. When King Herod of Judea had heard from the magi that the "King of the Jews" was born in Bethlehem, he gave orders to have all male babies in the area under the age of two slaughtered to get rid of the potential rival. To escape the massacre, the Holy Family—Joseph, the Virgin Mary, baby Jesus, and Salome, the midwife—fled to Egypt, where they spent four years changing locales every few months. Early Christians had regarded the trail of sites in which they had sought shelter as holy and had built churches near them as markers. We visited two of the sites, Abu Serga, a church built over a cave, and in Maadi, on the bank of the Nile, the set of stone steps from which the Holy Family departed for southern Egypt. Frank and I had a picnic on the well-kept grounds next to it, reflecting on the tenacity of the Holy Family, the early Christians, and the light and dark sides of humanity as a whole.

The final destination of our pilgrimage was where it all began, Israel. My dream of being in Jerusalem, visiting the Christian holy sites, and touching the Wailing Wall at the Temple Mount was to become reality. We arrived at the Tel Aviv airport, and the unpleasant exchange we had there with a security guard proved to be a harbinger of my impression of the country's state of affairs. As we went through customs while soldiers lurked about with rifles, a slight, young woman sidled up next to me and began interrogating us. What were we doing in Israel, and where were we going? We told her that we were planning to visit holy sites, but that did not appease her, and she continued her intimidation. Ignoring her, we purposefully marched ahead.

Our driver was an elderly Muslim gentleman. On the way to our hotel, he detoured to take us to a little church that contained the tomb of St. George. When we found it closed, he rang the bell of a house across the street. The keeper of the church, a young Greek Orthodox priest, came out and unlocked the door. The driver's gesture touched me, and I was able to let go of my annoyance from the harassment we encountered at the airport. Mustafa would be our driver until we reached Jerusalem.

As we toured the alternating lush and arid landscape peppered with old olive and cedar trees, Israel's importance to its inhabitants and to the world for thousands of years was palpable. We visited Nazareth, where Jesus grew up, and the Sea of Galilee, where He gathered His disciples. We swam in the Dead Sea, where I plastered myself with greenish-black clay with its high concentration of minerals. Jerusalem elicited awe at every turn, starting with the Yad Vashem Holocaust Museum. We somberly viewed exhibits of the Nazis' capacity for evil, which chronicled their oppression and extermination of Jews, more than half of the eleven million people Hitler annihilated. We then joined the throng of faithful at the Wailing Wall, and I placed my hand on it and left a prayer in one of the cracks. We walked the Via Dolorosa, where the fourteen Stations of the Cross marked the path of Jesus' suffering, from His sentencing by Pontius Pilate to His crucifixion and burial in what now is the Church of the Holy Sepulchre. Walking in the footsteps of Jesus Christ filled me with indescribable reverence.

For all of Israel's stunning beauty, rich historical heritage, and religious significance for Jews, Christians, and Muslims, I found the physical signs of the age-long, unresolved strife between Palestinians and Jews to be deeply disturbing. On the way to the Jordan River where St. John the Baptist purportedly baptized Jesus, I asked Mustafa about his views on the Israeli/Palestinian conflict. He didn't answer. As we continued along a barbed wire fence, he broke his silence by pointing to it, saying, "The land on the other side is Palestinian." He pointed up the hill where imposing white villas overlooked the countryside and continued, "See the houses up there? Those are Jewish settlements. Palestinians are not allowed to enter." I had heard justifications for and against land confiscation from both sides, but seeing the disparity made it hard to digest. I needed clarification. "But that's the most beautiful part. How can they come in and just take it when it's allocated to the Palestinians?" Once again, our driver retreated into silence as we drove through miles of flat barren terrain on a narrow road flanked by barbed wire fences dotted with signs warning, "Danger, mines." We arrived at the river just as a group of pilgrims were being baptized. Two Israeli soldiers carrying rifles stood guard.

On the drive south from Jerusalem to Bethlehem, I was not prepared for the aversion that overcame me as the separation wall emerged into view. From far away, what looked like a benign, horizontal white line blending in with the surrounding buildings grew as we approached into a solid concrete wall the height of a three-story building. The Israeli government claimed to have built it for protection against Palestinian suicide bombers. It went on for miles and miles, cutting off thousands of Palestinians from the rest of the West Bank, which they could only enter at Israeli-operated checkpoints. Relentless in its expansion, it had gobbled up Palestinian land, dividing communities and obstructing vistas.

Before entering Bethlehem, we stopped at Rachel's Tomb, one of the holiest Jewish sites, where one of the most beloved Biblical matriarchs was buried. Located in the Palestinian autonomous zone within Israeli-held territories, it looked like a high-security prison. A small, rectangular building with a white dome, the tomb was surrounded by the looming concrete walls. It was accessed by a long walkway between two walls topped with barbed wire and a watchtower manned by the Israel Defense Forces and Israeli Border Patrol. In the land where "love your neighbor" was the common thread among the three religions laying claim to it as their foundation, the confiscated Palestinian land, the barbed-wire fence warning of mines, the wall, and the military-guarded tomb were emblematic of separation and of the Israeli government's fear and power.

Although the history of the conflict is complicated on many levels, most ordinary citizens on both sides appeared to be willing to live together harmoniously. Each side's hardliners, however, both inside and outside of Israel, whether it was Iran threatening annihilation, the Palestinians refusing to consider peace resolutions, Jewish oppression of occupied Palestinian citizens, and those of both sides instigating wars and violence, have produced a palpable culture of fear. At a checkpoint in the wall where Palestinians passed through to get to their jobs on the Israeli side, we observed soldiers aggressively interrogating them in the same bullying manner with which we had been treated at the airport. I couldn't fathom having to live with this intimidation on a daily basis.

We heard diametrically opposed historical renditions of expulsions, occupations, and disappearances of the Jewish people; differing views of the emergence of Palestine; divergent opinions about which side instigated which war; and contradictory versions of who does or does not deserve statehood and the right to self-determination. Absorbing the various narratives, I wondered if I would ever know the truth. What was clear was the cyclical pattern of oppression built on fear/tension and frustration/attack/ retaliation. Each side had a right to self-determination, whether the solution was a two-state system or Jews and Palestinians living together peaceably in one state. I left Israel fantasizing a national holiday where Israelis and Palestinians would come together for a day to share their hopes and fears and put themselves in each other's shoes. It might prove that there were more similarities between them than differences.

What started out as a bucket list of sightseeing had turned into a spiritual pilgrimage. I had stood in the church I had dreamt of since childhood, which had played a major role in transforming ancient Greek civilization into a Christian one. I knelt where Buddha attained enlightenment under the Bodhi tree, visited revered Muslim holy sites, was blessed by Hindu priests, prayed at the Wailing Wall, and walked on sacred Christian ground. The experience was transformative. I felt a connection with the whole of humanity, past and present.

It hit me on the plane flying home. Not only did Frank and I not have one altercation, but any fear of it happening was gone. What we shared on this mother of all trips had strengthened our union. I felt a gush of love for the wonderful man sitting next to me. I thought of Hayal and how she had come into our lives—I could not have dreamed up a better "daughter." Another love wave lapped across my heart chakra. There was an excitement deep, deep inside of me that I couldn't put my finger on. I was sixty years old—a badge I was proud of—and the happiest I had ever been. I was charged up. There was an urgency, of course. Work was waiting for me at home—I had a book to write!

CHAPTER 18

Eleni

College fit Hayal like a glove. We returned home to find her ensconced in her classes, thriving as a student. Fascinated with how the human body functions, particularly the brain, she was majoring in molecular biology with a minor in philosophy. She possessed a wisdom far beyond her years and a deep empathy toward people and nature. One time she was watching a video on DNA strands and found them so beautiful she started crying. When she came home on college breaks, we would spend hours talking, processing her past, and musing about the future. In her formative years, Hayal had lacked love, support, and guidance, and these were things I could freely give her. Yet somehow, she had formed strong moral convictions on her own. She was an old soul, the daughter my mother always wanted, and I knew that Mother had sent her to me. I began thinking of Hayal as mine.

I had one house rule—I got to tell her whatever was on my mind and give her my solicited or unsolicited opinion on anything I wanted, but the choice of what to do with it was hers. Putting all of the responsibility on her made Hayal regularly ask for advice.

During one of our powwows about life and love, Hayal announced that she wanted to be baptized in the Orthodox Christian Church. Fr. Stephen had told me that she had approached him with the same request when she was at the shelter. He was the first person in her life she had truly trusted, and it made sense that she wanted whatever it was he was having. He told her, however, that getting baptized was not as simple as joining a club, but required a deep, spiritual commitment. Now that she was getting unconditional love from us, it was equally understandable that she wanted to be part of our "club." I called Fr. Stephen for advice. "This is the right time," he said excitedly. His church was Albanian Orthodox, and he suggested that the baptism take place in the Greek Orthodox church where our friend, Fr. George, who had also married us, and Fr. Stephen would be co-celebrants. We decided on a Sunday in mid-March.

Although I had been resolute about not having children, I had wondered from time to time what it would be like to be a mother. I would then digress, imagining having given birth to little monsters, and that would zap the fantasy. I didn't need kids of my own, anyway. I loved my brother's kids and had a special bond with Yianni, the middle child, who sometimes lost out on attention that was heaped on his older and younger siblings. There were also strong connections with my friends' children and those of my cousins in Greece. My life was rich and full as it was. I couldn't help it, though. Every once in a while, I would fantasize about having a daughter to love the way my mother had loved me, someone to whom I could impart the wisdom that my mother had passed on to me regarding life's challenges, cooking, God, and matters of the heart. There was no such thing, however, as a grown-up, ready-made daughter to be had. When Hayal asked if she could call me "Mom," an unexpected surge of love and joy overwhelmed me. I said yes she could, but not until after the baptism.

Both sacraments, the Orthodox Christian wedding that unites two people and the baptism that unites a person with "the Body of Christ" (the Church), are rich in symbolic rituals. The baptism includes an exorcism, which denounces evil, the anointment of Holy Unction, which commits the person to serving Christ, and the Sacrament of Chrismation, which imbues the soul with the Holy Spirit. Since it is mostly infants who are baptized, their "rebirth" is expressed by dunking them three times in a baptismal font filled with water. A new, white garment is then donned to represent the newly begotten purity.

"I don't want anyone else there," Hayal said when she learned that she would be crouching in a trough wearing a white top and pants while the priest poured water on her.

"This is not a party," I informed her. "We're not sending out invitations. However, if someone wants to witness the sacrament, I suggest you get out of the way of their spiritual path." Hayal agreed.

Godparents, or sponsors, are part of the sacrament. This was instituted when Roman Emperor Nero was persecuting Christians, and godparents would step in to ensure the child's spiritual growth in case the parents got massacred by wild animals in the arenas. Frank wanted to sponsor Hayal with me, but the church requires the godparents be Orthodox Christian. It also recognizes baptisms in non-Orthodox religions, and therefore a convert to Orthodoxy is not re-baptized. Since Frank was Byzantine Catholic, he only needed to partake in the Sacrament of Chrismation, the Holy Spirit part, to become Orthodox.

One Chrismation ritual is the naming. The godparent selects the name of a Christian saint, which the priest bestows on the person entering the Church to signify a new spiritual identity. Frank chose Paul to honor his father and brother. I wanted to name Hayal Anna after my mother but decided on Eleni after St. Helen (Agia Eleni in Greek), mother of Emperor Constantine the Great, the first Roman emperor to convert to Christianity, and after whom Constantinople was named. Both were canonized as saints for bringing Christianity to Western civilization. Known as St. Eleni of Constantinople, she was also born in what is now modern Turkey. Hayal immediately related to her, declaring, "That's me. I am Eleni!"

Fifteen people had asked to come and witness the baptism, including my friend Mary from Portland. Following the ceremony, Frank and I were hosting a luncheon at a nearby Greek restaurant. Shopping for a white dress for Hayal to wear after the ritual felt as if we were planning a wedding. The ceremony was very much like one. After his Chrismation, Frank and I sponsored Eleni. She went by that name from then on. We were no longer godparents or sponsors. As far as we were concerned, we were her parents, and she was our daughter. After she changed into her white dress and returned to the sanctuary for the completion of the sacrament, I read a letter I had written about what constitutes a family, that bloodlines were not a requirement. Christ had conveyed to his disciples that if two or more people came together in His name, they would be considered a church. I avowed that a family is forged when two or more people come together in the name of love. Everyone was moved to tears. Eleni and I embraced, and I kissed her as Mary snapped photos. It was a moment of indescribable joy shared by all. I finally got what my soul had always wanted but I had been blind to: motherhood.

One of the photographs Mary had taken was of me kissing Eleni after I read her my letter. It was Eleni's favorite. There was a floor-standing electric candelabra behind us. The photo was grainy, and somehow the glow from the lights was split into two cloudlike orbs, one over Eleni's head and the other over mine. Eleni had it printed and framed, and she gave it to me for my birthday to commemorate our bond. I proudly displayed it in the parlor and showed everyone our "halos."

Shortly after the baptism, my friend Fairley and I attended "An Afternoon of Forgiveness," a presentation given by Mariah Fenton Gladis, a world-renowned Gestalt therapist who lived and taught in a Philadelphia suburb. Fairley had told me Mariah's story. Mariah was only thirty-three years old when she was diagnosed with ALS, Lou Gehrig's disease, and was told that she had two years to live, at most. On the same day she had essentially been given a death sentence, her boyfriend Ron took her out to dinner and proposed marriage. Thirty-two years later, Mariah was a living force, teaching and healing. I knew I was in the presence of greatness. Paralyzed by the disease, she maneuvered her electric wheelchair as she carefully constructed words that, at times, needed translation. With her blazing red hair and blue eyes, beautifully dressed and perfectly made-up, she looked positively glamorous. Along with Gestalt-trained psychiatrists and assistants, she led weekend workshop retreats. One was coming up. Inspired, I asked Frank if he would accompany me to it, and he agreed. The experience was transformative. I marveled as I watched Mariah be fully present as she worked with people carrying emotional pain by reenacting the past trauma and creating an "exact moment of healing." Was it Mariah's technique that healed people, or the love that radiated from her eyes? I needed this woman as my mentor, so I decided to enroll in her Gestalt training program.

Eleni began her junior year in college in the fall of 2014. Her English had greatly improved. She made the dean's list every semester. Of course, there were the usual dilemmas of college life as kids make their way into adulthood. Disciplined and mature, she would relate to me in utter amazement about the crowd that went to parties to get drunk and arbitrarily hook-up. Boys vying for her attention didn't know how to act around her, and her crushes would fizzle. There were roommate issues to iron out and quandaries over finding responsible and trustworthy friends with whom she could share her story. When her past reared up, she would repeatedly ask "why," as giant tears welled up and overflowed. She introduced me as her mom but would resist answering the questions that followed. I suggested that she use, "It's a long story," my comeback when I didn't want to get into the details of her past. Eleni had maintained close friendships in Turkey, and there were bouts of homesickness. An opportunity came along to apply to Bosporus University in Istanbul for the spring semester.

She was elated when she was accepted. We made plans to meet in Greece after school ended in May so that she could meet my relatives.

Eleni was planning to take the MCATs for medical school. The timing, however, would not allow her to apply with one name and show up for the test with her new one. In the midst of expressing her frustration while I was driving, Eleni blurted out, "Why couldn't I have met you sooner, and you could have adopted me!" A flashbulb went on. "Look up adult adoption!" Within a minute, Eleni was reading out loud from her phone about adults being adopted in the state of Pennsylvania. The next morning, I stopped by Family Court to obtain the form. A court date was assigned for less than a month after submitting the application. On December 13, 2014, the judge began the proceedings, pan-faced, by stating that this was going to be a long and arduous process. "Oh, no," Eleni muttered under her breath. He turned to her and asked if she wanted to be adopted by us. She said, "Yes." He asked us if we wanted to adopt Eleni, and we said, "Yes." "Done! Congratulations," he bellowed. We all posed for photographs. Just like that, Hayal Yalcinkaya became Eleni Hayal Demas and our legal daughter. When she became an American citizen, her name change became legal, too. We were overwhelmed with congratulatory greetings. Many of my friends thought the whole thing was a miracle.

For me, the miracle happened when Eleni became our spiritual daughter at her baptism, and we were blessed as a family, in the name of love, in the eyes of God. I had a photograph to prove it. One afternoon, my friend Angelique came over for coffee. The framed photograph of Eleni and me taken at the baptism was on the demilune table, opposite from where Angelique was sitting on the sofa. In the midst of chatting, she looked past me squinting, her gaze transfixed on the photograph. "What's that?" she exclaimed as she got up and bolted toward it.

"Oh, our halos!"

"What halos?" she cried out without taking her eyes off the picture, seemingly thunderstruck. "That's an angel!"

"Where do you see an angel?"

"Here!" she exclaimed as she pointed to the two wings that incorporated the balls of light above us I had been referring to as halos. I gasped, staring at it in disbelief.

"Angelique, do you see this face?" I asked incredulously.

"Yes," she let out in a low voice, riveted.

"See those high cheekbones? That's my mother's face."

Despite the graininess of the photograph, the image of my mother as an angel was unmistakable. Her eyes looked downward as she hovered over us. The detail that emerged next made my knees buckle. Only icons depicting angels are shown with scepters. There, hazy but discernable, just to the right of the face, was a scepter.

Of course, we live in a physical world. Here, familiar elements converged to portray a glorious figure of an angel that resembled my mother. Not everybody saw what Angelique and I found to be unambiguous. Some people saw the wings but not the face, some saw the face but not the wings, and others would stare and see nothing. It mattered not. I had my angel, and the name of my friend who had found it was Angelique.

Chapter by chapter, writing became easier and easier. My two resistances that had made me argue adamantly against writing a book, fearing solitary confinement and not having anything to write about, had melted away. I now welcomed the solitude and found out that I had a lot to say. Writing became a way to process the gifts presented to me, some against my will, that had resulted in my supreme happiness. It brought clarity as to how extraordinary people and events popped up at the perfect time to help, instruct, and save me, elevating my faith even more; how my faith, in turn, provided me with the inner knowingness that whatever was happening, regardless of how negative, stressful, and unwelcomed, was necessary for a positive end result and growth; how the Holy Spirit went from being some nebulous concept that I couldn't wrap my head around to being a constant companion, whom I have experienced with the same certainty that I walk on this Earth—ready, willing, and able to be instantly accessible and beneficent, asking nothing more of me than to be invited in.

If my will had prevailed, not only would this book never have been written, I would not have stayed married, let alone have gotten married in the first place, to someone who evolved into a wonderful and supportive lifetime companion. I certainly would not have had a loving daughter. What most amazes me is the discovery of how simple it really is. I learned that I only needed to remember to say please and thank you. I learned to pray for what is best and to rely on the perfect entreaty, the Lord's prayer—asking for help not to surrender into temptation and to be rid of the ego, the deceiver, which attempts to keep me from my true purpose; asking to be freed of guilt from my offenses and to free any guilt from those who offend me, as forgiveness is healing; asking for a will greater than mine for the essential sustenance I need for today because I may not know exactly what that is; asking for the Holy Spirit, the Kingdom of Heaven, to enter my heart and mind, for anything is possible when I connect with Divine Consciousness, our Creator who resides in sound, light, and vibration.

People ask me all the time why, if there is a God, there are natural disasters, disease, suffering, death, and evil. My simple answer is that these things are part of the deal of having an earthly experience. From the miracles that have happened to me and to those around me, I can say from my experience that God can indeed keep us away from harm, be it natural or human-made. I count on faith, prayer, and heightened consciousness. We have been provided with a beautiful planet on which to experience true happiness, free will with which to choose, and a heart with which to love. If we are injurious to others and continue to destroy our environment, we will create our own hell. If we choose to love one another and respect our bountiful natural resources, we will have heaven on Earth.

Confirmation that I was on the right path came in an unexpected form. For my last homework assignment at the end of my one-year Gestalt study, Mariah asked that we write a letter to ourselves from our spirit guide. Another writing assignment? I shelved the request. At the next to the final class, Mariah gently prodded, "I haven't received anyone's letter from their spirit guide. It doesn't have to be long." That took the pressure off. Driving home, I composed two cute short paragraphs from a cheerleading spirit guide along the lines of, "you go girl, rah-rah-rah, you're so breathtaking!"

As soon as I came home, I went straight to the computer to write my tight, little letter and get it over with. As I wrote, thoughts kept emerging that I felt compelled to include. Normally, I need an outline to organize my thinking. This time, however, I wrote whatever came to my mind. Suddenly, something told me to wrap it up and formulate a closing. I printed it. Instead of the two paragraphs I had initially composed, what came out was almost two pages. I read it, unable to move. They were the most profound and encouraging words I could possibly need, which I have included here. The letter told me how things were going to go down and advised me on exactly what to do. The tears streaming down my face were not a reaction to its eloquence, but from a knowledge that I had not created it. I was only the vessel through whom it was channeled.

Whether or not this book sees the light of day doesn't matter. The most important thing is that writing it gave me the essential clarity of my truth, which I wanted to share with you. If you need proof that miracles exist, well, dear reader, if you're reading this, you now know that they do. Here's to wishing you, too, a miracle-filled life.

Letter from My Spirit Guide:

Dear Sophia,

Hooray, you're getting there!

First of all, allow me to tell you how happy I am to have been commu-nicating with you. I was not so sure at first—did I really need another egotistic, defiant, cheeky wild child under my watch? Knowing some of this beforehand, we sent you a saint for a mother and sure enough, you had to test a saint. But that dream I gave you when you were 19 really helped you start paying attention, didn't it? I was pleased when I received that first heart-felt thank you, and elated when you caught on that there's no such thing as too much gratitude. So, the more of it you expressed, the more reasons I gave you to express it! That's just the nature of things.

As you became aware of these gifts, you thought yourself lucky for all those "coincidences." Your gratitude allowed me to start blessing you with matters a little more, shall we say, divine? Boy, has it been fun watching your reactions—remember your glee at what you got when you asked for a sign from your father who, BTW, happens to be stand-ing right next to me as I am transmitting? And I'll never forget how you described to your friends the sensation you had after you put Holy Unction on the lump on your eyelid, even before you became aware of its spontaneous disappearance. "It felt like a thousand angels were taking turns hugging me!" Wow, little did you know that's exactly what was going on!

I know it's cliché to say, "It hurts me more than it hurts you," but, as you now realize, putting obstacles in your way is part of the deal. I will not use the word graceful to describe the way you accepted some of these necessary challenges. But after the initial resistance and the kicking and screaming, "Why are you doing this to me, God?" you began listening to the answers as they became progressively louder and clearer. You have no idea how extra creative I had to get with our communication when it got choppy there with Frank, and you let the ego get the upper hand. Despite the mind commotion, you took in those words I sent you and cracked open the door just enough so that the light in you could see the light in him. I'm sorry that his wedding ring had to get crushed in the process, but you know Frank needs to see to believe, and now he can go down that road, too. You deserve to have your dream companion on this journey. Your shifting perceptions fill me with joy, and you should know that nothing makes me happier than to turn around and bestow you with another blessing. Some of my favorite moments are after hearing you say, "Oh God, it doesn't get better than this!" and my going one step further to wow you more . . . So, how was your Mother's Day, Sophia?

We were all wondering up here when you would stop feeling lucky with your coincidences and start using the word "miracle." I believe it happened about the same time that you decided to share your blessings and be truly helpful to your brothers and sisters. Finally, I could take a step back from pulling all the strings. You are surrounded with special earthlings, but I had to send you two ultra-high-frequency mentors to help me help you help others. Both having defied death as defined by science, they had to meet two criteria—be love-driven and be fully committed to helping remove the fetters that keep humans from achieving their true purpose. First, I sent you Fr. Stephen and then Mariah. Are you getting along with them okay? Hee, hee, hee . . .

Now that everything is in place, what about the book? Everyone is scared, Sophia, but few carry on. You are doing so, one toehold at a time. Keep focused on what is real, and you will meet your calling. In the world of scarcity, love has no meaning and peace is impossible. Love is seen as finite, so if another gains it, there is less love for you. In that world, so long as gain and loss are accepted, no one is aware that perfect love is in them. You know otherwise. You know that the more the love cup is shared, the more love there is to drink. You recognize that God is an idea just like you are, and so your faith in Him is strengthened by sharing. No loss, only gain. In the holy instant, you recognize the idea of love is in you and in your mind that thought it. You are learning that by keeping all of your brothers and sisters in your mind, you experience completion. Herein lies peace, for here there is no conflict. This makes you want to give more, for this is love. In the holy instant, the laws of God prevail and only they have meaning, while the laws of the world cease to have any. The more your will aligns with God's, the more boundless you are. In that instant you are as free as God made you.

Your mission, Sophia, is not going around changing people. What is there to change when perfect love resides in all beings? Only the veil drawn across reality needs lifting. No one who has not yet experienced the lifting of the veil and been drawn into the light behind it can have faith in love without fear. This faith, given to me by the Holy Spirit, I give to you, and you will give it by uniting your mind with mine so that together we can lift veils. Write the truth with love, and this will be communicated without language to all of your brothers and sisters. This is how awareness is raised, even if no one reads your book. For it is ideas that minds communicate. You only have to write about what enters your mind and not worry how others will read it. Don't worry about who will read your book. You have been directed to offer miracles and to let the Holy Spirit bring to you those who seek you. I promise you that legions of spirits up here and many hands in the world will help them recognize that perfect love resides within them.

I want you to know, Sophia, that you are, have been, and will be loved forever. It is a true pleasure working with you, and I'm tickled pink to know what lies ahead for you. Don't worry, be happy, and as you read these words, know that I am with you always.

With love,

Your #1 Spirit Guide

Consciousness and Quantum Mechanics

The more I studied quantum mechanics, the fuzzier my grasp on reality became. Until then, I had thought science was knowledge that was neatly explainable, testable, and proven. The concepts I was now learning, however, demonstrated that quantum mechanics describes the world more accurately, allows for more extraordinary possibilities, and provides greater support for connectivity of everything than does classical physics. It challenges our view of reality.

It is hard to digest, but in the world of quantum mechanics, nothing is solid. The entire Universe is basically sound, light, and vibration. Everything we see and don't see is made up of infinitesimal particles. An electron, for example, is a particle but also behaves as a wave, as demonstrated by the famous *Double Slit Experiment*. When electrons are shot through one narrow slit onto a wall, the electrons line up, mirroring the slit. If, however they are shot through two slits, instead of lining up in two lines, they behave like waves, vibrating and fanning out to form an interference pattern of undulating bands on the wall. When a measuring device is introduced to observe the electrons passing through the two slits, their wave function collapses, and they go back to behaving like classical particles, forming two lines. It's as if the electrons know they are being watched! Is it possible they are conscious? Phenomena such as this have some scientists joining the orbit of yogis, psychologists, philosophers, and theologians in studying the field of consciousness.

Two other concepts particularly caught my attention. One is *Bell's Theorem*, named after John Stewart Bell. It demonstrates that if two particles come into contact with each other, become entangled, and then separate, whether across the room or into opposite corners of outer space, whatever happens to one simultaneously influences the other. The key word is "simultaneously." It suggests that the action is happening faster than the speed of light and the once-entangled particles instantly influence one another, suggesting that this occurs in the realm of consciousness.

Another key idea, David Bohm's *Holomovement*, involves a holistic, perhaps even mystical, approach to the Universe in which past, present, and future can coexist. A contemporary of Albert Einstein at Princeton, Bohm saw physical objects and empty space as made up of sub-atomic particles that continuously undulate with information. He postulates that any part of the object contains all the knowledge of the whole, much like looking at a part of a hologram and seeing the whole image. He believes that the human body operates in much the same way, being interconnected microcosmically and macrocosmically. How right he was about the micro part—look at how molecules in a DNA strand behave! In the human genome, a decoded DNA strand contained in the nucleus of a cell can provide information about the entire body it is part of, as well as give clues to diseases and their cures. Bohm's view of quantum mechanics was all about the interconnectivity of the whole and confirmed my spiritual convictions.

Quantum mechanics turns science into a bunch of assumptions and theories about reality, requiring mathematical formulas to weed out the wrong ones in a kind of process of elimination in which nothing can be proven.

This makes reality foggy. You pick up a brick, and it feels solid. Quantum mechanics says it is not because, in reality, the brick is made of moving wave-particles. Is the world as we see it an illusion?

Bohm's position was exactly that. He believed that reality is relative to our interaction with the world and our perception of it. When a solid circle is viewed from a certain angle, it appears to be an ellipse until a scientist comes along and contends that, in reality, the essence of the circle is atoms, while a quantum physicist will argue that its real essence is moving quarks. Each perception is another layer of reality, but the truth—the reality of the circle—will elude us. Bohm asserted that our separateness is also an illusion, that in fact we are one with each other and the whole Universe. Sounds more like God's realm to me.

Werner Heisenberg, another pioneer of quantum mechanics said, "The first gulp of the natural sciences will make you an atheist, but at the bottom of the glass, God is waiting for you." If more scientists thought like Bohm and Heisenberg, there would be much more harmony between science and spirituality. I became exhilarated at the prospect that, according to quantum mechanics, anything is possible.

APPENDIX B

The Physics of
Consciousness

Quantum mechanics aside, sound, light, and vibration are also integral to many religious traditions and practices. All three realms are also used in healing. Here, I focus on Hindu philosophy and Orthodox Christian mysticism, as they are two teachings I am most familiar with. Sound and light are central in the scriptures and rituals of both religions. It is believed that the vibrations of sound open the heart, and light enters the mind. It is in these realms where the Hindu connects with Brahma, or Universal Consciousness, to receive enlightenment and experience bliss, and where the Orthodox Christian receives wisdom and knows God. It is within these realms that the miraculous occurs.

I had entered adulthood with reservations about the virgin birth, Jesus being both man and God, and His resurrection three days after He was crucified. I was dubious about miraculous acts performed by saints, even as inexplicable events occurred in my own life which I continued to stubbornly refer to as coincidence. After all, there have been plenty of miracle claims that were proven to be hoaxes. Ironically, it was studying the laws of quantum mechanics and learning about the yogis' understanding of

Universal Consciousness that brought me full circle to fully embrace the faith I grew up with—the Greek Orthodox Church—but with a deeper understanding.

Yoga, which means "connection," originated in India over five thousand years ago with the Vedas, the ancient scriptures that have not been attributed to any single person or religion but are said to have been "heard" by the rishis, or seers, and generationally passed on by oral teaching. This revealed knowledge is the foundation on which the Yoga Sutras of Patanjali and Vedanta, among other traditions, are based, and it is the root of Hinduism, Buddhism, and Tantra. Vedanta, which means "end of knowledge," is the psychology of consciousness. Advaita Vedanta teaches seekers how to peel away their self-constructed identities to reveal their true selves and the ultimate knowledge of a nondual nature of reality. It asserts that there is no separation between the self and Brahma, or Universal Consciousness.

With enough practice, accomplished yogis can experience Samadhi, a deep meditation resulting in Samaya, or "liberation" of self. When in this state, siddhis occur. These are extraordinary powers that purportedly include levitation, teleportation, invisibility, bilocation (being in two places simultaneously), and psychokinesis—the very activities popular physicists theorize about today. Although these powers seem miraculous to non-practitioners, they are considered normal occurrences as side effects of advanced yogic practices. They are not the goal of the yogis and are intentionally played down lest discussion of them evoke pride and arrogance, which would impede enlightenment. Therefore, yogis will not allow themselves to be studied performing such extraordinary feats, which explains why there is no substantial body of documentation.

Alan Wallace, a Buddhist scholar, says of these practices:

> *"In Buddhism, these are not miracles in the sense of being supernatural events, any more than the discovery and amazing uses of lasers are*

miraculous—however they may appear to those ignorant of the nature and potentials of light. Such contemplatives claim to have realized the nature and potentials of consciousness far beyond anything known in contemporary science. What may appear supernatural to a scientist or a layperson may seem perfectly natural to an advanced contemplative, much as certain technological advances may appear miraculous to a contemplative."

Historically, classical scientists debunked many of these phenomena as illusions. Fortunately, there are those, like Nikola Tesla, who think outside the box. In the late 1800s Tesla, a prolific scientific inventor, worked on harnessing and converting radiant "free" energy, the precursor of zero-point energy, into electricity. Swami Vivekananda traveled to Chicago from India in 1893 to introduce Vedanta and Eastern philosophy at the World's Parliament of Religions. These two influential men met at a party given by American actress Sarah Bernhardt. Upon discovering that they shared a common interest in cosmic energy, they forged a lifelong friendship. Tesla was impressed to learn about Vedantic Prana, the "life force," and Akasha, aether, believed by the yogis to fill up all of space, while Vivekananda sought a scientific formula that proved matter could be transformed into energy and validate the effectiveness of yogic techniques. Tesla tried unsuccessfully to create such a formula, the proof of which did not come until Einstein's Theory of Relativity a decade later.

The exchange of ideas between Nikola Tesla and Swami Vivekananda is a wonderful example of how opening our minds to perspectives diametrically different from ours can profoundly enrich our lives. The extent to which each man was affected by the other's thinking is made evident by the following statements:

Swami Vivekananda:

> *Religion deals with the truths of the metaphysical world just as chem-*
> *istry and the other natural sciences deal with the truths of the physical*
> *world. The book one must read to learn chemistry is the book of nature.*
> *The book from which to learn religion is your own mind and heart.*
> *The sage is often ignorant of physical science, because he reads the*
> *wrong book—the book within; and the scientist is too often ignorant of*
> *religion, because he too reads the wrong book—the book without. (The*
> *Complete Works of Swami Vivekananda, vol. 6, "Notes of Class Talks*
> *and Lectures")*

Tesla:

> *The day science begins to study non-physical phenomena, it will make*
> *more progress in one decade than in all the previous centuries of its*
> *existence.*

In his book, *The Tao of Physics*, Dr. Fritjof Capra, a physicist and edu-
cator, writes about how basic elements of Eastern philosophy, particularly
Tao, beautifully illustrate the interconnectedness and dynamic nature of
the sub-particle world of modern physics.

He asserts:

> *Subsequent to the emergence of the field concept, physicists have at-*
> *tempted to unify the various fields into a single fundamental field which*
> *would incorporate all physical phenomena. Einstein, in particular, spent*
> *the last years of his life searching for such a unified field. The Brahma*
> *of the Hindus, like the Dharmakaya of the Buddhists and the Tao*
> *of the Taoists, can be seen, perhaps, as the ultimate unified field, from*

which spring not only the phenomena studied in physics, but all other phenomena as well.

Why does it have to be one or the other, science or God? It seems perfectly compatible for science to explain the mysteries of our physical Universe and an omnipotent, omniscient, and omnipresent God to exist. If God is, He is not bound by the laws of nature since He created nature and science will never prove His existence. Experiments with telepathy and telekinesis, however, are providing clues that we can communicate through consciousness and that our thoughts can affect the physical world. If consciousness is in all realms and we can communicate with it, then why can't we communicate directly with Divine Consciousness?

If we insist on evidence, we do not have to look further than our planetary system and our existence on this fine-tuned Earth. If the Earth's axis were shifted by a few degrees, or if we were a bit closer or farther from the sun, life on this planet could not be sustained. This fact makes our world a miracle, not an accident. Dr. John Lennox, a highly regarded professor of mathematics at the University of Oxford and outspoken Christian proponent of scientific laws pointing to God, says it another way: "If fine-tuning is likely on the hypothesis of there being a God, then the existence of fine-tuning enhances the probability of there being a God."

In Chapter 7, I have retranslated the Lord's Prayer from Greek to English to reflect the nuances that have been lost in translation. The first line in Greek reads, "Our Father who resides in the heavens," plural, meaning all realms. I have revised it to, "Our Creator who resides in sound, light, and vibration." God exists in all realms.

Sound and light are fundamental in Vedic scriptures. The pranava, the syllable AUM, which is more of a vibration than a word, is considered so sacred as to be Brahma/God. When chanted, it is believed to illuminate, to unite one with God and the whole Universe. According to the

Upanishads, part of the Vedic scriptures, light is also Brahma. It denotes purity and enlightenment. By reading the scriptures, one gains Divine Knowledge, which brings liberation from ignorance. Sound and light are profoundly expressed in the following prayer from the *Mundaka Upanishad* (2.2.3-4), the English version by Sanderson Beck:

> *"The word AUM is the bow; the soul is the arrow.*
> *God is said to be the target.*
> *By the unfaltering it is to be known.*
> *One becomes united with it as the arrow.*

> *In the highest golden sheath is God,*
> *without stain or parts.*
> *Radiant is it, the light of lights,*
> *that which the knowers of the soul know.*
> *The sun does not shine there nor the moon nor the stars;*
> *lightning does not shine; how then could this fire?*
> *The whole world is illuminated by its light.*
> *God truly is this immortal.*
> *God in front, God behind, to the right and the left.*
> *Spread out below and above, God is all this great universe."*

The more I learned about Hinduism based on Vedanta, the more I found myself comparing it to Orthodox Christianity. Sanatana Dharma, a unifying theory first recorded in the "Rigveda," is a collection of wisdom of ancient yogis. Sanatana means eternal truth—oneness with God and the Universe, and Dharma is the path through which it is attained by adhering to a code of moral law—justice, practice, peace, being of service, and loving one another. This conviction is central to the teachings of Christianity and also shared by many other belief systems.

Apart from obvious differences, I found similarities between Hinduism and Orthodox Christianity. Both religions worship one God/Brahma, a God without form, Divine Consciousness, the Truth. Both religions provide a system of beliefs that make an unknowable God more accessible. In Christianity, the Holy Trinity—God, Son, and Holy Spirit—are seen as One. Christ the Son, accepted as the incarnation of God through faith, has a human face that makes it easier to commune with God spiritually and physically through the sacrament of Holy Communion. The Holy Spirit, which is experienced as love and resides within us, makes it easier to visualize that we are also one with God. In Hinduism, on the other hand, there are many deities and thousands of personifications of different attributes of one supreme formless God, allowing Hindus to put a face on whatever aspect of God they wish to worship. Devotees of both religions believe that we are One with God and He is One with us.

As in the Vedic scriptures, sound and light have also been ascribed deep meaning in the Bible. The Word of God is taken to have literally created the universe. Sound preceded light. This is described in John 1:1–5:

> *"In the beginning was the Word, and the Word was with God, and the Word was God. The same was in the beginning with God. All things were made by Him; and without Him was not any thing made that was made. In Him was life; and the life was the light of men. And the light shineth in darkness; and the darkness comprehended it not."*

Genesis 1:3–4:

> *"And God said, "Let there be light," and there was light. And God saw the light, that it was good; and God divided the light from the darkness."*

The Word of God also manifested the incarnation of Jesus. John 1:14:

> *"And the Word was made flesh, and dwelt among us (and we beheld His glory, the glory as of the only begotten of the Father), full of grace and truth."*

Light is also how Jesus describes Himself. John 8:12:

> *"I am the light of the world. Whoever follows me will not walk in darkness, but will have the light of the world."*

My favorite miracle involving transformative light is the conversion of Saul, a Pharisee of Jerusalem who persecuted Christians, and who later became St. Paul, a fierce defender of Christianity. The Pharisees were an ultra-conservative Jewish sect that fervently adhered to the letter of the Mosaic Law. Saul believed that the teachings of Jesus defied the law. On his way to Damascus to hunt down Christians, Saul saw a flash of bright light and heard a voice calling to him, "Saul, Saul, why are you persecuting me?" Falling to the ground, blinded, he asked, "Who are you, sir?" The voice replied, "I am Jesus, whom you are persecuting. Now get up and go into the city and you will be told what you must do." His stunned companions led him to Damascus, where after three days he regained his vision and was baptized. The conversion of St. Paul, from a zealot persecutor to an ardent believer, possibly the one person most responsible for Christianizing the Roman Empire, best illustrates my definition of a miracle: a change of perception that is transformational. It also demonstrates how some people need a more dramatic whack on the head with the cosmic frying pan than others to experience a change of mind.

Much like the accomplished yogis who experience siddhis (teleportation, bilocation, and other paranormal phenomena) while in a deep meditative state, it has been reported that some Orthodox monks also experience these powers while praying. However, I could not find anything documenting this, only hearsay and hand-me-down stories. Then, I met Abbess Aemiliane of St. Nina's Monastery in Union Bridge, Maryland. Her story is a firsthand account of a mystic experience. Originally from Kansas, she received a PhD in Education from Harvard and became a Greek Orthodox nun. In 1981, the collapse of two skywalks at the Hyatt Regency Hotel in Kansas City killed 114 people and seriously injured more than two hundred others. Mother Aemiliane was one of the victims. She was crushed and trapped under sixty tons of steel beams and concrete. Miraculously, she found herself out of the rubble and in the arms of a stranger who told her everything was going to be all right. She was paralyzed from the waist down and was told that she would never walk again. Three months later, she walked out of the hospital, albeit with two canes. When Mother Amiliane joined a monastery as a novice in Greece, she visited her spiritual mentor's elder, Archimandrite Aemilianos, Abbot of Simonos Petras Monastery of Mt. Athos. She recognized him to be the very man who had cradled her after the collapse at the Hyatt. After twice asking if it was him, he neither confirmed nor denied it. Mother Amiliane then realized that he was a mystic and that he had bilocated. When she was formally tonsured, she took the name of the man who had saved her life.

Perhaps we, too, can learn from yogis who meditate and mystics who pray.

Glossary

Coincidence—Unrelated events that accidentally occur simultaneously and have meaning to the observer. It is a way in which God communicates with us.

Consciousness—Our core awareness where God resides. Consciousness allows us to live fully in the present and experience oneness with God.

Cosmic frying pan—It is what God gloweringly hits us over the head with to help us change our perception and see the light, to achieve a grand "aha" moment.

Ego—Fear-based, it is the opposite of the Holy Spirit. Its function is to stir up low-frequency emotions—anger, suspicion, jealousy, hate, power grabbing, etc.—to keep human beings apart from one another and separate from God. Also referred to as an acronym for "edging God out," the ego perceives God's will to be the enemy.

Faith—The utter certainty of the existence of God with whom we can have a personal relationship and a complete acceptance that whatever good or bad comes our way is meaningful for our growth. It is knowing that we are being taken care of by a higher power.

Free will—The ability God gave us to choose freely what we want. Acting from the ego's perspective may bring about instant gratification, but it can also create chaos in our life, making it a living hell. The more we align our will with God's will, however, the more love, peace, and joy we will have in our lives.

God—An omnipotent, omniscient, omnipresent, nonjudgmental Being that is Love, who created all realms of the Universe in which He resides, and with whom each of us can have a personal relationship. Though I believe this entity to be gender neutral, I refer to God as "He," since it is used most commonly and sounds better than "It." I often interchange God with Universe, Higher Power, Higher Consciousness, Universal Consciousness, Divine Consciousness, Divine Intelligence, Cosmic Intelligence, and Source.

God's will—For us to love and help each other here on Earth. We think we know what is best for ourselves, but God knows better. Turning over life's challenges to God's will brings about exactly what is needed for each of us.

Grace—The state of being in perfect peace; when we feel truly loved, or intensely love another. The sensation that we are one consciousness, connected with everything in the Universe, and are one with God.

Holy monkey wrench—Any obstacle, bad news, accident, person, place, or thing that trips up our intended plan or desire, ends up saving us from misfortune, and redirects us on the right path.

Holy Spirit—The active part of God who waits until It is invited to enter our midst, whether by intention or action, who communicates with all living things, and whose purpose is to connect humans so that they may love one another and be restored to their oneness with God in a state of grace.

Inner voice—The voice through which our conscience speaks to us. It is the seat of our wisdom. The ego tries to use our inner voice to grab our attention and keep us separate and in constant turmoil. At a higher level of consciousness, the Holy Spirit is there to guide us. We get to choose. As our inner voice evolves, it ignores the ego and naturally transmits the Holy Spirit's wisdom so that we can receive exactly what we need.

Love—The glue that binds us into one heart with our brothers and sisters and into oneness with God. Love is a state of grace where miracles occur. The more love you give, the more you receive, and the more love there is to go around. Love is infinite and eternal. Love is the antidote to fear and is what disarms the ego so that we can experience oneness. When we feel true love, we meet God.

Miracle—A highly improbable and timely singular occurrence or string of events that goes beyond mere coincidence and, in many cases, defies natural and scientific laws. As a result, we experience profound change, whether it is healing, a desired achievement, or simply a change of perception that contributes to elevating our awareness.

Wishful thinking—The state of not being in the present moment—when we are either wishing that the past was different or that the future will make everything okay. It is as if we are sleepwalking. In this state we may recognize a coincidence but miss what it is communicating and keep from taking action.

Disclosure: I have chosen not to write about mysticism of the many other great religions of the world because they are not part of my experience and, therefore, I focus mainly on Hinduism, as I have studied it in depth, and Greek Orthodox Christianity, as it is the faith in which I was raised.

Acknowledgments

When a medium told me that I was going write a book, I argued with her that, first, I had nothing to write about, and second, I'm a people person with zero inclination to isolate myself and write. She patiently heard me out then responded, "Spirit says when she's ready, there are many spirits here to help her, as well as many hands on Earth." The medium was too right about the help. I thank them all. I can only surmise who the blessed spirits are up there pulling strings, but I know for certain who has helped me here on Earth.

What made it possible for me to sequester myself and write in solitude were the following people, who offered me uniquely inspirational environments in which to do so, and to whom I'm eternally grateful. Thank you to my cousins Kanello and Aikaterina Nikitas for their mountainous retreat in Lagathia in the heart of Peloponnesus, Greece; to Yianni and Charlotte Petsopoulos for their house on the Greek Island of Astypalaia, where the stunning view of the sea inspired, and I was divinely sun-kissed daily; to my long-time friend Christine Fleming for her airy home on a bluff overlooking the Pacific Ocean in Neskowin, Oregon; to my brother and sister-in-law, George and Gayle Demas, whose ultra-cozy and super-sweet little beach cabin in Rockaway, Oregon, was the perfect getaway to overcome writer's block; and, last but not least, to Mary Norris and Joyce Miller for their open-ended offer to stay at Yellow Head, their private, picturesque little island off the coast of Machiasport, Maine.

I consider all my friends to be treasures and their love and belief in me priceless, for which there are no words to express my gratitude. I have relished the constancy of my scrabble sisters, sharing life's ups and downs with them since 1985. I want to voice particular appreciation for Alice Zander, Voula Liacopoulos, Ginny Kramvis, Reggie Dalton, Karen Shaffer, and Rosa Lee Smith, whom I could call on at any hour of the day for spiritual sustenance. And particularly for Mary Dutton, my biggest spiritual cheerleader, with whom I've journeyed from our party-girl days in college, through our individual struggles with faith, to sharing our personal relationship with God on practically a daily basis.

I want to express my deep appreciation for the friendship and mentoring I had from Fr. Demetrios Constantelos, a foremost theologian and Greek scholar, whom I miss very much. I also thank Elliot Tammaro, a professor of physics, for confirming my examples and use of terminology in writing about quantum mechanics.

I am grateful to my husband Frank for his encouragement and license to write about sensitive aspects of our relationship. How fortunate I was to have him read each chapter before it went to Mary Norris, my initial editor, who conveniently lives directly across the street and whose critiques and direction have made me a better writer. I also want to thank Ray Ricketts, an English professor at NYU, who lives two doors from Mary, for his invaluable developmental editing assistance.

Lastly, my gratitude goes out to Emily Temple and the rest of my team at Mascot Books for their attention, professionalism, and enthusiasm that brought this book to life and made my publishing experience downright joyful!

About the Author

Sophia has enjoyed three diverse careers: a decade in architecture that included working with notable 20th century visionary Dr. R. Buckminster Fuller, running her own couture fashion business, and working as a mental health therapist in private practice. She also created *Living a Fearless Life*, a twelve-workshop program designed to help society's most at-risk women increase their self-esteem, which was piloted in the Philadelphia Prison System and implemented with groups of ex-trafficked and ex-homeless women and women in recovery.

Writing a book was never on Sophia's radar. She began experiencing miracles when she was nineteen, and whenever she described a miracle to friends, the response would inevitably be, "These things only happen to you." In 2011, after Sophia reconnected with a childhood friend, told her about the latest miracle, and received the same reply, something clicked—there was a ring of truth to it. Although many people experience coincidences and serendipitous events, the prodigious number of miracles that had happened to her was indeed remarkable. Sophia identified the common denominator that had precipitated each miracle. Her desire to share that discovery made writing a book the most natural thing to do.

Sophia lives a happy life with her husband, Frank, in Philadelphia, Pennsylvania.